## What People Are Saying about Gary Comer and *ReMission*...

"A rigorous, hope-filled rethinking of our central mission and what it will take to fulfill it. Every serious Christian will benefit by engaging with this important book."

—*Mark Mittelberg*
Bestselling coauthor, *Becoming a Contagious Christian*
Author, *Confident Faith* and the *Becoming a Contagious Christian*
training course

"'The biggest challenge of all is to turn the church back into a culture-penetrating entity.' Gary Comer has identified the single greatest struggle of churches today. We have lost our focus and our influence. This book is gold for the church today—helping us get back to our core mission."

—*Dr. Ron Edmondson*
Pastor, Immanuel Baptist Church, Lexington, KY
Author, *The Mythical Leader*

"It's not a secret any longer: local churches are in trouble. The overwhelming forces of secularism, pluralism, hedonism, relativism, moralism, institutionalism, consumerism, and isolationism are exerting a wrecking-ball effect on numerous churches. Of course, most church leaders are reacting strategically to combat these forces in an effort to turn churches around. However, as Gary Comer asserts in *ReMission: Rethinking How Church Leaders Create Movement*, most of them are going about it in the wrong ways. Contrary to what most church leaders think, mission is not the byproduct of being a healthy church. Instead, Comer declares that church health flows out of mission. Do you want to make disciples? Get people involved in mission. Do you want to have a healthy church? Get people involved in mission. Do you want to have a dynamic church? Get your leaders involved in mission. And read this life-altering and church-revolutionizing book!"

—*Gary L. McIntosh, PhD*
Professor, Talbot School of Theology, Biola University
Author, *Growing God's Church*

"Systematic, insightful, and paradigm-shifting. Gary Comer introduces a fresh way to engage your churches into the mission of God through his 'ReMission Model.' Work through this with your lead team and enter into a new day of missional engagement and kingdom transformation in your city."

—Daniel Im
Coauthor, *Planting Missional Churches*
Author, *No Silver Bullets*

"I love this book! It is the life message of the author, whom I have known for over fifteen years. I love his research and flavorful writing that helps us *rethink* what God has called us to be and do. He educates and motivates the leader to *realign* his role to those he leads. We need a fresh insight and visual to *recapture* the obscured 'pattern' to gain the right 'posture' that will *reopen* the hearts of millions to the 'process' of genuine transformation. His ideas must be talked about and applied to the present day church at the highest levels so that it can be lived out by everyday followers of Christ."

—Dr. David Mills
Pastor and founder, SERVE U International

"*ReMission* can help us and our congregations rethink the central calling as the people of God in our neighborhoods and beyond. We cannot afford to be distracted by all the programs and busyness of our church life; it is time to learn from the heart and strategic thinking of Gary Comer and recalibrate our hearts to the mission for which Christ assembled His church."

—Dr. Mike Fabarez
Senior Pastor, Compass Bible Church
Focal Point Radio Ministries
Author, *Exploring the Gospel*

"*ReMission* takes a bold step in moving pastors and churches into their community with the gospel. Gary Comer lays out a stewarding plan any church can follow."

—Joel Southerland
Director of Evangelism, NAMB

"Gary Comer delivers an in-depth and candid look at the complexity of reaching our communities with the message of Jesus Christ. He offers a practical and well-thought through process to help you regain mission and momentum in a way that can result in sustained new growth and new life."

—*Dr. Dan Reiland*
Executive Pastor, 12Stone Church, Lawrenceville, GA

"The church needs to revisit and recover its sense of mission, and in so doing, Gary Comer is convinced that it will recover vitality, unity and purpose. Jesus tasked his church with a sole, primary obligation: to go and make disciples. *ReMission* will certainly help His church recover that mandate."

—*Scott Espling*
Pastor, Relevant Church, CA

"*ReMission* is a wake-up call to our core mandate, and a masterpiece for strategic global evangelism. Gary presents an in-depth analysis of the current status of evangelism and diagnoses why evangelism has failed. His audacity to confront age-old methods of evangelism challenges us to re-think our mission strategies. *ReMission* gives comprehensive, tried and tested, practical methods on how to evangelize effectively today. This is a must-read for all church leaders."

—*Zachary King'ori*
Bishop, Kingdom Christian Ministry, Nairobi, Kenya

"In *ReMission*, Gary Comer questions and challenges some of the most sacred and deeply entrenched paradigms in the church. But don't get the wrong idea. Gary loves the church and is passionate about seeing new people find 'life-changing' faith. Thank God for Gary, his relentless curiosity, and his creative gifting to explore new ways to advance the kingdom."

—*Mike Barnes*
Pastor, Community Church Big Bear

"Gary Comer has an incredible heart for the church to be missional at its core. Through stories, practical advice, and paradigm-shifting challenges, he offers wisdom and leadership for the church to fulfill its role of empowering believers to live out the mission of God. If you are a leader in the church or just someone who cares about people knowing Jesus, this is a must-read."

—*Andrew Boganwright*
Sandals Church Campus Pastor

"This book is absolutely soul-stirring. There comes a time when the church needs to refocus, reignite, reinvigorate, reinvest, and rejuvenate its passion for the mission field. Gary Comer not only addresses this issue, he also provides the church, its leaders and its people, with the necessary tools to do just that. Don't just read this book—apply the principles contained within."

—*Leighton Ainsworth*
Pastor/Author of *Victory Over Myself*, UK

"Thank you, Gary! This field guide for re-missioning evangelism in today's context is a critically important work. In our radically altered culture, in which many have left evangelism to the paid professionals, either out of fear or the feeling of being ill-equipped, this book brings hope. I highly recommend it."

—*Kathi Allen*
Church Planting Coordinator, SWCP
A ministry of The Christian and Missionary Alliance

"Gary Comer's latest book, *ReMission*, is a home run. This is not only a tremendous resource for pastors, board members, and Christians who aspire to make a difference—it is a necessary one. The church has lost its focus and its ability to engage with our secular culture. This book will help the leaders of any church to recapture their focus on the mission of the church."

—*Dr. Brent Strawsburg*
Founder and president, Brent Strawsburg Apologetics
Author, *Footprints of Faith: Defending the Christian Faith in a Skeptical Age*

"In *ReMission*, Gary Comer offers both an astute analysis of the discipleship void in the church today, as well as rethinking a way forward. Change is needed in order for the church to flourish in following Jesus's commission. This book is a helpful addition to the dialogue that will bring change."

—*Gino Curcuruto*
Church Planter, The Table Philadelphia, Northeast Network Director

"It has been said that most people will resist change until the cost of maintaining status quo becomes too painful. Only then are they open to change. In *ReMission*, Gary Comer not only paints a painfully accurate picture of today's church, but he also expertly details the change needed to fulfill God's purpose for the body of Christ: leading non-believers to saving faith. *ReMission* is inspired, timely, honest, and encouraging. It will change your heart and mind."

—*Greg M. Dodd*
Author, *A Seed for the Harvest*

"Gary Comer comes to this place with a wealth of experience as a God-cooperator. His passionate love for the bride of Christ is obvious on every page, and on every page you will find practical and effective analysis, and instruction for retooling your context in order to be faithful and fruitful in this or any age."

—*Dr. Michael L. Wilson*
Professor (formerly with Access Asia)

"This book matters—I mean, it *really* matters! If leaders do not see a primary imperative in making missional disciples, the church in the West will be dead in the water. Gary Comer has produced an authentic, practical, and hard-hitting work that we would do well to read, understand, and implement!"

—*Gary Gibbs*
National Evangelism & Church Planting Director,
Elim Pentecostal Church, UK

"I have known Gary as a friend and partner in ministry for thirty years. He has constantly and consistently modeled authenticity and evangelistic effectiveness in his own life and ministry, and he clearly shares these concepts in *ReMission*. I look forward to applying these principles in a greater way in my own life, and sharing them with the church planters I serve."

—*Dave Reynolds*
Leader, Alliance National Church Planting

"Read this extraordinary book—the efficacy of your church or ministry could depend on what you glean from it. Gary Comer does not mince words. He challenges leaders to connect with the foundational focus of discipleship; transformation. *ReMission* brings one back to biblical values, and launches one forward toward fruitfulness."

—*Dr. Parnell M. Lovelace Jr.*
Lovelace Leadership Connection

"Once again, Gary Comer tackles the greatest need in the church today: Returning the church to a culture-penetrating force. He delivers a deep-dive on the root problem plaguing today's church. Practical help follows with tangible strategies for church planters and pastors to shape church culture and train members to read the needs of their friends and engage them in life-changing conversations. Read it to the end. The chapter on Muslims is stellar."

—*Eric Oleson*
Director of Southwest Church Planting

"The Christian community has a rich tradition of being on mission. Gary Comer's call to revitalize and reengage in mission by addressing how the methodologies currently being employed are out of context is quite timely. The cultural landscape has evolved and the approach the church takes must also evolve to continue to be relevant and effective for the kingdom."

—*Brian Lipscomb*
President, Elevation Story

"When it comes to evangelism, Gary will equip you and the people in your church to become effective witnesses for Christ. Knowing how to do evangelism will reignite your passion to seek the lost—which our Lord Himself gave as the reason He came into the world."

—*John Njoroge*
Ravi Zacharias International Ministries

"Gary Comer's *ReMission* is stocked with warnings, admonitions, and in-your-face realities. He offers practical, biblical solutions to problems that the shrinking, marginalized church is facing today. Read it if you dare."

—*Dr. Ken Priddy*
Executive Director, The GO Center

"Being the church instead of doing church! In *ReMission*, Gary Comer brings us back to the heart of God—others! Strap in to read it. He has sized it absolutely right."

—*John Blue*
Pastor, Mission Orange County

"Gary Comer understands that any mission without movement is meaningless! Yet, we need to ask ourselves to what extent movement defines or at least refines mission. As you read these pages, you will find that not only your community but also your calling will be challenged and empowered to not only survive, but to thrive, as God builds His kingdom in you and through you."

—*Jim Solomon*
Associate Pastor, First Presbyterian Church, Baton Rouge, LA

"Dr. Gary Comer's *ReMission* challenges us to think outside the pews of the church and assume a countercultural outlook to the existing church itself. He puts this responsibility on Christian leaders to create a missional culture—one that extends beyond their own circles. Through his provocative, innovative, and catalytic approach, coupled with relevant cultural examples, Dr. Comer presents what health in the body looks like—to bring together the strategy of the church with the vision of Christ."

—*Martin Alvarez*
Operations Director, Ethnos Asia Ministries, USA

"*ReMission* is not just a book title, it is a clarion call and deeply resonating theme that applies to every living, breathing Christian. Read these prophetic pages with an open heart and mind. And let God do the transformational wonders that happen when his mission is deeply rooted and thoroughly expressed in your life and ministry."

—*Will Mancini*
Founder, Auxano
Author, *God Dreams*

# ReMISSION

## RETHINKING HOW CHURCH
## LEADERS CREATE MOVEMENT

*Gary Comer*

WHITAKER
HOUSE

## ReMission:
### Rethinking How Church Leaders Create Movement

Gary Comer
soulwhisperministry.com.

ISBN: 978-1-62911-943-4
eBook ISBN: 978-1-62911-944-1
Printed in the United States of America
© 2018 by Gary Comer

Whitaker House
1030 Hunt Valley Circle
New Kensington, PA 15068
www.whitakerhouse.com

Library of Congress Cataloging-in-Publication Data (Pending)

1 2 3 4 5 6 7 8 9 10 11 ᵾᴶ 25 24 23 22 21 20 19 18

# DEDICATION

I dedicate this book to all church innovators—those who are
willing to look afresh, to think deeper, and to dare differently.

# ACKNOWLEDGMENTS

A book is born in the life of the writer. Yet inspiration connects with a community of people, each one contributing colorful threads to the larger tapestry. Of course, God is the orchestrator of every aspect and deserves the ultimate praise. Looking back, I can say that this book came into being through a series of divine provisions. I am fully aware that the ball easily could have dropped along the way; but, somehow, it didn't. For that, I first have to say, thank you, Lord Jesus!

Thank you also to...

My literary agent. I needed an agent as the bridge to the traditional publishing world. Fortunately, God had a faith-filled servant named Gary Foster who was willing to extend his hand, even as he warned me, "The odds are not in your favor." For your going against the odds to represent my voice, I am grateful, Gary!

Early inspiration. During my doctoral study with professor Gary McIntosh at Talbot Seminary, I made a pivotal decision to extract three chapters from my first book, *Soul Whisperer*. It made that treatise more focused, and it started me dreaming about a second book. As crazy as this may sound, *ReMission* completes the work that God began in me under Gary McIntosh's tutelage, which goes all the way back to 2009. My writing will forever be linked to this man, who had the belief to speak these powerful words: "You could be an author one day."

My editors. While I was serving at Relevant Church, pastor Scott Espling was first to give me valuable shaping input on a number of chapters. No other person has affected my projects as much as my editing friend Don Toshach. More than just a talented wordsmith, Don has been a content filter and collaborator; and because Don has not held back from giving me his most candid feedback, God has used him as an instrument of refinement. For the results, I am bound at the hip to this man. Don, if any accolades come from people's words or voices, please take a bow!

I am also enormously indebted to Courtney Hartzel, Whitaker House's editor who received Re-Mission as her assignment. What a beautiful job of taking this project and honing its use of language and heightening its clarity. Courtney, you gave it the polish that makes it shine in so many places. Thank you!

Whitaker House. Christine Whitaker, thank you for fielding my calls and questions, and for guiding this whole process with such professional care and wisdom. In that same vein, I want to thank the managing editor, Tom Cox, for his guidance and sharp eye with the production and promotion aspects.

My family. My beautiful and supportive wife, Robin, is the one who knows me best, and, amazingly, she still loves me! She has stood behind my crazy dreams, even when the path was markedly long, and far from easy. We have learned to cling to hope and to remind ourselves, "The story is not over." Matthew and Nathaniel—my college-age sons, whose lives and faith have affected mine so profoundly—have also helped me see mission concepts within their spheres. To my treasures of pride, I love you!

The Soul Whisperer Ministries team. Pat and Althea Roman, some of our dearest friends, have supported our ministry vision, giving us the chance to chase big dreams. I could never thank you two enough! To my co-laborers: Greg and Dayna Hardee, and Joshua Tinsley: Thank you for partnering with me in the call of helping churches raise their game. Dayna has served as a sounding board for those raw, vulnerable parts of the writing, and she often gave me the courage to put it out there. "Hold to your voice," she'd say. I have to thank my designers: Tasha Montgomery, of AmpersandInk Designs, who did a fabulous job with the proposal and book graphics; Kris Van Houten, for his digital talents; and Caleb Childers, of Malachi Films for his video expertise.

Endorsers. Twenty-nine top-level ministry leaders answered the call to read this book and then write their thoughts of it. JR Woodward, having picked up one of my blogs for his Missional Times newsletter, was willing to give my manuscript a look and then to write a beautiful foreword. JR, you were one of those miraculous provisions! Many notable individuals, such as Daniel Im and Ron Edmondson, did not know me personally and yet reviewed the book anyway. When I made my pitch, saying, "I know this is coming out of the blue," Dan Reiland, the executive pastor of 12Stone Church, shot back: "Sometimes, 'out of the blue' is good."

Sandals Church. Captured within the pages of this book are many stories that came from my five years of serving in the thick of it with you all. Special thanks to Matt Brown, Dan Zimbardi, Andrew Boganwright, Dan Crowley, Don and Helen Roseberry, Derek I. (full name withheld to safeguard anonymity), Adam Atchison, Brian McCoy, Gary Overholt, and Lori Albee.

Southwest Church Planting and the North American Mission Board (NAMB). To my close friends Director Eric Oleson, and National Christian and Missionary Alliance (CMA) church-planting director, David Reynolds: Your friendships have undergirded my resolve to fight this out for his glory! I also appreciate the partnership with the NAMB, and the churches where we have trained and served.

Serve U International. Over the past decade, I have been blessed to journey all over the world with Pastor David Mills. Serving on this international mission board has broadened me to speak into the global climate. And how amazing to serve alongside fellow board member Roy W. (full name withheld to safeguard anonymity), whose mission impact will one day be seen to measure at the highest of levels. I have been blessed by my mission experiences and by the opportunity to observe partners with such wisdom on reaching the ends of the earth.

Friends. Finally, I want to thank a few additional friends: Parnell Lovelace, with the Great Commission Research Network; Martin Alvarez, of Ethnos Asia; John Njoroge, serving with the Ravi Zacharias team in Kenya; and lifelong friends Jim and Stephanie Boyd, church planters in Alaska.

—Gary Comer

*"Praise be to the L<small>ORD</small> my Rock,
who trains my hands for war, my fingers for battle."*
—Psalm 144:1

# CONTENTS

Foreword.............................................................................................19

   1. Name-Dropper ............................................................22

   2. Designing Skyward ......................................................38

## PART I
## CULTURE: SHAPING THEIR INTERFACE

   3. The Pattern .................................................................59

   4. The Permeation ...........................................................75

   5. The Posture .................................................................93

   6. The Process ...............................................................116

## PART II
## CHANNEL: EMPOWERING THEIR INFLUENCE

   7. Tipping the Tower.......................................................139

   8. Pinpointing the Flow .................................................158

## PART III
## COURSE: CHARTING THEIR INSTRUCTION

   9. Your Path Design.......................................................181

  10. Step In.......................................................................195

  11. Step On .....................................................................215

  12. Step Up .....................................................................232

  13. Step Out....................................................................250

  14. Leader Legacies .........................................................279

**AFTERWORD**

    In the Trenches of ReMissioning....................................................297

**ADDENDA**

    A.  Conversational Lines to Reach Muslims......................................317

    B.  The Top 10 Mission Skills ("Must-haves" for All Christians) ...332

    C.  The Path Model.........................................................................334

About the Author.............................................................................336

# FOREWORD

*The deepest motive for mission is simply the desire to be with Jesus where he is, on the frontier between the reign of God and the usurped dominion of the devil.*
*—Lesslie Newbigin*

It is time to take an honest look at the church in North America, as well as to examine the churches we serve. For though there are more mega-churches today than ever before, there are fewer people who self-identify as Christians. As a result, we are not seeing God's kingdom become a greater reality in our neighborhoods and cities. If we are going to be the church in a life-giving way in our current context, and flourish in our missional calling, we need to assess ourselves as leaders and examine our methodologies in light of God's coming future.

An honest assessment of reality will alert us to the fact that making simple cosmetic changes to our current programs is not sufficient. Better-produced Sunday experiences will not help us meaningfully engage the people to whom God has sent us. We need more insightful and incisive changes if we are to see the church flourish in all the ways God desires.

What is needed? We need reoriented leaders and a re-missioning of the church.

While leadership includes communicating, casting a vision, and creating culture, far and above all else, leadership is about being an example. In particular, we need leaders who desire God and his kingdom, and who embody what it means to join him in the renewal of all things. We need to lead people into mission, which requires more than just *instruction*. People need leaders who are *immersed* in mission, who lead lives worth *imitating*. For more is caught than taught, and people are more likely to do what we do, not just what we say. As Gary Comer says, "Who *you* are as a leader, and who *they* become as disciples, will shape the outcome of the entire movement."

Besides reorienting our lives as leaders, we also need to re-mission the church. This is what Gary Comer helps us to do in this book. He guides us by helping us to make challenging assessments and to engage in the work of "rethinking and redesigning." We need to consider the *pattern* that Jesus set for us, and allow his example to *permeate* our way of life. This means that "form must match formation." We must move past pure lecture and cognitive learning to cultivate laboratories where people engage in experiential learning, where their *posture* is "profoundly honest, deeply humble, grace oriented, and missionally focused."

Cultivating a missional culture also requires creating a *process* that allows us to become a community that welcomes people into God's family and helps shape people to become mature disciples who *live in* the world *for the sake* of the world *in the way* of Christ. Gary gives us some guidelines to develop a thoughtful process by which we help people live on mission.

By nature, the church is movement. If we are not experiencing movement, we need to examine the reasons why. Too often, our approach to leadership creates bottlenecks to mission. Gary helps us to move from being what he calls "vertical leaders" to "horizontal leaders," so that through the power of the Spirit, we can unleash the full potential of the body of Christ. We need to equip our fellow priests to build deep relationships and learn to share the good news in a way that connects with the heart and soul of those who don't yet know Christ. This requires us to grow in our ability to understand people's true need and to share the gospel in such a way that speaks to their life.

As a prophetic evangelist, Gary calls us to develop a path of instruction and a form of discipleship that help the whole body steward the Great Commission well. He tells us, "If your church or ministry does not have a steady stream of living, breathing new believers coming into the faith, growing as disciples, and reaching ever-extending networks of people, you have veered off course." If you realize this to be true of the congregation you are leading, you will find this book extremely valuable, for it is clearly born out of the experience of someone living out the Great Commission well.

Some might argue with Gary's proposal that healthy spirituality flows out of mission instead of mission being the by-product of health. In my experience, Gary is right on with his statements "You have to go to grow" and "If we do not have mission, we do not get Christlike people." For when we walk with people and immerse ourselves in mission together, in this place of liminality, people are drawn to spiritual practices as a way to sustain themselves on mission and to live out a risk-taking kind of faith. On the other hand, if the community to which I'm inviting the non-Christian to become a part is unhealthy, I'm likely to feel hesitant to bring in others. So, you will need to decide which comes first: the chicken or the egg? Either way, mission is necessary if we are to live out our calling as the sent people of God.

Gary Comer writes in a way that pulls us into what he has to say. He captures us through stories and offers proverbial wisdom on how to cultivate an evangelistic culture where everyone learns to share his or her faith in personal and dynamic ways. This is a book I will recommend to all those with whom I work. It's a timely message for all. I have found that nothing breathes new life into an old or new congregation better than new people coming to faith. This is probably one reason why Paul told Timothy, "*Work at telling others the Good News, and fully carry out the ministry God has given you*" (2 Timothy 4:5 NLT).

—*JR Woodward*
National Director, The V3 Movement
Author, *Creating a Missional Culture*
Co-author, *The Church as Movement*

# —1—

# NAME-DROPPER

> It's unbelievable how much you don't know about the game you've
> been playing all your life.
> —Mickey Mantle

I was not always a name-dropper. However, growing up in a rural retirement hot spot named Fallbrook in northern San Diego County, I became close friends with Stuart Milner, son of Martin Milner, star of a popular TV show called *Adam-12*. (If perchance you are drawing a blank, it was a '70s series about two LA beat cops.) Other than Martin Milner, I have shaken hands with only a handful of celebrities, and I've known even fewer "bigs" in the church. Looking back, I see how my humble upbringing kept the practice of name-dropping at bay. Yet, as the domino falls, all this changed in 2012, when something occurred that would label me a "name-dropper."

It began when Columbia Pictures released the movie *Moneyball*, which was nominated for six Academy Awards, including best picture. If you watched this premiere film and paid attention to the early story development, then you saw "Mt. Carmel High School" emblazoned on the front of the jersey worn by Billy Beane, the young general manager of the Oakland Athletics. Brace yourself. Are you ready? I played high-school sports against Billy Beane—not only baseball, but football and basketball, too. I remember having to face the super-tall, All-American ace pitcher, as he was depicted in the movie, and not faring well at the plate. Surely, he would not remember me—just another K in the books. Decades later, after experiencing his own dream-ending curveball, Beane became famous in another way.

*Moneyball* tells his story—it depicts his painful and mystifying disappointment as a professional baseball player, followed by his rise to become one of the most innovative Major League general managers the game has ever known. Based on the book *Moneyball: The Art of Winning an Unfair Game*, by Michael Lewis,[1] Beane's life, as depicted in the movie by the same name, illustrates what happens when *hard assessment meets innovative thinking.* Beane spurred one of baseball's most thrilling seasons, when the Oakland A's took a lowball budget and a hodgepodge roster of rejects, and made one of the greatest runs in baseball history. As the winning streak continued, culminating in a record-setting twenty consecutive victories, one fan held up a sign that read, "We May Never Lose Again!" As it turns out, the A's did lose in the American League championship series, and their Cinderella story fell short.

In spite of the letdown, and even though Billy Beane, in the aftermath, chose to decline the lottery-level offer to become general manager for the Boston Red Sox, his story surpasses all others, in my opinion. What other baseball front-office executive do you know whose life story has been retold in both a book and a full motion picture (with his character played by Brad Pitt, no less)? As for his impact, alongside number-crunching statistics guru Peter Brand, Beane transformed the way people think about America's national pastime. Due to Beane's influence, such teams as the Arizona Diamondbacks, the Boston Red Sox, the Cleveland Indians, the New York Yankees, San Diego Padres, the St. Louis Cardinals, the Toronto Blue Jays, the New York Mets, and the Washington Nationals now employ full-time sabermetric analysts.[2]

But make no mistake: Beane was the pioneering trailblazer who went first. Consider what it took. He alone had to size up their unwinnable predicament, overcome the traditionalists, push back the naysayers, squelch his own doubts, and hold faith in a previously untried system that he was

1. Michael Lewis, *Moneyball: The Art of Winning an Unfair Game* (New York, NY: W. W. Norton & Company, 2003, 2004).
2. Keith Woolner, "Aim For The Head: Aim For The Front Office," *Baseball Prospectus* (May 4, 2007). http://www.baseballprospectus.com/article.php?articleid=6187 (accessed September 9, 2011).

convinced could beat the system! That description, in my view, captures Major League leadership. For this, Beane deserves the notoriety and accolades he's received. So, I drop his name close to mine...often.

What may not be as crystal clear is that you, as a church leader, face a similar predicament. Do you realize that the deck is stacked against you and against the success of your group, mission, or church? We could lay down on the table quite a few cards that do not line up in your favor. Though I write to Christians on all continents, let me begin in my own backyard.

## THE NEW PLAYING FIELD

Right now, in the second decade of the third millennium, gospel influence is waning in Christianity's North American stronghold (not to mention in other regions). Though I could amass a great amount of support for this claim, which could include the free fall of "mainline" attendance, let me just note one *Washington Post* article citing LifeWay Research on America's largest denomination—the evangelical Southern Baptist Convention (SBC). SBC gathered in 2015 to report multiyear declines of baptisms and members (204,000), the largest in over a century.[3] This snapshot is symptomatic of a careening culture where overwhelming forces of secularism, pluralism, hedonism, relativism, and moralism, as well as insider issues of institutionalism, consumerism, and isolationism, throw nasty curveballs.

As we, like Billy Beane sizing up the next season, look ahead to what is coming on the horizon, I wonder whether we are even remotely prepared for the wave that is building. In a doctoral-level class I attended, the professor gave a sci-fi-like forecast of the future church: a global population of 9.7 billion projected by 2050, with detailed data on numerical expansion in every major U.S. city, and with an escalating infusion of immigrating families beyond Christian moorings.[4] Afterward, I was not the only one who felt as if he'd been socked in the stomach. The imminent need of reaching increasing numbers of people from ever-distant, non-Christian starting

3. Thomas S. Kidd and Barry Hankins, "Here are three reasons why Southern Baptists are on the decline," *The Washington Post* (June 16, 2015).
4. Bob Rowley, "Reproducing Clinic 101: An Introduction to Church Multiplication" (presentation at Talbot Theological Seminary, La Mirada, California, June 11, 2010).

points caused me to feel ill. During a break, feeling queasy, I walked outside to pray.

At the time, I was beginning to dabble with new thoughts on where the church needed to go. In response to a proactive paper I had written on creating evangelistic synergy, a leader inquired, "Are we really that bad?" Her honesty resonated with me. In deference to many tremendous churches and ministries, from a general perspective, I find it hard to imagine the church with a larger and more complex challenge. I get that it's a big statement. So, without going into elaborate layers, let me back my contention with five quick bullet points that encapsulate more precisely what we are facing.

+ First, we are in a mass cultural transition; and, as usual, the church is lagging. As to adjustments, we have not expanded our peripheral vision nearly enough to include the pervading post-Christian target.

+ Second, the rising populace is exceeding the scale of our workforce and the range of their skills. In what is now a globally pluralistic era, we will need to reach divergent worldviews. The frontier is at our doorstep, and yet the vast majority of church members are unprepared for the required engagement.

+ Third, we have gravitated away from the unsaved, both as individuals and as the church at large. Our spiritual formation patterns tend to undercut mission from a sociological point of view. Oddly, that which is spiritually good detracts us from the calling that is great.

+ Fourth, churches remain stuck in the dark ages of yesterday's evangelism—overly simplistic paradigms that are unappealing to church members and have lost their efficacy. For these reasons and more, whole sectors of today's church have abandoned the big "E" altogether.

+ Fifth, many surveys, including the telling American Religious Identification Survey (ARIS), indicate that the irreligious sector—popularly called the "nones"—is growing in a rapid, European-like shift, and sizable percentages of people are no longer coming in through the front door of the church.[5] Compounding this trend from the inside, we also have the "dones"—those who have left or are leaving their local steeples for good, sending dire signals about church, its leadership, programmatic machinery, and a disillusioning vacuum felt by those within its walls.[6]

## RE-MISSION DIALING

Moving from the wide-angle view to a zoom lens, the biggest challenge of all is to turn the church into a culture-penetrating entity again. This feat will require Beane-like recalibration. We'll need to earmark every one of the above bullet points for mission overhaul: how we relate to the culture, how we go to wider circles, how we reinterpret spiritual formation, how we reframe evangelistic engagement, and how we reach a drifting populace outside and stop the bleeding inside. It is a daunting challenge, but I believe there's a way to do it.

As to this process, which I have termed *ReMission*, it is my conviction that nothing else will be of greater benefit to the health and vitality of your fellowship. The term *re-mission* is pregnant with meaning. Most of us hear it and think of remission in cancer patients. I certainly am tapping into that sentiment, and more. From Middle English and Old French, *remiterre* means "to let go; to cancel free their punishment; to give relief from suffering; and to restore to a former status or condition." The first three descriptors match the grace ministry of the gospel: the letting go of one's past, the cancellation of the debt and penalty of sin, and the relief of suffering (at the level of both the individual and society). Beautiful! Each of these elements will play out in this book for the inspiration of you and the people you lead. But it's the fourth description—the restoration of the status and conditioning of the church—that is my primary focus within these pages.

What I am eliciting is the responsibility of church leadership to hone its methodology in order to achieve Christ's ultimate aims for his body. It

---

5. American Religious Identification Survey (ARIS 2008), principal investigators Barry A. Kosmin and Ariela Keysar, Trinity College, Hartford, CT. The sampling of 54,461 indicated an almost doubling of non-religious identifiers from 8.2 percent in 1990 to 15 percent in 2008. Available at www.ebony.com/wp-content/uploads/2012/05/aris030609.pdf.
6. Josh Packard and Ashleigh Hope, *Church Refugees: Sociologists Reveal Why People Are Done with Church but Not Their Faith* (Loveland, CO: Group, 2015), 2.

is apparent that in the life of the average church member, the church is not succeeding with either mission intent or extent. Scores of pastors I have talked with want to see their people become more missional and mobilized, but these pastors are stumped on how to pull this off. I don't believe it's possible to make prolific disciples using the methods of many churches today. How can anyone countermand what I am saying when what we are doing is not achieving the vibrant mobilization we so desperately need? Of course, I am talking in aggregate terms. Yet the facts and faces say the same thing. Whether I'm looking at statistics or looking into the eyes of the people I am training, it is clear that we have mass numbers of receptacles, yet few effective representatives. *ReMission* seeks to restore the status and conditioning of church membership as a movement. Like the restoration of someone from illness to health, it is what we are meant to be.

> SCORES OF PASTORS I HAVE TALKED WITH WANT TO SEE THEIR PEOPLE BECOME MORE MISSIONAL AND MOBILIZED, BUT THESE PASTORS ARE STUMPED ON HOW TO PULL THIS OFF. I DON'T BELIEVE IT'S POSSIBLE TO MAKE PROLIFIC DISCIPLES USING THE METHODS OF MANY CHURCHES TODAY.

It's now that I'm going to divulge my whopping billion-dollar idea: *Health flows out of mission rather than mission being the by-product of health.* Not only is this notion crazily counterintuitive in its leaning; it is perhaps antithetical to what you have thought or been taught. You may have heard this mantra: "Make disciples, and you will get mission." I'm arguing just the opposite: *Do mission to get disciples.* Now, you don't have to agree with me immediately, or ever; but I earnestly plead that you would hear me out. In the chapters ahead, I will lay out my reasoning, and maybe—just maybe—I will succeed in moving the pendulum of your thinking.

There is power in seeing something with stark-naked clarity. I love how Jesus took all the possible issues he could have addressed with the young rich ruler and synthesized them all down into a single phrase: *"One thing you lack"* (Mark 10:21). The guy had a mountain-sized pile of errant views, and Jesus boiled it down to a single malady. If we take a sweeping panorama of modern Christendom and boil it down to the crux of our collective issue, I submit that the "one thing" the church needs is *ReMission*. As it was to the enslaving idolatry of the young ruler's heart, the antidote is deeply spiritual and life-revolutionizing. Had the rich young ruler heeded Jesus' instructions to release his worldly goods and bless the poor, he would have been blessed beyond measure, being invited into the greatest call and cause ever offered to man—the call to join Jesus in his kingdom work. The weight of the invitation to "Come, follow me" would haunt him for the rest of his days. Thinking he could merely add eternal life to his shareholdings, he missed true life altogether.

GIVE YOUR PEOPLE VIABLE MISSION,
AND YOU WILL HAVE GIVEN THEM
A MEANS TO SPIRITUAL LIFE AND HEALTH
AS THEY BECOME TRUE DISCIPLES OF JESUS.

Give your people viable mission, and you will have given them a means to spiritual life and health as they become true disciples of Jesus. But allow your people to maintain the ideological foothold that what they truly need is to satisfy themselves, spiritually speaking (in a consumeristic sense), and you will have a bunch of huddled, dysfunctional, intellectual sickos on your hands, all of them drowning in endless, self-aggrandizing stanzas of *Oceans*—but whose lives are not worthy of Christ or his gospel. To carefully qualify, I am not saying we don't need internalized growth; I'm saying we need a whole other kind of growth in order to be vitalized.

The theory I am putting under scrutiny has been tested before. Past experiments with renewal have sought to correlate the relationship between spiritual nurture and mission impetus. During the '60s and '70s, thousands of books addressed the subject—titles such as *Journey Inward, Journey*

*Outward; A Quest for Vitality in Religion;* and *Dry Bones Can Live Again.* Elton Trueblood, in his book on renewal, *The Company of the Committed,* speaks of a "valiant band for Christ" who would revitalize the church and culture, stating: "We have around us many new frontiers, but the most un-explored of all frontiers is that of loving fellowship."[7] The main idea he pos-tulates is that intensive spiritual renewal inside the Christian community will generate inner passion that will propel believers outward for Christ.

In retrospect, did it happen? No! You've got to hear the reason curtail-ing the anticipated mission bounce. The participants receiving the spiritual inputs never felt "whole" enough. Howard Snyder, in his groundbreaking work *The Problem of the Wineskins,* identified the problem of turning in-ward.[8] As soon as people focused upon themselves and their own growth, they couldn't break the ingrown cycle: *I have lack. Feed me. A little bit more. Still more.* Can you see it? Unhealthy. Sick. Anemic.

Fast-forward forty or fifty years, one finds valuable extenuating per-spective to be added to the mission empowerment equation. (The funda-mental difference I have with all the renewal books is not the heart but the "how-to.") I am not a polemist merely seeking analysis, but an analyst and a practitioner seeking a solution. With eyes on the prowess of God's people, I will get practical to help you grow and expand your reach.

I may take some shots for my upside-down thesis that *doing mission is the means to becoming a bona fide disciple,* but in the famous words of history, "Here I stand." If we do not have mission, we do not get Christlike people. Just so we are clear: When I use the words "mission" or "missional," I am speaking inclusively of evangelism (granted, some people prefer the term "making disciples"). By my definition, the mission of God (*missio Dei*) extends to those who are outside the existing body of redeemed followers in full line with God's prescribed purposes. Otherwise, in God's bookend-ed "last-days" age for salvation, we were preaching to the choir. (See Acts 2:14–21.) In chapter 3, "The Pattern," I will delve into my theme with far more development on this qualitative discipleship. For now, I am scratch-ing the metal, hoping to get a small amount of paint to stick.

7. Elton Trueblood, *The Company of the Committed* (New York, NY: HarperCollins, 1979), 7.
8. Howard A. Snyder, *The Problem with the Wineskins: Church Structure in a Technological Age* (Dovers Grove, IL: Intervarsity Press, 1975), 17.

The truth that I am going after is known in the general world. Why does the counselor see the need for counselees to *get out of themselves* and go serve somebody else? Because he knows that if the counselees remain focused on their own problems, they will remain stuck! Why does the process of recovery from alcoholism involve the twelfth step of reaching out to help another? Because this outreach step is a critical aspect to maintaining sobriety. Why does the physical therapist insist that his patients exercise? Because they need to build muscular strength. How many sermonettes and Bible studies will be enough to finally prompt Christians do what Jesus called them to be doing all along? And how can we describe any tree as "healthy" that does not produce its intended fruit?

THE DYNAMIC WORK OF THE SPIRIT, EMPOWERING EVEN BRAND-SPANKING-NEW BELIEVERS, OCCURRED AS THEY WENT ON MISSION FOR HIM. SO DID MUCH OF THEIR LEARNING.

Commenting on an article about evangelism in *Christianity Today,* one reader posted, "The church (overall) in America is dying because we don't focus or spend time with God. If we did, the Holy Spirit would come to control our lives and we'd be passionate about what Jesus is passionate about."[9] There it is! This individual has bought the classic argument for renewal—hook, line, and sinker: *Wait upon God to transform you before you do mission.* With the assumption that there is more for God to do, renewal—or its close cousin "revival"—is the missing piece.

At first glance, this appears to be precisely the same thing that played out with the disciples who gathered in the Upper Room until the appointed time of Pentecost, when God poured forth his Spirit. Yet the Upper Room

9. Jack, February 15, 2016, comment on Ed Stetzer's "Amplifying Evangelism—The Future of Outreach and Mission: When evangelism meets pluralism, what's the Christian to do?" *Christianity Today,* (February 12, 2016). Available at: http://www.christianitytoday.com/edstetzer/2016/february/amplifying-evangelism-future-of-outreach.html?start=1 (accessed March 22, 2016).

was a once-in-history exception for Spirit-void believers. This is apparent from the fact that every time thereafter, when Luke uses his fave-phrase "filled with the Spirit," he is referring to gospel mission. The normative pattern in the Bible is not *Wait to be filled*, it's *Filled to fulfill*. Can you see the difference? God's filling happens in and for his continuing work.

To me, this distinction is significant. The dynamic work of the Spirit, empowering even brand-spanking-new believers, occurred as they went on mission for him. So did much of their learning. From what we see in the early writings, they were not focused on themselves; nor were they spiritually dry, as we sometimes claim to be, or barren of missional fruit, like so many of our members.[10] No longer were they seeking a "green light" from God. Instead, they saw their lives as an extension of his. Perhaps their close proximity to Jesus' earthly life had something to do with that. But what we do know is, gospel messaging was instrumental to their lives and growth in every possible way. It is why I tell churches and Christians, "You have to go to grow."

It is also noteworthy that the pioneering thrust of the early Christians, which bloomed in vitality to a virtual takeover by the fourth century, occurred bereft of church buildings and control centers.[11] In the embryonic stages, they didn't even have Bibles. My gosh! What did they have? They had mission. They had a message that many were willing to die for. Can anyone tell me that we are healthier than they were? Before you dismiss my premise prematurely on the grounds of its being imbalanced, please know that I am all for Bible study; in fact, my published works prove that I am a major advocate of discipling others and tooling them to develop spiritual intimacy with Christ. But when it comes to diagnosing our greatest issue, we've got it backward. And it's killing us.

## NEW ARCHITECTURE NEEDED

The reason we do not see waves of prolific missional Christians rising from our ranks today is that our problem is systemic, rooted deeply

---

10. Michael Green, *Evangelism in the Early Church* (Grand Rapids, MI: William B. Eerdmans, 1970), 166–193.
11. Rodney Stark, *The Rise of Christianity: How the Obscure, Marginal Jesus Movement Became the Dominant Religious Force in the Western World in a few Centuries* (New York, NY: HarperCollins), 56–57.

in church tradition and popular market culture. Like chemotherapy, this book will attack the virulence head-on. I believe the developmental process explained herein works regardless of a church's platform or cultural positioning. I am not charging you to be something that is not befitting of your vision; I only want to see your church, group, or agency have exceptional impact.

> WHAT WE MUST AVOID AT ALL COSTS IS BECOMING JUST ONE MORE ASSEMBLY OR ASSOCIATION THAT MERELY TALKS ABOUT THE VALUE OF MISSION WHILE BEING INEFFECTIVE AT CARRYING IT OUT.

What we must avoid at all costs is becoming just one more assembly or association that merely talks about the value of mission while being ineffective at carrying it out. *ReMission* is about what you galvanize in and through your people for real effect. I am not swinging for air! Follow the precepts I will lay out in this book, and your church, group, or agency will raise its game. The formational concepts and skills introduced in these pages apply to everyone: the newbies, the rejects, the underdogs, the misfits, the maturated, the movers, and all. In truth, I don't think there is anything under heaven more important than our present subject. We get to experience what the psalmist writes, *"My heart is stirred by a noble theme"* (Psalm 45:1). When it comes to Jesus' call, you won't get half-measures here. My heart burns. Like the pen needle of a tattoo artist, may it sear you!

Let me be up-front at the outset—it will take smarts, sweat, and capital to erect this kind of "outfra-structure." It's easier to do a service. The challenge becomes plain as you see few Christian entities functioning at even a Minor League level. When I examine a church for the purpose of consultation work, what I typically see is a hybrid of attractional structure (aimed at reaching people via the service) and renewal-based thinking (the belief that feeding the flock will foster outward seeding). As much as this mainstay has its strengths, the combination is also the source of our anemia—and, you might say, our need for an enema. Attraction is limited; renewal is a lie. The remedy to both is found in developing new mentalities and revamped training with the capacity to summon our greater potential: *ReMission*. Throughout this book, I will share insights gleaned from an architectural icon, the Roman Aqueduct, to inspire conceptual thought. As to what could be released through the body, take heart—the twenty-first-century church is the untapped mother lode of transformative springs!

To show you just what we are up against, however, I offer this caveat to something I believe in very strongly. Just because a church has a discipling program in place and emphasizes the process of making disciples does not mean that it is effective. The aim is right, but when I observed these types of efforts during a case study of a major congregation in a sampling of community group members, the figures I tallied were sobering when it came to reaching people outside the church.[12] As one person said, "Discipling disciples is one thing; making disciples is quite another."

You don't have to take my word for it. Go survey a sample of your regular, presumably "mature and healthy" Christians, and ask them to tell you the last time they led someone to Christ. Whom have they been reaching toward or discipling of late? What names and exciting stories can they offer? And how deep is the thrust of their mission zeal? Granted, there will always be a few shining exceptions; but unless your ministry circle stands above the rest, the results you find will not buoy any optimism. Based on the compilations of researcher Ryan Kozey of *Christ Together*, 73 percent of Christians had no effectual sharing relationships with anyone outside God's family. Asked to give the number of people they were reaching toward, the most common response—what they call the "mode"—was zero.[13] (Multiple reasons exist for this isolating ineffectiveness, not just a lack of

---

12. Community Group Outreach Survey, Riverside, CA (July, 2014). The survey, conducted with a sizeable congregation, revealed missional growth and progress of the members but limited measurable impact on reaching unbelievers.

13. Ryan Kozey, "Your Church on Mission: What's It Going to Take?" (presentation at Southwest Church Planting Forum, October 29, 2014). The *Missional Behavior Survey* by Ryan's network, Christ Together (with a sampling of tens of thousands), provides a telling picture of the body's evangelistic anemia. Waiting for publication.

love for the lost.) Evangelistic disciple-making remains our weakest pulse, hands down.

Even if the broad base were suddenly engaged, another barrier exists. Hear the words of a leading player from a prominent church in Texas, who, after eyeing my book's first chapters, sent these comments to my assistant:

> I have been encouraging our pastor to come up with a vision for our church especially after The Global Leadership Summit. What I have also mentioned is that a vision will be worth nothing unless you give our church body the skills and competencies to carry it out. This is the most difficult piece of execution. I get the sense in our church that our people don't know what to do even though their hearts would like to engage.[14]

She nailed it! Her insight is worth repeating, in paraphrase: *Vision without skills and competencies accomplishes nothing.* And she was right—it's the most difficult part. To close that gap, coded numerically within the narratives of *ReMission* are 10 skills all Christians should learn and practice in order to influence others for the gospel. To fuel the movement further, take notice and teach them! But be sure to put them into practice in your life first. Believers need worthy role models as they endeavor to live out mission.

This woman's characterization straddles the spectrum where statistics have plateaued or declining churches outnumber growing ones four to one (80 percent not growing); and among the 20 percent of elite performers, much of the growth is from Christian transfers.[15] Though the megachurch phenomenon expands, actual growth (conversion) is not keeping up with population expansion.[16] This explains why the Pew Research Center has projected that Islam will surpass Christianity as the largest world religion, because they are basing it on natural growth (families born into the

14. Sandi Dillon, e-mail message to author's assistant, October 2, 2015.
15. Jared C. Wilson, *The Prodigal Church: A Gentle Manifesto against the Status Quo* (Wheaton, IL: Crossway, 2015), 35.
16. Sally Morgenthaler, "Worship as Evangelism: Sally Morgenthaler Rethinks Her Own Paradigm," *Rev!* (May/June 2007), 49–51. Available at: http://nancybeach.typepad.com/nancy_beach/files/morgenthaler_article.pdf.

religion), not having Christian conversion-growth as a significant factor in play.[17] If you think this factoring criterion is being made in error, you are mistaken. As a church-planting coach for a prominent denomination, I routinely perused reports from the planters. Given that church planting is often hailed as the leading thrust of Christ's movement, you would think the data would be brimming with fruitfulness. Not so! Most church plants were reaching few. Some plants' results over months and even years were nil.

> **THOUGH EVERY CHRISTIAN CHURCH SHOULD BE A PLACE OF THE WIDEST INCLUSION, CHRISTIAN CULTURE HAS BEEN BECOME KNOWN AS ONE OF CLOSED MINDS AND CLOSED DOORS.**

Mind-set also troubles me. Though every Christian church should be a place of the widest inclusion, Christian culture has been become known as one of closed minds and closed doors. Yes, we praise God that we are reaching some—and we rejoice when even one is willing to join. However, conversions and new memberships are becoming rare. Even with our fancier stage sets and worship bands, the unsaved are not beating paths to the church doors. I value the belong-before-believe concept, and urge churches to leverage love within all their gatherings. That said, we have come to the place of thinking that if they don't come to us, we can't reach them. I am afraid that this view is creating its own self-fulfilling prophecy, with a dangerous isolationism resulting. It is a dagger to gospel mobility. I surmise the early church would have foreseen the self-imposed limitations and squashed it! Can we not reach anyone unless he or she comes to us? Does that barrier jive with our Bibles?

---

17. Bill Chappell, "World's Muslim Population Will Surpass Christians This Century, Pew Says" *NPR* (April 2, 2015). Available at http://www.npr.org/sections/thetwo-way/2015/04/02/397042004/muslim-population-will-surpass-christians-this-century-pew-says.

The new reality we must contend with is that increasing percentages of unsaved people are outside what I call the "joining circle." These are people who, even if invited by a friend, will not attend church—at least, not initially. Involved with CRU (Campus Crusade) at his college, my son Nate invited five of his disbelieving friends to an event and got five no's in reply. But are these five individuals willing to have a conversation with him? Absolutely. At Sandals Church, we addressed this issue directly, seeing how easy it was for unreached friends to skirt an invitation to church and have it go nowhere. We have to learn how to step up to a new plate. Though rarely intentional, codependency on pastors and church services is unhealthy for members, hindering movement and growth. We must reexamine the parameters and retool accordingly.

Please know I am not alluding to church members merely telling others about the gospel, but rather redefining what it means for ordinary Christians to have dynamic, relationally oriented spiritual influence where they live. This is where the church's greatest potential lies. It is where the culture is headed, so we must maximize it. And one more thing: Is it not all too common that the believer, once churched, finds himself separating from the lost for what can become years ad infinitum? What I have been picturing might sound overpitched, but there's striking truth here!

——

During our watch—right within our sight of the shore—a tide is rising *outside* us. I am referring to those people in arm's reach of us on a daily basis: irreligious, skeptical, indifferent, progressive, pleasure-seeking, moralistic, forgotten, God-accusing; those who are ethnically aligned; and our coworkers and neighbors hitched to a variety of other faiths and fragmented "Cuisinart belief systems" of their own making. From a gospel penetration and cultural impact meter, the church does not resemble a movement. Please tell me, has there ever been a time when we needed that kind of resurgence more than now? So, I am asking: Who is going to remedy this? In our historic moment, who is going to course-correct? Who, if not you?

Just as Billy Beane had to think outside his box, are you willing to think afresh with me about how to take on a seemingly unwinnable scenario? The time is ripe for innovative leadership. When I read Stetzer and Bird's *Viral Churches*, a book all about church planting and expansion, I appreciated the refreshingly candid comments placed inside a later chapter regarding the declining North American church: "We are in the midst of a missiological mystery here in the West." And then, "Do not hesitate to innovate, and adjust your methods. You might find the key to the breakthrough that we all desire."[18]

What are these experts hinting at? Simply this: A silver lining exists. Hard realities bust boxes. Fact-facing sparks creative problem-solving. Leveraging dilemmas into a pivot is God's way; he knows blessing cannot come bereft of human impasse and struggle. Do breakthroughs occur that way in your life? They do in mine. I believe God wills to take his church to new levels. I wrote this book to help church leaders and mission-focused members envision what could happen when *hard assessment meets innovative thinking*. In each of the succeeding chapters, I will be making hard assessments to springboard your growth. You will get the chance to weigh my analysis and the corresponding *ReMission* principles. So, put on your thinking cap!

Friends, we can meet the challenge before us. We can elevate our capacity for gospel impact. But we will have to let go of the old models that are no longer enjoying the effect that they did in years past, and we must embrace the new ideas that arise from our present realities. We must venture into entirely new avenues of thought. I believe with all my being that you can become the mission catalyst that not only your church, but "the Church," needs!

---

18. Ed Stetzer and Warren Bird, *Viral Churches: Helping Church Planters Become Movement Makers* (San Francisco, CA: Jossey-Bass, 2010), 180–81.

# —2—

# DESIGNING SKYWARD

I have been afflicted with the belief that flight is possible.
—Wilbur Wright

From early school days, I have fond memories of the Wright brothers' story. Two words grab my imagination: *Kitty Hawk*. Being there to witness the first airplane flight would've been so cool! Just like many of the big things in life—raising godly kids, maintaining personal purity, fighting for your marriage, growing a vibrant church, reaching a secular world—what is earnestly sought is not easily achieved.

At the crest of the 1900s, the dream of manned flight was alive but still tantamount to fantasy. A mode of transportation we take for granted today was then a perplexing puzzle, a conundrum so difficult that it continually defied the human capacity to solve it. It was this challenge that led Wilbur Wright to request all existing knowledge on the matter from the Smithsonian Institute, believing in faith that the hour for human flight had neared.[19] Revisiting the historical account, I could not avoid the imprint of profound lessons—ones I will remember all my life.

In the end, it was not power that did it. The main competition had devoted their time to developing an exceedingly powerful engine. As with a stone skipped across the water, all you needed was enough force, so they thought.[20] Nor was the answer money related. The government-sponsored group had spent what was, at that time, a small fortune—$70,000 (an

19. James Tobin, *To Conquer the Air: The Wright Brothers and the Great Race for Flight* (New York, NY: Simon & Schuster, 2003), 1–4.
20. Ibid., 52.

amount that would be millions of dollars today), in comparison to the Wrights' menial $1,000 outlay.[21] Nor do we find the determiner tied to commitment level. Lots of people wanted to fly. Contenders from all over the globe—Germany, France, Brazil, and England—had tried with resolute zeal. One person had even died trying. Yet, up to that point, no one had been able to build a vehicle that could propel human beings through the air for any mentionable amount of time.

The secret was not lying in a Smithsonian vault or in the popular ideas regarding flight that were floating around at the turn of the century. What finally broke it open—what unlocked the mystery and released the boundless potential—came down to a single innovative concept: *interlinking design.*

Leaving guesswork behind, the Wright brothers discovered something no one else had. Regarding mechanized flight, the leading voices were plain wrong! Repeating successes at the lowest levels of altitude and distance, the Wright brothers alone, of all living people, had attained an understanding that would revolutionize our globe. Author James Tober recounts that at the New York City debut in 1909, "Wilbur told reporters, 'I have not come here to astonish the world.' But his impromptu flight around the Statue of Liberty did precisely that."[22]

## HARD ASSESSMENT: OVERSIMPLIFICATION

Examining the Wright brothers' achievement from a leadership lens has value, especially because, as you will see, it closely parallels our topic at hand. In fact, I propose there are two things that happened in the Wright brothers' story that must happen in ours, if we are serious about *ReMission.* The right mentality is a powerful thing. What did Orville and Wilber Wright do, exceptionally, to bring about this breakthrough?

In hindsight, it seems rather obvious now that putting the emphasis on power was a major mistake. Had the Smithsonian's lead guy, Professor Langley, assessed the problem more accurately, his name might have been the one made gloriously famous for having first achieved flight. The Wrights, on the other hand, learned to view the conundrum of manned

21. Ibid., 192.
22. Ibid., 215.

flight comprehensively. From their analysis, the flying machine problem was threefold: lift, control, and power. By first inventing a wind tunnel to test their research (which was conducted over a period of four years), they calculated the wing curvature that would create optimal lift, and then configured the apparatus to make aerial control possible. Make sure you get this difference. The key, for them, became harnessing lift for the purposes of balance and control. Engine power was the least of their concerns. Only after the procurement of stability and steering would the engine even be needed.[23] To this day, our modern world seems to think that all our problems are best solved with more power. Not so.

If you asked me to diagnose what is wrong with or missing from the church in the missional sense, you could pose it this way: Why is it that studies show a solid 75 percent of attending members are disengaged from God's prime mission thrust? (Christ Together's data and LifeWay's 2015 SBC research concur.[24]) And why do most Christians, knowing the gospel full well, reach so few with it? Dream with me here. Can you imagine what could happen if we could flip those numbers? It can happen. Immediately, two questions arise.

First: *Have we properly sized up the problem?* When I observe up-front leaders try to solve the mission dilemma through a sermon series or by giving simplistic answers in a quick plug or sound bite from the stage— believing that all their people need is to hear: (a) "Love others," (b) "Share your story," (c) "Live the faith," (d) "Be incarnational," or (e) "Just go tell them about Jesus"—I see a failure of leadership, however well-meaning. Paraphrasing author Garry Poole, "Let's not give two-cent answers to billion-dollar problems."[25] If mobilizing the whole church is our aim, the missional development of its members is a billion-dollar problem. If we fall short in sizing up the problem, no wonder we're still on the ground. Church leaders often fail to estimate the intricate levels of human insight, practical training, cultural reads, structural development, and experiential engagement necessary for members to become effective mission vessels. I

23. Ibid., 74.
24. Kidd and Hankins, "Here are Three Reasons Why Southern Baptists are on the Decline," June 16, 2015.
25. Garry Poole, *Seeker Small Groups: Engaging Spiritual Seekers in Life-Changing Discussions* (Grand Rapids, MI: Zondervan, 2003), 106.

will argue that these are all integral, not ancillary, to developing Christlike character and launching a gospel-centered mission. And in this, the church has made a huge mistake.

> CHURCH LEADERS OFTEN FAIL TO ESTIMATE THE INTRICATE LEVELS OF HUMAN INSIGHT, PRACTICAL TRAINING, CULTURAL READS, STRUCTURAL DEVELOPMENT, AND EXPERIENTIAL ENGAGEMENT NECESSARY FOR MEMBERS TO BECOME EFFECTIVE MISSION VESSELS.

In my experience of teaching an anti-human trafficking group how to come alongside victimized individuals and discern a pertinent gospel message—a skill that would sing healing hope to their souls!—one leader relayed, "I have no skills." Pause to imagine the vacuum she felt. I wasn't shocked. I've heard the same sentiment repeated a thousand times. Please note this person had been in the church for years—a solid, progressive, Bible-teaching church, by the way. She had heard innumerable biblical messages and yet remained virtually clueless as to how to go about the very thing the Bible was calling her to do. She, and most of the others in that training group, for that matter, did not understand how to seed the gospel effectively within their unique mission subculture, nor did they comprehend the faith-formation process of discipling a nonbeliever. I present to you this example of nonexistent mission quotient (MQ) only to say, once again, that there is a big gap to close.

Our second question is this: *Have we properly addressed the problem?* The realization of human flight required a design that dealt directly with the difficulties. In other words, the Wrights figured out exactly what problem needed to be solved. They addressed critically what others had neglected. Their competition: the brilliant minds of Langley and Maxim (from England), with their teams, failed to fathom the multidimensional scope of the answer. How many times have I seen church leaders miss or cut out factors that are crucial for developing people effective at sharing the gospel? Don't even ask. As I have attempted to articulate, the inertia we face is formidable. Oversimplification has been our nemesis.

## FROM GROUNDED TO SOARING

The first change of thinking we must make is to drop any notion that the problem can be solved by only one message, one effort, one push, one emphasis, or one program. If we minimize it, like Langley did, we will falter. Instead, let's take a bigger, more comprehensive approach in addressing the dilemma. That type of holistic thinking, by itself, will point us in the right direction and give us a realistic shot at a solution. Who *you* are as a leader, and who *they* become as disciples, will shape the outcome of the entire movement. What the Wrights did "right" was choose the proper approach to their obstacle. And, certainly, they had an inherent drive toward curiosity and discovery that unlocked innovation. Those are the kind of leadership qualities that we would do well to model in our own lives.

WHO *YOU* ARE AS A LEADER,
AND WHO *THEY* BECOME AS DISCIPLES,
WILL SHAPE THE OUTCOME OF
THE ENTIRE MOVEMENT.

In that vein, before we venture further, please don't overlook the significance of the word "brothers" in the story of the Wrights. Human flight was achieved through the highest level of *collaboration*. Are you asking yourself, *Who is it that I must invite to this study?* Mission infusion occurs in a team environment. Your act of inviting will honor and bless your people. The ideas and discussions about your church, group, or organization will be rich, and it is best that they be shared among the key players and colleagues, so that permeation may flow down and throughout each artery of the body. To facilitate this process, I have included some important questions and takeaways for your troop at the end of each chapter. Strap on your collective flight suit and goggles, and get ready to climb higher together, my friends!

All this is to say that I have no stomach for spinning wheels on the tarmac. I didn't write this treatise so that your church or mission would stay the same. But if you're not with me in sizing up the problem, you might miss the significance of the following sections that discuss the tackling of that problem. These three sections—(1) Culture: Shaping Their Interface, (2) Channel: Empowering Their Influence, and (3) Course: Charting Their Instruction—were not selected at random. I am not just trying to fill pages in a book. No, each section counts in a compounding way.

I've thought this through. What if you impart influential skills that are bereft of cultural shaping? Your efforts may crash and burn. Shaping their interface, or developing the ingrained values of relating, undergirds the skills of those you are training, boosting their influence in the most powerful of ways. Will we achieve a high rate of engagement and sending, apart from an intentional mission path? I don't think so. Remember Langley: Leave out one section, and you'll lack an integral part of the whole. Wasn't that a recipe for failure? Can you imagine a professional golfer focusing on only one part of his game? You wouldn't expect to see him in the winner's circle anytime soon.

Making progress in every arena is the only way to secure your group's missional development. "Oh, but I want it simple," some say. A singular sound bite? Simple? Sorry, it's just not possible. Raising a potent movement, like achieving human flight, is not easily accomplished. It demands a sophisticated, multifaceted design; skilled implementation; and, truthfully—let's just say it—smarter leadership to get it done. Don't be dismayed by the ascent of your climb. Something thrilling lies before you. You get to experience the adventure of doing the difficult! If you go hard after it, one day, your people will rise up and thank you that you did.

Besides taking a comprehensive approach, there is something else that is absolutely critical within the story of the Wright brothers. The four years they spent mastering the curvature of the wing symbolizes a massive leadership learning curve. I often wonder if leaders are clear on what God's task requires of them at the innermost level. What degree of stature and perseverance will it take to lead outward? Is it etched in our minds with crisp convictions? Do we even know? With great reverence for the path that God has taken you down already, I hope to use the chapters ahead to connect your leadership journey with mine. I want you to see how our paths might beneficially intertwine. Is that not the purpose of the body? I benefit from you, and you from me. Let me bring you into my story a little.

## THE MISSION CURVE

My wife and I began to zero in on the uniqueness of our firstborn son by the time he reached the age of four. Matthew's peculiar patterns started to emerge with greater clarity and confusion, leading two concerned parents to the doctor's office. Learning about Asperger's syndrome has been an education—not just about our bright, beautiful boy, but also about life, about people, and about ourselves. One big revelation was recognizing how much my own tendencies leaned in the same direction. In that way, Matthew and I have a bond. We are wired similarly. My mind, too, is always spinning. I like to say, "Why stay in the moment when there are so many other places to be?" Like Matthew, who is incredible at completing puzzles and whose mind sees pictures, I, too, am a visual thinker.

In search of understanding, my wife and I attended a lecture by autistic-born professor Dr. Temple Grandin called "Different Kinds of Minds."[26] When Dr. Grandin entered her forties, she had an epiphany that others did not see the world as she did. (If only more Christians could appreciate this insight.) From her research, she outlined four distinct types of minds: visual thinkers (photo-realistic), pattern thinkers (mathematical), verbal thinkers (a category populated by many church pastors), and auditory thinkers. Having autistic wiring herself, she identifies as a visual thinker. Her hand-drawn designs of how to better handle livestock not only landed her a prestigious job but also made her one of the nation's leading animal welfare advocates. She has authored multiple books, including *Thinking in Pictures*. As she talked about the various mind strengths and the reasons we need one another, I again noted how much I am like my son.

26. Temple Grandin, "Different Kinds of Minds" (presentation at University California Riverside, May 21, 2013).

In midlife, when God initiated the greatest redirection of my life—and, ironically, when I was most tempted to believe he was doing nothing—God began to unveil to me the purpose behind my pictorial way of thinking. I wrote my first book, *Soul Whisperer*, which features diagrams based on original drawings I'd done on paper or whiteboard to illustrate how influence unfolds in the human-spiritual dimensions. Writing from the position of outreach director at my church, I authored a four-book *Missional Engagement Series* using picture concepts to help churches do mission.

Returning to Dr. Grandin, another notable contribution of hers was distinguishing between "top-down" and "bottom-up" thinkers. Bottom-uppers form concepts from real examples. They pay attention to detail, scrutinizing how things work in the nitty-gritty. Top-down thinkers form a concept first, then make related applications. In this way, top-downers tend to get disconnected from the way things actually occur. This disconnect, by the way, is a weakness of many church leaders (who don't do details!), which I, from my experience as a consultant, will expose periodically and attempt to rectify for you or your team, when possible. Ergo, Dr. Grandin's argument: We need one another.

Leaving the lecture that night, I personalized her analysis. Like Dr. Grandin, I am a bottom-up type. Building and designing from the bottom up involves seeing how something works with great specificity. This realization explained why I had struggled in earning my doctorate, while much of the content I was ingesting came from top-down, theoretical thinkers. I found myself questioning how these "experts" could champion the call to mission but remain, for the most part, unhelpful. One guy wrote a whole book on evangelism that was devoid of any stories about him actually doing evangelism. I'm not kidding. No *real people* were reached. Perusing his pages, I was bewildered. How could he write without actual, living, "HD" experience? My reaction mimicked that of the authors of *The Missional Quest* when they discovered that pastors and leaders who had read works by the missional camp's intellects (Alan Hirsch and Michael Frost) were still scratching their heads on how to get the conceptual theory moving in their contexts.[27] This lingering haze is precisely the predicament the

27. Lance Ford and Brad Brisco, *The Missional Quest: Becoming a Church of the Long Run* (Madison, WI: InterVarsity Press, 2013), 11.

church faces. If we do not redress the missing linkage between *what the church is* and *what the church does*, in living expression, we will not see what God longs to see lived out and fulfilled by his people.

The potency of good design, and its invaluable, enhancing contribution, is that it pictorially breaks down concepts and builds up from the bottom. That is what the Wright brothers did that others did not. If I can help you do more *picturing* and *bottom-up thinking*, I believe you will become a better leader. You will be able to empower your team and people more fruitfully, guaranteed! When you see what is occurring or needs to occur, you will rise as a leader, especially in the mission realm. There's much work and reading to do in order to reach our destination, so I charge you with holding on to these two concepts: (1) picturing and (2) bottom-up thinking. These practices will serve you well as we move forward. Throughout this book, I will introduce a variety of thematic terms—a technique of mine that will signal critical takeaways.

I DON'T CARE WHO YOU ARE, OR
HOW GREAT YOUR CHURCH, GROUP, MODEL,
OR MISSION IS; THE FACT REMAINS THAT
*IT CAN BE DONE BETTER.* YOU CAN LEAD BETTER.

Also inherent in its function, design always assumes we can do things *better*. Like the architect who knows he could have gone in another direction, design deals with potential options and outcomes. When I bump into a leader who is design-intuitive, I feel energized and excited over *what could be!* Without wading deeper, perhaps we should all acknowledge something about our situations. I don't care who you are, or how great your church, group, model, or mission is; the fact remains that *it can be done better.* You can lead better. Your people can execute much better. The church and its mission arms can do things with far greater influence and effect amid our increasingly shifting and lost world. Fixing our eyes on higher bars, we will find that improvement will be our modus operandi.

Fortunately, I do not have to wax on endlessly. How do I know that? Because you're reading this book! However, there is a trick to perform that will not occur by a mere wave of the wand. You see, visionary design cannot be merely ornamental to your leadership; rather, it must permeate your deepest core. I reckon that's a full-fledged cover-to-cover challenge. I hope you're ready for the whole ride. As to what God wants to do in you—I'm praying for magic! And now, my esteemed leader friends, let's now explore more of God's call on your life—the place of mission—and what this book will require of you.

Since you selected this book, I can surmise what's sitting before you, and perhaps your expectations.

+ Church planters—trying to get those ducks to line up, crank out another sermon, and survive another week. I've been there, twice. You're reading in the hope of its blessing your church, as in:

+ Pastors and staff—adding some new branches to your missional tree.

+ Campus ministers—wanting to better capture the coed crowd.

+ Organizational heads—aiming to project an optimal futuristic arc.

+ Group leaders—looking to turn community influence in missional directions.

+ Church members—seeking a rich kingdom-building conversation.

+ Missionaries—needing to draw in distant hearts from distant lands.

+ Missional warriors all—seeking to stomp out injustice for Jesus, everywhere.

In each case, wherever God has planted you, bring your brain—that powerful gift to be developed and stewarded. Upping the ante, here's one more for your traveler's checklist: Please pack your character, too! I have choice words on this topic, appropriately placed at the beginning of our journey. In the chapters ahead, you will find that your personal qualities matter. Design and character are inextricably linked. *ReMission* is ultimately about your own transformation. I surmise you didn't pick up this book with that idea in mind. Let me contextualize why I say so.

## LEAKY CHANNEL

Years back, when the results of Willow Creek's study entitled *Reveal: Where Are You?* first leaked, it was fascinating to gauge reactions across Christendom. Echoing voices were all too eager to offer their interpretive endorsement of the findings and, with puffed-out chests, gloried in declaring, "I told you so! See, you were wrong—you needed something more meaty like what we have at our church (of seventy-five)." In a blog, Ed Stetzer sums up how respondents embellished and even lied about what Bill Hybels and the report actually said.[28] Lied. Good job, Ed, for taking us to the mat!

> MANY CHURCH LEADERS APPEAR TO BE EITHER TOO INSECURE OR TOO ROMANTICALLY ENAMORED OF THEIR OWN MINISTRY TO GO TO THAT PLACE OF SEEING WHERE THEY ARE SUCCEEDING AND FAILING, AND BEING RECEPTIVE TO CHANGE.

Though salient insights did surface from the study, which examined Willow Creek and six other Willow Association churches and revealed a significant "self-feeding" discipleship gap with younger believers, and surprising levels of dissatisfaction with the older,[29] what *Reveal* also laid bare was that the Willow Creek group was willing to be honest. By taking off the rose-colored glasses to assess the results within their model, and simultaneously opening themselves up to scrutiny, they exemplify what every church and organization needs. You would think this kind of rigorous

28. Ed Stetzer, "Weeping for Willow's Disciples," *Christianity Today* (July 7, 2008). Available at: http://www.christianitytoday.com/edstetzer/2008/july/weeping-for-willows-disciples.html.
29. Greg Hawkins and Cally Parkinson, *Reveal: Where Are You?* (Chicago, IL: Willow Creek Association, 2008). Available at: https://www.willowcreek.com/ProdInfo.asp?invtid=PR35413. I fear the distorted interpretations of this report have created an unintentional result away from open evaluation, particularly at the large church and organization levels. See also: "What Reveal Reveals: Criticism of Willow's latest self-study does not undermine its value" *Christianity Today Editorial* (February 27, 2008), http://www.christianitytoday.com/ct/2008/march/11.27.html.

self-evaluation would be common, especially in ecclesiastical circles, which should be topping all lists for the most transparent of places. Yet many church leaders appear to be either too insecure or too romantically enamored of their own ministry to go to that place of seeing where they are succeeding and failing, and being receptive to change.

In my experience with consulting, I have visited churches in desperate need of help whose leadership believed they were fine overall. One pastor, whose church was struggling and reaching no one, stated the proverbial, "I know what I'm doing. I've been at this for twenty years." Meanwhile, at the other end of the spectrum, churches growing at a robust clip clamored incessantly for new insight. Look at the contrast from a consultant's diagnostic view. One is stymied and closed off to input; the other is growing and hungry for more. Do the math!

In an interview I did with church revitalization guru Ken Priddy, he compared church decline scenarios to the recovery movement, saying, "If the church leaders are not at the place of hitting bottom, they will continue to think that they know how to heal their broken church." In recovery circles, they say, "It's your thinking that got you here." According to Priddy, church leaders must own their failure. They must come to the place of brokenness, recognizing that they can't do it their way anymore.[30] Granted, you may be far removed from that despairing place, but should we not all possess this same humble, teachable spirit? Can you imagine what God could do with the exceptionally erudite leaders who would result?

Why do some people remain sponges for new wisdom, while others assume they've got it locked? It's a mystery. What is not a mystery, however, is how the leader's refinement pays huge dividends. When consulting, I often think, *If the pastor is willing to endure evaluative pain from me or another, speaking into their life and leadership, then the church will grow exponentially.* The equation goes like this: Leader's pain = church's gain. Or how about this language: "Your two-hundred-person church could grow to six hundred, if only you were willing to drop the pride and get help." But, time after time, church leaders lag in their learning vigor and settle for mediocrity. I recall when this occurred in my second church plant. For some reason, perhaps because I had planted a church before, I rested in my

30. Ken Priddy (church revitalization leader) in discussion with author, August 17, 2010.

knowledge, thinking I had it in the bag. To me, acquiring new knowledge was not imperative; and, as a result, my church paid the price.

## TIME AFTER TIME, CHURCH LEADERS LAG IN THEIR LEARNING VIGOR AND SETTLE FOR MEDIOCRITY.

Hugh Halter and Matt Smay have distinguished between the two primary church leader types: (1) Sodalic = "Scattered" – Go, and (2) Modalic = "Gathered" – Teach and obey. They estimate that a sizeable 90 percent of their readers operate in the modalic side.[31] They point out that, given this imbalance, and also considering the inherent challenges of a post-Christian era, we need Sodalic strengths.[32] Let me qualify: It is my professional opinion that no area requires greater levels of learning than mission. You may be thinking, *What else is there to know?* Evangelism. Mobilization. Disciple-making. Missional living. Church planting. Global missions. Don't we have that all sized up and dialed in already? I am here to tell you that not only are we not very effective today, but we know little of the revolutionary changes that are beckoning. The curvature is just beginning for where we need to go as a new missional epoch emerges. If God's leaders don't experience a mass L-curve (*ReMission*), their church or group will not rise above an impaired vision.

Compounding the "settling" conundrum is what the Heath brothers describe in their *New York Times* bestseller *Made to Stick*: "Once we know something, we find it hard to imagine what it was like not to know it."[33] For some rather odd reason that seems common to all of us, we human beings tend to have a difficult time unlearning what we have learned. How ironic

---

31. Hugh Halter and Matt Smay, *And: The Gathered and Scattered Church* (Grand Rapids, MI: Zondervan, 2010), 133.
32. Ibid., 133–34.
33. Chip Heath and Dan Heath, *Made to Stick: Why Some Ideas Survive and Others Die* (New York: Random House, 2007, 2008), 20.

that it's the old schemas that block new growth. With the ancient aqueducts, an ongoing problem was calcium buildup caused by lime leaching from the soil into the springs.[34] Can you see it? There's a residual attitude that occurs when knowledge builds up within leaders to the point of blocking the flow of fresh ideas and perspectives.

I have faced this type of calcification head-on, having participated in countless discussions about evangelism. One day, after hitting a wall with a certain church leader, I zeroed in on the word *intransigence*, which is basically a refusal to change one's views. It is why I feared the revisionist ideas expressed in my book *Soul Whisperer* were doomed from inception. At the time, my seminary had warned me that no one would publish a book on evangelism, and certainly not from a "no-namer" like me. Even though negativity shrouded the subject, no one seemed to be saying what I was saying: "Maybe we need to scrap it (our mode of thinking) for a whole new approach with a distinctly better skill set." Do you see this tension playing out with the pastor who rejects an idea put forth by an associate, saying, "I know what's best; I've been doing this my whole life"? The result is that the potential for innovation vanishes. There's no rethinking or changing course. In other settings, such a reaction by the leadership would be unthinkable; but in the church, it's all too common.

In contrast, consider the concept of "reengineering," which has gained wide acceptance in the business sector. (We will consider this topic in greater depth in later chapters.) Authors Michael Hammer and James Champy define the term this way: "'Reengineering,' properly, is the fundamental *rethinking* and radical *redesign* of business processes to achieve dramatic improvements...."[35] We're not talking patchwork remedies to provide a temporary fix, but rather about tossing aside prior assumptions in order to invent an entirely better way to do something. The authors continue, "We must ask the most basic questions...Why do we do what we do? And why do we do it the way we do it?"[36] Notice how one question relates to purpose, the other, to processes. Get this: The business culture has accepted the

---

34. A. Trevor Hodge, *Roman Aqueducts & Water Supply*, 2nd Edition (London, England: Bristol Classical Press, 1992, 2012), 109.
35. Michael Hammer and James Champy, *Reengineering the Corporation: A Manifesto for Business Revolution* (New York, NY: HarperCollins, 2001), 32.
36. Hammer and Champy, *Reengineering the Corporation*, 35.

idea that it is necessary to continually reengineer and redesign in order to remain viable. Leaders in business understand how quickly past practices become obsolete.

> THE BUSINESS CULTURE HAS ACCEPTED THE IDEA THAT IT IS NECESSARY TO CONTINUALLY REENGINEER AND REDESIGN IN ORDER TO REMAIN VIABLE. LEADERS IN BUSINESS UNDERSTAND HOW QUICKLY PAST PRACTICES BECOME OBSOLETE.

The church, however, is a different story. With dire ramifications, intransigence only compounds futility in a fast-changing culture that is increasingly fractured, global, differentiated, and suspicious. Remember Billy Beane in the movie *Moneyball*, making a passionate appeal in the boardroom: "You are not even seeing the problem. We've got to think differently. If we try to play like the Yankees in here, we will lose to the Yankees out there!"[37] As stuck in the ruts as we can be, and though perhaps it is still more the exception than the rule, many are open to new thinking, or, in business verbiage, *reengineering*. By escaping our status-quo trappings, we can embrace the shifting ground by reassessing, rethinking, and redesigning. Adapting more quickly and moving from static to dynamic principles and practices will help us hit real-time targets. Later on, I will highlight the distinction between these two concepts—static versus dynamic—to enhance your training. This change will increase your effectiveness in sustaining the motivation of the people you lead, keeping them on the edge of discovery and dependent upon the Spirit in all their mission endeavors. That's *ReMission* at its best!

The layers of innovations that have been built upon the Wright brothers' initial breakthrough to get us where we are today in the realm of aviation shows the rate and scope of change needed to meet the shifting culture of tomorrow. If you, as a church leader, have not already made it part of

---

37. *Moneyball*, DVD, directed by Bennett Miller (USA: Sony Pictures, 2011).

your culture's DNA, please work toward empowering ingenuity. You may want to make a few bold changes to get everyone accustomed to the new pace. Make sure they know clear well that anyone who is looking afresh at the challenge, as well as looking upward to God for inspiration, will be celebrated, even if the results of his attempts fall short of complete success. Let's kick down new doors! Get this type of mentality ignited in your members, and then watch out.

## OUR PIVOTAL TIME

Finding himself unexpectedly in the company of a group of U.S. fighter pilots, Scott had to think fast on his feet. Seizing the moment with his esteemed guests, speaking rather off the cuff, he asked which country's aerial fighters were rated second. Their reply surprised him.

"Actually, America is number two."

"Really?" he mused.

"The number one fighters in the world are in Israel," they shot back, then proceeded to give three reasons why. The first reason they identified was backing. Israel's air force receives a total commitment of resources. The second reason they cited was urgency. Israel's pilots get up every day to train, knowing that, any minute, it could be "game on" for the survival of their people. The third reason they offered was sharpness. If you are an Israeli fighter pilot, you retire at twenty-six. Research has revealed that once a person gets past his mid-twenties, contemplation of other concerns lessens his risk-taking edge. What a fascinating peek into the psyche of modern Israel and its frontline responders.

> IN THE CURRENT MISSION MALAISE, WE NEED MEN AND WOMEN WHO ARE PIONEERING ON THE EDGE AND INSPIRING OTHERS TO DO REMARKABLE FEATS.

From Scott's retelling of this conversation, I couldn't help but notice that the church could afford to make serious strides in all three areas:

*backing, urgency,* and *sharpness.* Yet it was the third term, *sharpness,* that was pinned to my psyche. How many of today's leaders have lost their edge? As pastors, regional leaders, mission gatekeepers, and seminar/conference promoters, it's easy to regurgitate our past training and sling out that old, leftover hash. We feel safe with clichéd teachings and corralled expectations. We stop believing we can break new ground that would far exceed where we've been and greatly surpass where others have settled.

I am not trying to push your competitive button here; but when it comes to our piloting mind frame, shouldn't we be pushing the envelope? In the current mission malaise, we need men and women who are pioneering on the edge and inspiring others to do remarkable feats. Are you ready to ratchet up your ranks of the faithful? Because, if you are, character-wise, it will take every bit of your leadership stature: honest evaluating, teachable humility, administrative initiative, creative imagination, dynamic adaption, expanding vision, courageous passion, pace-setting skills, and relentless persistence. The concepts we will discuss in *ReMission* require it all! Have you come to grips with the fact that the flow will rise only as high as you're able to go?

———

We have conducted some preliminary triage, and now we need to put things in order. Having properly assessed the problem, we will take a comprehensive view at tackling it. We have also looked within, getting our own hearts ready to catalyze missional formation.

Let's now enter the specs of the design. I will begin with "The Pattern," the cornerstone chapter of four culture-shaping pillars.

## *REFLECTIONS*

1. Do you agree that your specific calling must intersect with the Great Commission in order for you to be in the center of God's will? How so? Elaborate.

2. Why do you think some leaders keep in the learner's pocket, while others settle? Make a mental list. What traps have you fallen into, and how have you managed to escape them?

3. Do you agree that the learning curve for mission is just beginning? Why or why not?

4. How would you rate your personal mission quotient right now? Be brutally honest.

5. On a scale of 1–10, with 1 being the lowest and 10 being the highest, what level of leadership do you offer your people in the missional sense? If they were to rate you in this area, would their rating match yours?

## *REMISSION TAKEAWAYS*

1. It is important to invite your team into this learning discussion to begin the process of permeation into the body.

2. Due to the complexity of the mission-development conundrum, the mobilization challenge must be approached in a comprehensive, multifaceted fashion.

3. Both your learning and character curve must be high if you expect to raise the standard of your people.

# —PART I—
## CULTURE:
## SHAPING THEIR INTERFACE

# —3—

# THE PATTERN

Celebrity-worship and hero-worship should not be confused. Yet we confuse them every day, and by doing so we come dangerously close to depriving ourselves of all real models. We lose sight of the men and women who do not simply seem great because they are famous but are famous because they are great.
—Daniel J. Boorstin,
*The Image: A Guide to Pseudo-Events in America*

It is a highly celebrated work of art by one of the most celebrated artists of all time, so one can understand the controversy when the Uffizi Gallery in Florence, Italy, announced that it was planning to restore Leonardo da Vinci's *Adoration of the Magi*. The museum curators hoped to clean the canvas of the soiling that had accumulated over the centuries so that viewers could see the painting in its original colors. Adding to the tension was the invitation they extended to Dr. Maurizio Seracini, a Florentine man—whose innovative use of technology and revisionist ideas have threatened the art world's establishment—to assess what needed to be done.

Museum officials removed the bulletproof glass protecting the painting, thereby granting Seracini full access to the masterpiece so that he might determine if restoration were even possible. With all this hype and buildup, you can easily envision the firestorm that occurred when Seracini rather abruptly postulated that the famous painting admired through the centuries was not the work of da Vinci. What an outcry followed! How could anyone make such a claim? There were reasons.

Upon close examination, from naked eye to microscopic lens, Seracini found that the top paint layer had been applied much later than the drawing underneath, and that elements of the undercoat were missing, as if wiped from the canvas. And there was more. Seracini noticed some water stains on the back panel, the location and puddled pattern of which indicated that the painting had been lying facedown for quite some time. The idea of a painting of this magnitude, by a master artisan, lying in such a position and being exposed to water, is unthinkable. It sounds immediately suspect, until one considers the fact that da Vinci was to have done this work when he was only twenty-eight years of age, and little known as an artist.

Intrigue builds as we consider what might have occurred. The piece had been commissioned by some Augustinian monks for the purpose of an altarpiece. Yet what if the vision of the young artist went beyond the monks' traditional expectations? Could it be that when the artist delivered a more "revolutionary," radical reinterpretation of the scene they had requested, they found it unfitting for their worship space, and rejected it? That would explain what the hard evidence seems to point toward—that when the artist left the city in the late 1400s, the monks put his sketch in storage, where it would eventually fall to the floor, facedown.

Decades later, when da Vinci had made a name for himself, the discarded drawing would have become valuable and salable. With da Vinci in Milan, and not planning to return to Florence, Seracini theorizes that the piece must have been given to another artist, or artists, to finish—picking it up off the floor, rashly cleaning its frontal (and scratching off some of the paint in the process), drawing over the figures (as a kind of censorship, to make the piece acceptable), and completing the work.

If you have marveled at this masterpiece in the Uffizi, as I have, the hypothesis feels irreverent, at first. But the story, like this artwork, is not finished. Seracini's commission was to see if this iconic work of art could be restored to its original condition. If the top layer was the work of an unknown artist, who displayed a rather poor brush technique for his own rendition, what was the true inspiration that he covered up? What did da Vinci envision in his depiction of the adoration that perhaps was not appreciated in its day, and that we have never laid eyes on?

Using ultrasound and infrared technology, Seracini exposed for the first time the *underdrawing*. Intersecting 2,400 image frames into a mosaic, suddenly, he enabled us to see the true lines, strokes, and vision of the original artist. Exhibited digitally in the Uffizi, this original version encompasses a vast, multiscoped human audience with ferocious war imagery in the background. Almost thirty new faces and figures emerge, with far greater feeling and emotive dimension, and we see much more intimately the personal portrait of the young artist himself that he included in the painting. A sense of awe comes over those who view this version. Finally, after centuries of cover-up, we have seen the real artistic genius of da Vinci![38]

The premier da Vinci expert in the world, Dr. Carlo Pedretti, authenticated that the underdrawings match da Vinci's handiwork. Before, we looked at an imposter's replication; now, finally, we see the true masterpiece!

## HARD ASSESSMENT: DISCIPLESHIP OBSCURITY

If the purpose of *ReMission* is going to take root in your culture with resounding effect, it must involve a qualitative kind of restoration. By shedding false layers of tradition and misapplied priorities, we must recover the original discipleship vision of Jesus—what I now like to term "the underdrawing." To reignite the mission ethos effectively, we must reclaim the power of emulation.

In his introductory remarks to *7 Men and the Secret of Their Greatness*, Eric Metaxas posits that emulation used to be a learning hallmark, with books like *Plutarch's Lives* and *Foxe's Book of Martyrs* being regular fare. But with the damage to leadership authority brought on by events such as the Vietnam conflict and the Watergate scandal, the general notion of nobility was ripped asunder. In Metaxas's words, we went from "the extreme of being naïve to the other extreme of being cynical."[39] Is it possible that, being inside the cultural wake, we are not cognizant of how much emulative distancing has affected us, whether as individuals or institutions?

---

38. *The Da Vinci Detective: Two Great Art World Mysteries Solved*, DVD, produced and directed by Nigel Levy, *Smithsonian Networks* (UK: Darlow Smithson Productions, 2006). Available at: https://www.amazon.com/Vinci-Detective-Mike-Coles/dp/B002D0L0PY.

39. Eric Metaxas, *7 Men and the Secret of Their Greatness* (Nashville, TN: Thomas Nelson, 2013), 14–16.

Consider that we lead or attend churches where so much of the focus is on helping us increase in biblical literacy, cope with problems, interpret personal pains, connect in fellowship, grow spiritually, have our needs met, and otherwise realize an earthly life that is good and right, full and satisfying. Yet the greatest question—the most powerful question—deals with vision: *What does it mean to be a Christ follower?* We must courageously scuttle all props and scrape off our own plastered-on layers to address that question.

My concern is not only that we have lost emulation, but also that we have lost a true representation of the Master leader. After all, Jesus was the most mission-focused person who ever walked the earth; and yet so many Christians look nothing like him—in mind, manner, or method. Any leader, professor, pastor, parishioner, artist, writer, lyricist, or designer who is going hard after the reclamation of Christ's precedent is doing great good for today's church.

JESUS WAS THE MOST MISSION-FOCUSED PERSON WHO EVER WALKED THE EARTH; AND YET SO MANY CHRISTIANS LOOK NOTHING LIKE HIM—IN MIND, MANNER, OR METHOD.

Though this book offers neither an exhaustive look at the life of Christ nor a singularly focused presentation of Christ's methodologies, I will offer a mosaic of biblical images throughout the text in an attempt to capture him more fully. To put you at ease, I am not talking of anything digressive of orthodoxy. This is not Reza Aslan's bestseller *Zealot*, a theological revision of Jesus as a religiopolitical leader built on a multitude of false assumptions relegating Christ's divinity to a concoction of the Gospel authors.[40] No! Jesus is fully man and fully God, the infinite, sinless one made flesh—the only one qualified to be sin's substitute. What I am saying is,

40. Reza Aslan, *Zealot: The Life and Times of Jesus of Nazareth* (New York: Random House, 2014).

we have not dialed into the locus of power found in his mission persona. Because of this, we lack the missional know-how that he possessed and practiced in all his earthly encounters. It is those patterned characteristics that remain veiled in obscurity.

Seeing through the counterfeited coverings, we expose the underdrawing. We do this first for ourselves, and then for others to see. Can any of us afford to miss the true picture and vision of our Master?

## UNDERDRAWING DISTINCTIVES

At the outset of his earthly mission, Jesus spoke, on an empty stomach, words full of implications. When the disciples, returning with food, were shocked to find him talking to, of all people, a Samaritan woman, he seized the moment to declare, *"I have food to eat that you know nothing about"* (John 4:32). That little line was big. The mission of the Father was the deepest hunger of the Son. It was his food, the sustenance that kept him going every waking, hungry minute.

As much as we hope to take on the true character of Christ, such as he displayed to his disciples that day, a massive gap exists between him and us. Jesus came to lay down his life as an atonement for our sins, but every day, he was working to advance the kingdom for his Father. (See John 5:17.) Upon closer inspection, we will find that his ways are not our ways. This means that when we use the words "disciple" or "Christlike," we must filter our usage through his missional life. Contrarily, there are believers who think of themselves as true representations of Christ, when they are truly nothing of the sort. Jesus articulated his vision for emulation with an array of verses. Consider how, in John 14:12, he linked following with fulfilling: *"Whoever believes in me will do the works I have been doing."*

A student-to-master motif colors the entire New Testament. Jesus lived it out with the Twelve. Paul voiced the same value when he wrote, *"Follow my example, as I follow the example of Christ"* (1 Corinthians 11:1). The imitation theme threads all the way back to the communal relationship of the members of the Godhead. In a deep and beautiful way, the book of John captures the intimate relationship of a *leading* Father and his *shadowing* Son. Consider, for example, Jesus' words in John 5:19–20: *"Very truly I tell you, the Son can do nothing by himself; he can do only what he sees his Father doing, because whatever the Father does the Son also does. For the Father loves the Son and shows him all he does."* Jesus passed to us the baton of emulation when he said, *"As the Father has sent me, I am sending you"* (John 20:21).

Being on mission leads to spiritual regeneration (the full-infilling sense and scope of it), where the deep loving connection with our heavenly Father is established. As Jesus says, *"It is the Father, living in me, who is doing his work....I am in the Father and the Father is in me"* (John 14:10–11). In essence, mission is the reception and reciprocation of God's boundless love for humanity.

Yet a widespread observation of missional platforms shows that the present form of church is not even close to emulating Jesus' missionary nature. Author R. Geoffrey Harris highlights this gaping divide with these words:

> The Gospels reflect the fact that mission is the essence of the Church's life and not just an aspect of it. The life of Jesus is invariably represented as being enacted in the world at large (and not in religious settings), among ordinary people of all sorts (and not just among believers) and, in particular, as reaching out to those beyond the normal scope and influence of the religious establishment. Jesus' early nickname, "friend of sinners," is transformed in the Gospels from a term of abuse into a badge of honour and respect.[41]

Contrary to Christ's example, we have come to define "disciple" by such criteria as knowledge, behavior, and fellowship, whereas Jesus saw discipleship as the embodiment of his heart, actions, skills, and fruit. Anytime we stray from God's intention (some might call that sin, by the way), the result is ill effects. Because of this misappropriation, we now have a pandemic of isolated Christians feverishly studying their Bibles but neither living what their Bibles are calling them toward nor seeing Scripture through a lens that distinguishes Jesus' methods in a transferable way.

---

41. R. Geoffrey Harris, *Mission in the Gospels* (Eugene, OR: Wipf & Stock, 2004), 227.

WE NOW HAVE A PANDEMIC OF ISOLATED
CHRISTIANS FEVERISHLY STUDYING THEIR BIBLES BUT
NEITHER LIVING WHAT THEIR BIBLES ARE CALLING
THEM TOWARD NOR SEEING SCRIPTURE THROUGH
A LENS THAT DISTINGUISHES JESUS' METHODS IN A
TRANSFERABLE WAY.

Can you imagine Christ going on a food run because he would rath-er hang with his "bros" than have a conversation with a lost woman at a Samarian well? Zap that story from our Bibles. This is exactly what is hap-pening at the engagement level of Christian lives. How many conversations have they bypassed because they lack their Master's mission focus and sav-vy? How many potentially redemptive relationships never had a chance? How much learning and gospel opportunity was missed? How many thrilling extension stories, like that of the Samaritan woman who won over a whole town for Christ, have been nullified? Where is the church's burgeoning vitality?

Recovering the pattern established by Jesus Christ may take drastic measures. The houses in our neighborhood have a history of forming leaks in the slab foundations. As if five claims to our own insurance company were not enough, there was the night that my lovely bride turned on the water in the tub and then fell asleep. After waking to a strange, eerie sound, we stepped into a bedroom lake! Due to the water damage and mold pros-pects, repairers had to gut entire sections of our house. The family room, situated below the master bath, was stripped clean—all the drywall, ceil-ing, and flooring gone. As it says in Ecclesiastes 3:3, there is *"a time to tear down and a time to build."*

You have to look hard at your groups, ministries, and church. You might have to stop what you've been doing and start all over. When my friend Aaron and his team realized their church's recovery ministry had become ingrown and unreflective of Christ's heart, what did they do? They shut it down and then rebooted the whole ministry around mission. As church leaders, we ask big, bold questions. Are we helping our people become missionally viable where they live and breathe? Is it their lifeblood?

## ULTIMATE CLARITY

Clarity bolsters conviction. Let's be clear about Jesus' ultimate intention. Acquiring head knowledge was not his vision. As Paul wrote, knowledge "puffs up," whereas love edifies. (See 1 Corinthians 8:1.) The reason Christ calls us to mission first is because mission is, first and foremost, about love. Love is the MO of Christ's disciples. Knowledge is important, but it is subservient to love. Spiritual rhythms, likewise, are important but subservient. When we make "ultimate" anything that is meant to be "subservient," we get off track.

The tricky tangent can apply even to something as treasured as God's Word. Wasn't this the case with the Pharisees when Jesus confronted them, saying, *"You search the Scriptures because you think that in them you have eternal life. These are the very Scriptures that testify about me"* (John 5:39)? Where is life? In the Scriptures or in Jesus? As high a view as I hold of the full breadth of God's inspired Word, I also believe that certain ideas surpass or eclipse others, being preeminent (in the academic world, this is called "prioritism"[42]). When Paul wrote, *"Now these three remain: faith, hope and love. But the greatest of these is love"* (1 Corinthians 13:13), he was acknowledging that there is something ultimate, or in highest position, for which to strive.

Similarly, the author of Hebrews honors God's past revelations but emphasizes the final, superior authority of Christ when he writes, *"But in these last days he has spoken to us by his Son"* (Hebrews 1:2). Why is this so significant? He continues, *"The Son is the radiance of God's glory and the exact representation of his being"* (Hebrews 1:3). Nothing before Jesus gave us the full, true picture of God the Father. (See also John 1:18.) In other words, the Son is the pinnacle of God's progressive revelation.

To use a wedding ring as a metaphor, the Scriptures are the band and settings; Jesus is the jewel. When a recently engaged woman proudly puts her left hand before you, what are you looking at? Seminary professor and

---

42. Christopher R. Little, "The Case for Prioritism: Part 1," *Great Commission Research Journal* (Winter 2016).

theologian Daniel Kirk blogs, "Jesus is the thing. Scripture is the sign that points toward the thing. Scripture provides a series of portraits so that we will know the real thing when we see it."[43] This is no small point. If you do not get your aim straight and locked on, the disciples you lead may become casual observers or legalistic learners[44] rather than followers, and the degree to which they conform to the image of Christ may become wishy-washy. And then, just like a discarded masterpiece, something priceless will have been lost.

For anyone tempted to think this nuance is trivial, we have to ask a series of questions. Why is it that we have so many Christ-followers disengaged from the world in a missional sense? No relationships with those outside the faith—is that not oxymoronic? Why do we have so many believers running around with judgment on their agenda? Have you been on Facebook lately? Why do we have masses of impotent messengers of the gospel? Jesus was laser-level effective in all his interactions.

## WHY IS IT THAT WE HAVE SO MANY CHRIST-FOLLOWERS DISENGAGED FROM THE WORLD IN A MISSIONAL SENSE? NO RELATIONSHIPS WITH THOSE OUTSIDE THE FAITH—IS THAT NOT OXYMORONIC?

If we truly followed Jesus, we'd have to reconcile ourselves to his life and his words in the following passages: *"For the Son of Man came to seek and to save the lost"* (Luke 19:10), and *"For God did not send his Son into the world to condemn the world, but to save the world through him"* (John 3:17). We'd have to give credence to rectifying injustice like he did. (See, for

---

43. J. R. Daniel Kirk, "Jesus is Ultimate" (December 2, 2015). http://www.jrdkirk.com/2015/12/02/jesus-is-ultimate/.

44. Another descriptor that applies is "amateur politicos." To that end, I would interject that it was an apolitical Jesus who told Governor Pilate, *"My kingdom is not of this world"* (John 18:36). Not that we don't have a place and role in politics as citizens; but, in the archetype of Christ, the political agenda will never take precedence over the greater call of kingdom advancement. If politics conflicts with the message of Jesus, as it can do, and often does, the gospel loses.

example, Luke 4:18–19.) We'd have to pay attention to the way he interacted with the world, not how we have resigned ourselves to do that. We'd have to assimilate the way he crossed social, cultural, racial, and religious lines to reach people. Ready to join that yoga class, visit your local mosque, or hang out at your neighborhood block bash? Then you'll have to learn to apply Christ's full range of gospel communication skills. Most Christians, neglectful of Jesus' mission pattern, have no clue what those armaments even are, and, therefore, have no arsenal from which to draw. We can miss the real thing, the true picture of discipleship, the underdrawing.

It's not enough to tell people to be like Christ. You have to break it down and make it something realistic to pursue and practice. I define it with skills. Most popular recovery programs have 12 steps. I've slimmed them down to 10 *ReMission* skills. Otherwise, people won't get it. They won't understand who they are supposed to be or how to engage. Will we need 2,400 image frames for the restoration? Nah, not that many. But we will have to show our people a multiplicity of images on how Jesus related to people from all walks of life if we expect them to follow him in fulfilling his work.

The theme of emulation lives in more than Jesus' words and divine prerogative. In the villages of seaside Galilee, Jesus healed two men by performing an almost identical sequence of steps seen in the seventh and eighth chapters of Mark. Certainly, he could have been more efficient. We know, from his healing of the centurion's servant in Luke 7, that he could have healed these guys from a distance. Why would Jesus go through the painstaking effort of a multi-sequenced pattern in which he employed—count them—six actions? I am not going to repeat a chapter I wrote on his varied techniques, but I will only point out that the back-to-back repetition constitutes a signature, of sorts. Like LeBron James's slam dunk, Dirk Nowitzki's one-legged fall-away jumper, or Stephen Curry's stepback three-pointer, a signature move is something you keep using because it consistently works.

In pulling both men away from the crowd for an intimate moment, Jesus established a signature method. He proceeded to hold hands with the men; apply his own spit to their affected area(s), whether the ears and/or the tongue; cast his gaze skyward; call out with passion; and lay his hands on one of the men. Twice! What's with the shtick? The answer is telling. Jesus was not merely healing their bodies—he was invoking their faith. He repeated the process for his onlooking, record-keeping followers. It was his way of saying, "Watch me. This is how it's done!"

After studying Jesus' ways of imparting the gospel, I didn't want people to merely tell of the gospel (a technique that's not effective with most!); I wanted them to be like Christ, drawing people into belief through a faith-formational process. This is why I wrote, in my book *Soul Whisperer*, "Spiritual formation coming out of mission, not preceding it, is what the Bible pictures."[45] As you know by now, that idea is the driving theme of this book. It's when Christians begin emulating the heart, actions, and skills of Jesus that they begin to form the right spiritual projection. It is then that we see the *ReMission* of the body. Jesus' skills are not mere techniques; they are character qualities. By the biblical definition of seeking others' interests above our own, it is the quality of love. (See, for example, Philippians 2:3–4.) When he walked with others, he was a companion. When he touched, he showed empathy, understanding, and sensitivity. When he pointed to the Father, he showed his heart fully expressed in outward inclusivity. This is what it means to be Christlike. It is God's ultimate at its spiritual core.

**IT'S WHEN CHRISTIANS BEGIN EMULATING THE HEART, ACTIONS, AND SKILLS OF JESUS THAT THEY BEGIN TO FORM THE RIGHT SPIRITUAL PROJECTION. IT IS THEN THAT WE SEE THE *REMISSION* OF THE BODY.**

So, what of our own spiritual nurture? Is that not important? Our teachers/formation leaders teach us many things. They force us to slow down. They imbue spiritual rhythms that make a difference in how we live so that we can abide and bear fruit. They increase our knowledge. I know the value of the spiritual-formation gifts. We need them. But we

45. Gary Comer, *Soul Whisperer: Why the Church Must Change the Way It Views Evangelism* (Eugene, OR: Wipf & Stock, 2013), 24.

must behold and embrace something higher that has the potency to rectify a relentless disease of self-absorption. If we are ever to be healthy and right, we must fulfill our commissioned purpose. We need *ReMission*. It is our true North Star.

We could put it all together this way: Spiritual rhythms are the equipment of the soldier. He must eat to fight. He must rest to fight. He must be fit to fight. He must train to fight. But none of these rhythms is the ultimate, in and of itself. Each is subservient to a greater assignment: fighting to win the war. Being ultimate, the gospel mission not only obeys the foremost call of God; it expands God's glory in the most exponential way, and is the only means to include others in the fullness of his love and resources.

Too often, we lack this clarity. Anytime we venture away from God's vision, the consequences are dire. If our eye is "off" or "dark," then how great is that darkness? (See Matthew 6:23.)

## TEETER-TOTTER LEADERSHIP

A pastor invited me to address his congregation. I hoped to see his church move together to love and to reach their community. I had written a mission vehicle for Sandals Church called *Launch Point*, designed to guide community groups in engagement, and I thought it would be a great venture for his people. My time and talk were well-received, as my truth-telling wife affirmed. Yet, some weeks later, when we talked about implementation, all that the pastor was willing to do was to have his people participate in prayer walks in distant neighborhoods. (Note: They were not even walking their own neighborhoods.) With his trademark pastoral concern, he reasoned, "I want their hearts to be prepared." I wanted to say to him, "Are you telling me their hearts would not be prepared if they were trying to reach actual people?"

Now, let me just say that I am all for prayer. Intercession plays a major part in redemption. I think prayer walks are a great way for churches to increase vision and get their people thinking about reaching others. But I could not end that conversation without telling the pastor that if prayer walks were all they were going to do, they would not reach anyone. Jesus did not commission us to pray; he commissioned us to go and make disciples. Though God may opt to bypass us, as he did with Saul using supernatural voice and light from heaven along the Damascus Road (see Acts 9), by definition, the endeavor of evangelistic discipling is a work of God requiring human agents. It does not happen incognito.

Though it may have gone undetected by others, the pastor's response fell gravely short. His members needed to stretch themselves missionally, but he lacked the courage to call them into engagement. Although he had sent them out there in prayer, in reality, he was failing in faith, not willing to trust God to develop and use his people in the prime discipleship directive. Believe me, this pastor was no outlier. Many pastors and church leaders fit all too nicely into his camp. I will add that what is most amiss in him is his view of Christian discipleship. He is coddling church attendees rather than making them into disciples.

Evangelism was central to Jesus; thus, it must be central to us. From Christ's example, my definition for evangelism is this: *Partnering with God in the process of shaping the mind and heart to believe and follow.*[46] Please note how the four dimensions offer clarity regarding what Jesus is calling your people to be and to do. Use it! Parsing it down will prove helpful: (1) Partnering with God (that is spiritual and exciting), (2) in the process (that means it's an ongoing relational work), (3) of shaping the mind and heart (that requires knowledge and skills) (4) to believe and follow (that's our end goal). This agency of the Father working intimately through each follower occurs when believers come alongside unsaved people they know or are getting to know in order to help them reach a place of belief and followership. Learning to apply Jesus' heart, manner, and skills within the engagement is what their discipleship is all about. Sure, they have other gifts to develop and employ, but Christ excuses none from the gospel, which is his declarative main thrust until he returns.

Think with me what championing a mission pattern will mean to those under your wing. You are like the father in Anthony Doerr's Pulitzer Prize-winning novel, *All the Light We Cannot See.* Living in Paris at the cusp of the Second World War, this father, a locksmith by trade, has crafted a massive micro-sized model of his own town. With more than just buildings, the level of detail is stunning. Why would someone put painstaking effort toward producing such a thing?

---

46. Ibid., 149.

Tuesday after Tuesday fails. She leads her father on six-block detours that leave her angry and frustrated and farther from home than when they started. But in the winter of her eighth year, to Marie-Laure's surprise, she begins to get it right. She runs her fingers over the model in their kitchen, counting miniature benches, trees, lampposts, doorways. Every day, some new detail emerges—each storm drain, park bench, and hydrant in the model has its counterpart in the real world.

Marie-Laure brings her father closer to home before making a mistake. Four blocks three blocks two. And one snowy Tuesday in March, when he walks her to yet another new spot, very close to the banks of the Seine, spins her around three times, and says, "Take us home," she realizes that, for the first time since they began this exercise, dread has not come trundling up from her gut.

Instead she squats on her heels on the sidewalk.

The faintly metallic smell of the falling snow surrounds her. *Calm yourself. Listen.*

...Six blocks, forty buildings, ten tiny trees in a square. This street intersects this street. One centimeter at a time.

Her father stirs the keys in his pockets. Ahead loom the tall, grand houses that flank the gardens, reflecting sound.

She says, "We go left."

They start up the length of the rue Cuvier. A trio of airborne ducks threads toward them, flapping their wings in synchrony, making for the Seine, and as the birds rush overhead, she imagines she can feel the light settling over their wings, striking each individual feather.

Left on rue Geoffroy Saint-Hilaire. Right on rue Daubenton. Three storm drains four storm drains five. Approaching on the left will be the open ironwork fence of the Jardin des Plantes, its thin spars like the bars of a great birdcage.

Across from her now: the bakery, the butcher, the delicatessen.

"Safe to cross, Papa?"

"It is."

Right. Then straight. They walk up their street now, she is sure of it. One step behind her, her father tilts his head up and gives the sky a huge smile. Marie-Laure knows this even though her back is to him, even though he says nothing, even though she is blind....

They are halfway up the rue des Patriarches. They are outside their building. Marie-Laure finds the trunk of the chestnut tree that grows past her fourth-floor window, its bark beneath her fingers. Old friend.

In another half second her father's hands are in her armpits, swinging her up, and Marie-Laure smiles, and he laughs a pure, contagious laugh, one she will remember all her life.[47]

What, we should all ask, possesses us for the Father's precious ones? We could leave them in their rooms, as so many are now. Isolated. Diminished. Ineffectual. Blind. Or we could believe in them by giving them something tangible to wrap their minds and hands around, something pictorial to illustrate how to navigate their divine purpose in the real world. Yes, you can give your people a human model that is potent enough to lessen fear and strengthen their poise, and substantive enough to handle the mission maze outside their door. Like a father devoted to his blind daughter, or Paul exhorting his timid protégé Timothy, *"The goal of our instruction is love"* (1 Timothy 1:5 NASB).

———

If we agree that Christ has provided an iconic pattern for his people to emulate, then how are leaders to accomplish that qualitative formation? In the next three chapters, we will delve into the details of how to shape a Christ-likened culture that matches Christ's interface with the world. As you will see, there is need for hard assessment, deep thought, and clear action.

The next chapter addresses what is critical for this quality of *ReMission* engagement to have even a chance. The good news is, God has placed the power for permeation within your grasp.

47. Anthony Doerr, *All the Light We Cannot See* (New York, NY: Simon & Schuster, 2014), 40–41.

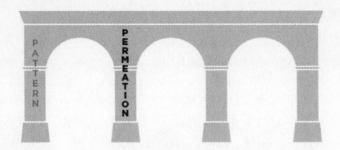

## REFLECTIONS

1. In what ways do you see the church losing sight of Christ's original vision for his disciples' emulating him? Offer specific observations from the lives of others.

2. Do you agree with the author that Christlikeness ought to be
   defined in missional terms? Why or why not?

3. When you think of evangelism, can you see the difference between Christ's personal faith-drawing pattern and the predomi-
   nant "telling" mode of today?

## REMISSION TAKEAWAYS

1. Jesus' skills are character related, requiring people to develop
   and grow in spiritual qualities.

2. Emulating Christ is the preeminent goal of the Christian faith.

3. If you do not break down Christlike skills (ten in the book),
   your people will not know who they are to be or how they are to
   follow Christ, missionally speaking.

# —4—

# THE PERMEATION

It so happens that the work which is likely to be our most durable monument, and to convey some knowledge of us to the most remote posterity, is a work of bare utility; not a shrine, not a fortress, not a palace, but a bridge.
—Montgomery Schuyler

On June 6, 2015, at the self-proclaimed halibut fishing capital of the world—Homer, Alaska—a strange meteorological event occurred. It was not something perceptible to the casual tourist or passerby, but at 10:56 a.m., out on what they call the Homer Spit, two newly relocated church planters took a photo of the horizon that included two faintly visible mountains in the distance. When these pastors later inquired as to the names of those two peaks, a local corrected their claim, clarifying that those mountains were not visible from the Spit. Doubt ensued as to what they had actually seen, but their corroborating photograph soon erased all traces of skepticism.[48]

Yes, Mt. Fourpeaked and Mt. Douglas—out of sight, geographically, from the Homer Spit due to the curvature of the earth and their respective distances of ninety-five and eighty-seven miles—were clear as day to the human eye and the camera lens. What these two men witnessed and photographed makes no sense at all, until you understand the term *refraction*. From mid-seventeenth-century Latin *refringere*, "to break up," the term is defined in the dictionary as "the fact or phenomenon of light, radio waves, etc. being deflected in passing obliquely through the interface between one

---

48. Photograph, Brian Moore (Faith to the 49th, Facebook), 6-6-15.

medium and another or through a medium of varying density." In simpler terms, what had appeared on that day was the collision of one cold medium of air with a warmer, less dense front, which deflected the light in such a way that it resulted in a towering mirage.

If perchance you are still shaking your head regarding this explanation, I will only make things worse by saying that the same phenomenon was the definitive conclusion of British researcher Tim Maltin to explain the mystery of what really occurred on the night the *Titanic* went down: refraction resulted when the cold air of the Labrador Current met the warm air of the Gulf Stream. By combing painstakingly through volumes of eyewitness testimony and ship records, Maltin assembled a preponderance of evidence: the descriptions of "refraction" by those aboard other vessels in the vicinity; passengers' reports of frigid air suddenly coming upon them; the unusual brilliance of the stars; the blurring of the water's horizon with the sky; the fact that the captain of the nearest ship, Stanley Lord of the SS *Californian*, perceived the gigantic liner (one-sixth of a mile long) to be a smaller steamer; the failure of the lookouts, who could spot "bergs" thirty minutes away, to see the massive iceberg before it was right upon them—all this seems to point to the phenomenon detailed in the Smithsonian documentary *Titanic's Final Mystery*, and we must now entertain the notion that it was an optical illusion that contributed to the sinking of the great ship.[49]

## HARD ASSESSMENT: REFRACTED LENS

From close observations made and corroborating data collected over more than two decades of ministry, I have become convinced that one pervasive factor affecting today's church is refraction. Pastors look out at their beloved congregations and get a romanticized view of what is actually occurring.

This distorting tendency has many props. Perhaps the most obvious is how deeply invested the pastor and the church leadership are to the body of believers they oversee. Whether they planted the church or not, it is their baby; and what parent doesn't wear rose-colored glasses when it comes to

---

49. *Titanic's Final Mystery*, directed by Nigel Levy, written by Nigel Levy and Tim Maltin, Smithsonian Channel (US/UK: Airborne TV & Film, 2012). Available at http://www. smithsonianchannel.com/shows/titanics-final-mystery/0/141474.

his or her children? When a church's corporate accomplishments and community prominence are added to the mix, who, may I ask, is able to resist the lens-skewing effects of pride? Granted, each leader must assess this issue personally. You may be the rare exception. Your eyes and ears might be spot-on and ruthlessly honest.

Honest evaluation, by the way, is the quality I admire most in a leader. The apostle Paul captured this virtue with a penetrating verse: *"I say to every one of you: Do not think of yourself more highly than you ought..."* (Romans 12:3). Great leaders are set apart by their ability to maintain a humble perspective. High-level leaders are not so caught up with themselves or with news clippings about their ministry that they lose objectivity. To the contrary, the exceptional leader is searching for deeper insights on what is really going on. The axiom popularized by the movie *Friday Night Lights* is their motto: "Clear eyes, full hearts, can't lose." Even when they see good things happening, they realize that their church is only scratching the surface of who Jesus wants them to be and what he wills them to do in the world. They might even have the ability to see sweeping deficiencies. And they can make cold, hard assessments about themselves, too.

> GREAT LEADERS ARE SET APART BY THEIR ABILITY TO MAINTAIN A HUMBLE PERSPECTIVE. HIGH-LEVEL LEADERS ARE NOT SO CAUGHT UP WITH THEMSELVES OR WITH NEWS CLIPPINGS ABOUT THEIR MINISTRY THAT THEY LOSE OBJECTIVITY. TO THE CONTRARY, THE EXCEPTIONAL LEADER IS SEARCHING FOR DEEPER INSIGHTS ON WHAT IS REALLY GOING ON.

When I first met Matt Brown, the senior pastor of Sandals Church, I was researching how churches followed up with newer believers. Matt told me immediately, "We are doing nothing to address that." He did not appease me with glowing words about his greatly renowned church. He did not rattle off a church-promo spiel but rather offered a straight-up assessment. Of course, that meant he was able to perceive how things could be improved.

So, are you ready for some hard assessment? It's a critical issue that is, in my view, pandemic in scope. It strikes me as something that is authentically true in an almost universal way—that *church leaders overestimate the impact of their teaching.* I submit to you that this type of refraction hinders church mission in the biggest of ways. It is the iceberg slicing across the steel hull and compromising the outward movement of God. As it was on that fateful, frigid night in 1912, there seem to be numerous aspects contributing to this phenomenon.

It's not just the low-memory retention of message hearers (an average 5-percent recall of what was said), or the fact that so many people attend church services only sporadically. The root is sly in that it stems from an honorable conviction. Ironically, pastors and teachers are only following what they have been repeatedly taught. They deliver messages from God's Word, ones they have worked diligently to prepare with full faith in the two-edged sword that is able to cut between soul and spirit, joints and marrow, and never return void. (See Hebrews 4:12; Isaiah 55:11.) Thus, it is with solid theological footing that they feel satisfied that the people within earshot of their voices are well-equipped to do God's will and execute his mission here on earth.

This inference might be accurate if it were not for another, overarching principle in play—one not usually seen or understood, that will invariably stymie the transference of vital equipping to the members of your ministry body. But when it is understood, Bible teachers can see how they must make course corrections in order to achieve the growth they are aiming for. The principle is this: *Form must match formation.*

This concept is fundamental to the message of *ReMission.* If the goal of teaching is to generate a greater understanding of God and theological truths, then the form of up-front preaching matches the formation. Similarly, as we all know, making an evangelistic appeal works from up front, as well. In both cases, the listener can gain what he or she needs from the pastor's verbal explanation of God's Word. Most Bible-teaching churches help their people to understand theological truths about God and the gospel of grace, along with relevant life applications. For this, I credit most pastors and teachers with a job well done.

Yet when you shift the goal of teaching to creating a missionally effective Christian—one who embodies the way and manners of Christ, and who possesses the cultural literacy necessary among gospel influencers in today's post-Christian world—the form of preaching does not match the formation. Not even remotely so. In my assessment, this explains the existence of the gap between pulpit and pews. The statistics do not lie. In sum, Christians know the gospel, but few of them know how to steward it.

## CHRISTIANS KNOW THE GOSPEL, BUT FEW OF THEM KNOW HOW TO STEWARD IT.

What this tells us is that another kind of formation is missing and necessary, one that does not occur from merely listening to someone talk about the Bible. What I am referring to is practical knowledge—the know-how of engagement, the kind of learning and life-skill development that enables relational spiritual influence to flow to others. This is what Jesus possessed and imparted to his disciples through his three years of close-proximity friendship and engagement training.

Let me state the principle another way: *You can't produce mission formation if the format doesn't involve experiential practice.* As one person wisely said, "You cannot become what you are not in the process of becoming." It's like surfing. You can't learn to surf just by hearing someone talk about it. Even if your instructor is a pro, learning to surf occurs only by getting out in the waves. Feel, positioning, technique, and conditioning are all critical; to think anything otherwise is laughable. This mission rule applies to other biblical values, as well. Thus, if you are teaching people about the value of community, and yet your form of gathering is not leading people into deeper, more honest relationships, then don't be surprised when none of your listeners "gets" the community thing. I once watched a membership course implode at a major church, not because the content was bad, or that the presenter wasn't ably prepared, or that the church wasn't truly behind it. No, it died, and rightly so, because the form did nothing to produce the desired formation. The class attendees sensed this disconnect and stopped coming. When the pastor realized what was happening, he threw in the towel. Call it a format failure.

Granted, teachers who are sodalically gifted (that is, gifted in sodalic enterprises, or starting new ministries and churches; the opposite, "modalic," refers to strengthening extant ministries and churches) will do slightly better to inspire people to move outward with their faith; but even they will hit the ceiling of this principle fairly quickly. You can't overcome it by an exceptional teaching ability, no matter who you are or how gifted people perceive you to be. Missional formation, or discipling people to be like Jesus in manner and message, does not occur in a non-skill, non-practice, non-participatory way. Nowhere is this principle more vital than in the most difficult area of development: evangelistic disciplemaking.

I realize that my proposition may elicit a reaction from the most didactic of devotees, who are likely to reply with the usual line trotted out by most Bible teachers: "All we need is the Word! We just need to preach— nothing less, nothing more." Can you hear the refrain: "If only people knew their Bibles…"? I realize how valid that sounds to some. But it's refracted, not accurate. Possibly arrogant. Definitely unhelpful. All told, it is hurting the church. We need *ReMission* in this area to revitalize the whole body.

I would also argue that this view is not biblical. We have a way of selectively truncating our interpretation of Scripture according to our gifting, so that we see what we want to see, and fail to prize what is there within the full range and discipline of hermeneutics. The Scriptures have an exhaustive content about mission dynamics, and yet pastor-teachers often fail to appreciate how crucial these details are for their people to learn, and how this understanding must be developed along unconventional lines. The difference between lecture and laboratory is skill acquisition. Hands-on learning. Situational feedback. Heightened self-awareness. Follow-up coaching. Compounding insights. Your people need to learn it and then live it to get it.

Refraction obscures the need for mission formation. So, for permeation to succeed, you must first decide to peer through a non-refracted lens and get clear on how missional formation actually comes into fruition. Then, you must add the training and engagement features that raise and route your entire church body. This book will help you in the critical areas of approach, character, skills, and structures. But none of those will be set in motion unless you have the proper lens. The humility that is needed to avoid overestimating the influence of teaching is rare. Only exceptional leaders make this honest assessment of themselves. For the sake of the gospel, I pray that you are one of them. To illustrate the importance of this skill in the mission equation, let me share with you a conversation I had with a church leader from another continent.

## TRAINING OF A DIFFERENT KIND

While I was training a group of church leaders in rural Kenya, African pastor Zachary King'ori asked me to address some pastors in the city of Nairobi. Enthused over my mission precepts, he contextualized their situation, saying, "In the cities, people are where they are regarding faith, not by chance but by choice." Can you appreciate the delineation he was making? It was not refracted. His statement is generally true of our time.

THE BULK OF "OUTSIDERS" ARE ALREADY AWARE, AND WARY, OF OUR BASIC MESSAGE PITCH, AND HAVE THUS BEEN INOCULATED TO OUR OVERUSED, OVERSIMPLIFIED APPROACHES.

People in cities and suburbs all over the world are cognizant of the Christian church and its message. Most of them know something about Christmas and Easter, at least, and have even witnessed Christians getting the word out. Many of them are also bombarded with Christian messaging on Facebook, Twitter, and the other various forms of global media. It's not as if they live in the pre-Christian times of the early church or reside in such remote areas that they have never heard of Jesus or the Christian faith. It's not because they haven't heard that they don't believe; it's because they have chosen not to.

What does this reality mean for the church? First, we can misinterpret the starting place of potential believers. The bulk of "outsiders" are already aware, and wary, of our basic message pitch, and have thus been inoculated to our overused, oversimplified approaches. (No wonder the bullhorn doesn't work anymore, except to push potential seekers farther away!) This fact highlights the great error of the traditional telling paradigm, which identifies the problem as people not having heard the gospel message. Certainly, there are people groups in various regions of the world who haven't heard the gospel. Our lead church-planting catalyst in India enumerated 309 unreached people groups in West Bengal alone. Mission entities such as New Tribes and Frontiers are going after the farthest pockets on the planet. Praise God! But here we are, talking about major population centers.

Though we do get hungry inquisitors from time to time to whom we must explain Christ's intervention and then lead to faith, for many others, our messaging challenge has changed. As I premised in *Soul Whisperer*, we must make a radical shift: "It's not about telling, it's about helping people to hear."[50] This process of inception, of implanting the gospel in a way that draws interest and intrigue, ushering the receptive person into a greater understanding of, and desire to follow, Jesus, is a skillful, structured art. It requires that believers learn what facilitates relationally oriented influence. In my view, each Christian must have ten major skills in his or her tool kit; these I have coded numerically, from 1 to 10, and I will use this codification going forward.

Keeping to the wisdom of my astute African friend, and in an effort to whet your appetite for what lies ahead, I ask you: What is the "choice" unbelievers are making? That is a great question, and it's one we must answer if we are to accurately appraise our current playing field. Here is my short answer: Disbelieving individuals inhabiting major population centers have made the conscious choice (though it may seem unconscious) that their self-directed life is better than the Christ-offered one.

---

50. Comer, *Soul Whisperer*, 13.

| Their Self-Directed **LIFE** |  | The Christ Offered **LIFE** |
|---|---|---|

For our secular friends, the choice appears to be a slam dunk. (Of course, there are some individuals who choose not to believe for rational or emotional reasons.) Who is going to show genuine interest and compassion for them, and not just treat them like a project? Who, might I ask, is going to intercept and help them reinterpret their thinking? Who is going to help them see that their choice is not even close to being the true, best one?

Inlaid by God, the Scriptures give us the tools to answer this call. When God commissioned Paul, he prescribed for him the role *"to open their eyes"* (Acts 26:18). When Jesus spoke to the Samaritan woman, was he not filling her eyes with what he could offer? *"If you knew the gift of God and who it is that asks you for a drink, you would have asked him and he would have given you living water"* (John 4:10). One thing is certain from the context: If Jesus had not presented her with the metaphor of "living water," she would not have come up with it herself. He had to create a provocative picture to make it plain for her to see.

For those who are concerned about the gospel's having an appeal to self-interest, please note that when Jesus spoke of "living water," he was not watering anything down. It was truth. Gospel messaging includes, and typically begins with, the benefits of faith, eventually leading to wholehearted repentance. If we are to follow Jesus' pattern, we will help others to see the benefits of a relationship with him. (This is Skill #1: The Gospel Key.) The challenge of equipping believers to do this, however, looms large in the church. Most believers have never learned the skill, let alone practiced it; nor have they seen God use them to lead others into the faith, as Jesus did. They need an entirely new skill set. It takes specialized training to develop within our most valuable asset, God's people, the capacity to penetrate a drifting culture with a life-intervening message.

CHRIST-FOLLOWING CHURCH MEMBERS
DO NOT DEVELOP THE RELATED SKILLS AND
ENGAGEMENT EXPERIENCES ESSENTIAL TO
CHRISTLIKE GROWTH FROM LISTENING TO
A SERMON OR SERIES OF MESSAGES.

Again, Christ-following church members do not develop the related skills and engagement experiences essential to Christlike growth from listening to a sermon or series of messages. I tested this concept one day, listening to a message from a top-notch communicator. He made seven solid points about mission. It was a great talk. What did it actually accomplish? In my view, nothing. Avoiding negativity and insubordination in my attitude, I asked another leader for his opinion, and he offered the same assessment. The people under his leadership who had heard the same message all left there knowing what they had already known: They should reach out with the gospel. But as they scattered out the door into their mission field, not one of them knew anything more about how to go about doing that.

At the cusp of the seeker revolution, Rick Warren stated that he'd dumped all but two of his prior messages for their impracticality.[51] Would I suggest that you shift all your messages to focus on the theme of mission? At this point, you might guess that the first thing I would say is this: Even if you did that, the form would fail you. But, perhaps surprising from someone who places such an emphasis on mission, I would say no. Pastors have ten primary things to accomplish when addressing their congregations, and all ten items are important. What I am suggesting is that you employ a serious training mechanism in your church or mission entity. Pastor-teachers have a lead role to prime the pump and point to the great assignment, but there is far more to be executed than inspiration. Let me say it straight: We are too far removed from the rabbinical discipling model of Jesus. In generic terms, our goals of renewing attraction to the gospel to the point where people attend a weekly service and join a small group

---

51. Rick Warren, "Purpose Driven Preaching" (presentation at The Purpose Driven Church Conference, Saddleback, California, 1994).

Bible study do more to encourage inward consumption than to empower outward expansion.

IF WE OVERESTIMATE THE POWER OF THE PULPIT OR UNDERESTIMATE THE NEED FOR TRAINING, THE HOT AIR OF PREACHING WILL HIT THE COLD AIR OF MISSIONAL MISUNDERSTANDING, LEAVING US WITH THE UNSETTLED WEATHER OF APATHY, CONFUSION, AND MISSION DISCONNECT.

If we overestimate the power of the pulpit or underestimate the need for training, the hot air of preaching will hit the cold air of missional misunderstanding, leaving us with the unsettled weather of apathy, confusion, and mission disconnect; the result will be that little, if any, of our mandate is actually accomplished. In sum, we fall short in discipling people for mission, and the fruit, or the lack thereof, will show. A pastor was telling me the other day how Barna research indicated that millennials are leaving the church because they are not being equipped. Note: The research is right! Various field-study factors exist for winning the hearts of younger constituents, with their active participation as countercultural world-changers as one underlying theme, and a huge part of it.[52] My warning is that Barna's finger-to-the-wind data should not dictate our marching orders, lest millennials see through our lack of conviction that reinforces what David Kinnaman has called the struggle between "the church as it is (market driven consumerism, hyperindividualism) and what they believe it is called to be."[53] Ouch! I repeat my theme: Renewal is failing to realize calling. Whether or not you agree with my analysis, let me ask you: Why is

52. Exponential, "5 Things Millennials Wish the Church Would Be: New Barna Research Reveals the Questions Church Planters Should Ask to Authentically and Effectively Engage Young Adults" (June 30, 2016). https://exponential.org (accessed July 2, 2016).
53. David Kinnaman and Aly Hawkins, *You Lost Me: Why Young Christians Are Leaving Church…and Rethinking Faith* (Grand Rapids, MI: Baker Books, 2011), 77.

it that we have so many biblically literate Christians who are missionally ineffective disciples?

Allow me to illustrate with a brief parable.

A Bible teacher charges his people to take the gospel to the world. Each person gets handed a spear—the only weapon he or she will have to use for the gospel. But something's wrong. Though the shafts of the spears are straight, sturdy, and strong, the spears have no points.

Not deterred by the apparent oversight, and in full obedience to their leader's charge, out into the world the people go, bounding forth with spears in hand. It is not long before the people realize that they lack the means to accomplish their noble task. Some try to use the spear, but because it lacks a piercing tip, it does not capture anything, managing only to bruise and bludgeon. After a few such episodes, these individuals come to reckon that this weaponry must be meant for others who possess a much greater agility than they.

Not long after, the teacher is again handing out more spears! Hearing the impassioned words of their leader, the people reassess their thinking and decide that the spear shafts must indeed work. So, out again with enthusiasm they go! But the tip-less reality cannot be overcome. Thus, the results are the same as before. And then there's another message given… and then another.

The core understudies, however, already aware of their tip-less plight, deaden themselves with passivity, saying, "Fool me once, shame on you. Fool me twice, shame on me." Their excited urgency wanes. The promised adventure of the Christian life didn't pan out, at least not for them.

Adding to the shortfall, that which is well-received from the pulpit with shouts of "Amen!" may actually prove harmful to their efforts at witnessing. Such is the case when all they pick up is how "righteous" and right they are, and how "unrighteous" and wrong others are. They unwittingly turn into judgmental jerks! Or perhaps all they really got was another push to go out there and boldly get in others' faces with the gospel (a tactic that does not encourage receptivity), targeting strangers (an approach that is highly ineffective in today's relational climate) with an emphasis on eternal life (a theme that seems irrelevant to present-day thinkers). All that those well-meaning words did was set them up to fail, missionally.

There is a better way.

## A TALE OF TWO MISSIONS

As God would have it, at the time when one leader was saying no to the mission on-ramp, another leader was saying yes. Our response to mission tells a story. A group invited me to come introduce my book *Launch Point* and set them off on their journey. I don't know if I have ever given that inspirational pep talk without at least a degree of doubt regarding what will happen. Gospel mission is a lump-in-the-throat, gut-check challenge for everyone.

After completing a few weeks of the training laid out in *Launch Point*, the leader dropped me an update. After some back-and-forth deliberation about possible projects (a fantastic exercise that moves a group beyond the typical "one-hit wonder" thinking into thoughts of ongoing mission development), they decided to partner with the L.A. Dream Center to do outreach in their area. The project would involve serving at a local refuge shelter, with the idea of developing relationships of spiritual influence over time.

Meanwhile, I received via text message a praise report from one of their participants, Pam, who had begun pursuing a relationship with a Muslim friend. She and her husband, Steve, had shared a meal with Haani and Mohammed. The conversation had come alive when Mohammed expressed an interest to hear more about Jesus, and they had ended up sharing the whole gospel with him. Pam and Steve were thrilled!

When I later learned that Haani had not returned any of Pam's calls or text messages, I became concerned about Pam's pace. Pace is vital to the efficacy of mission. Understanding this dynamic, which can prove a tough read, helps us avoid the too-much-too-soon syndrome, where, in our zeal to share, we may overwhelm an individual and threaten our relationship. It's the equivalent of shooting oneself in the foot.

Seeing Pam at a party a few days later, I coached her, "Focus on building the relationship. If the relationship is solid and feels safe, it will be able to hold the conversation." (Here I touched on Skill #2: Safety.) Establishing safety enables our friends to be, believe, and express anything and everything, without threatening the relationship in any way. Most Christians are terrible at safety; in fact, they are often the antithesis of grace and patience, getting all hot and huffy when someone expresses an opposing point of view. The result is that love is lost and vital dialogue shuts down. During one of my trainings, a woman broke down in tears when she realized that her reaction to her son had pushed him further away. Believer-evangelists need to be taught how to extend safety lines to open up a conversation—lines such as, "We don't have to agree on everything. I don't expect that. I am just glad that, as friends, we can share our real thoughts with each other. I value your honesty and will always treasure our friendship."

I encouraged Pam to persevere. The fact that her Muslim friend had not responded to her text messages was not the end, I hoped, but just the beginning. I told Pam to keep praying, loving, and reaching out. There was a bigger story to pursue.

Then I got another report from the group leader, Dayna. It had to do with an unexpected development on the day they did their outreach. A man without any form of identification showed up with an object lodged in his foot. The volunteers praised God when a worker spoke up and said he was a doctor. He examined the man's foot, and then he and several other team members took the man to the doctor's office for treatment. A conversation over the course of the drive revealed that the injured man was a leader of the Mongols, an infamous biker gang. He disclosed some rather disturbing things he and his fellow Mongols had done, much to the disbelief of Dayna and the other workers.

After the man's foot had been treated, the group got back in the car to return to the shelter. Dayna, mindful of the *Launch Point* training she had received, circled back to continue the earlier conversation and applied some of the skills—namely, Skill #3, Drawing, which takes the dialogue to a deeper place. Following up with some second-tier questions, she asked the man, "Can you tell us more about your experiences?" and "How are you feeling and coping with it right now?" He went further into his story. By the end of the trip, the conversation had gone so deeply into his life and needs, resulting in such wide spiritual openings that Dayna ended up leading him to Christ! He reported, "There have been times when I could have done it before, but I knew I wasn't going to change my ways, so I didn't." Dayna and her fellow workers were overjoyed.

Then I heard about another group member practicing Skill #4: Framing, or the way we create ongoing conversations. After initiating a dialogue about faith with his daughter's boyfriend, this man took things deliberately slowly, not going too far or too fast at first. At a natural stopping point, he extended an invitation to continue the conversation at a later time. (One of my axioms is, "We need to have a conversation about having a conversation.") Over the next several weeks, two more talks occurred, each one going further and becoming more personal. During the third dialogue, his daughter's boyfriend surprised this man by inquiring, "How does one become a Christian?" and then, "Can I do that?" After the father had made some clarifications, Pat came to Jesus.

Most of the others in this group had never seen anything close to the fruit of conversions. Mitch, who works with the Yamaha racing crowd, was well-positioned inside this subculture; but, over the years, he had not led anyone to Christ. With his Christian presence on public display, he felt convicted by *Launch Point* to up the ante with certain relationships, some of which were of the "hardcore" variety. In one unprovoked, flurried exchange, when a guy was railing about God and the existence of "other alien worlds," Mitch found that a spiritual response just rolled off his tongue: "I am just glad I know the One who said, 'I am that I am.'" His racer friend paused to take it in. Mitch has continued working the process, seeking God to provide more inroads.

Finally, there was the medical worker who had a meaningful conversation at the hospital with a young female cancer patient named Kai. It was the caring persona of this missionary-in-disguise that drew the attention of Kai, and when Kai heard her talk openly about her faith, she jumped to join the group. Her journey with Christ had begun. Amid news of a frightening prognosis, she found new faith, new friends, and new, transcendent joy!

The quality of these various engagements stimulated reflection on my part. I recalled the night that I sat before this group, appealing for them to launch out and engage for the gospel. And now I was pinching myself over what had transpired. I have seen the dominos fall time and again. It's as if God is just waiting for us to take a step, to move forward with his plan; and when we do, he is ready to bless and confirm our prime calling.

As I mentally categorized these stories—a Muslim couple, a Mongols' leader, an unsaved boyfriend, a member of the racing subculture, a frightened patient looking for hope—it struck me that none of these things happened to people at the church where prayer walks were the only mission. Not only that, but the missional discipleship of the members' lives didn't happen, either. Contrast that to the vital spiritual health of Christians doing what they were meant to do: learning and developing new skills, sharing joys, drawing inspiration from one another's experiences, growing in faith, depending on the Spirit, and empowering new believers. It's exciting, fulfilling, and the best that the Christian life has to offer!

When I think of the pastor who declined engaging his people in mission, I believe he had a wrong view of discipleship, as well as an insufficient view of how to bring about his congregants' personal spiritual growth. Can you see it? You need *pattern* and *permeation* principles at work to achieve *ReMission*.

## STRUCTURING YOUR MISSION FORMATION

Most congregations today have two primary growth vehicles: a large, communal worship service during the weekend and individual meetings of small groups during the week. It doesn't take an engineer to know that a two-legged stool will not stand. Try it! You'll find that the seat lacks balance and weight-bearing capacity. In the church, we must add the third "leg." In order for permeation to succeed, leaders must create within their cultures the balance and the weight-bearing capacity for gospel influence to flow through lives all the way out into the neighborhood, community, and world.

This bridging support will not automatically happen from more of the same up-front instruction and routine fellowship. You need missional training coupled with engagement experiences. Hiring mission trainers who understand relational influence dynamics is doable for many churches, but please don't rely on seminars, workshops, and consultants who are still trying to convince church leaders that confrontational evangelism is still effective in today's culture. Even the smallest of churches can afford to equip their people adequately. Make the investment. Plan for a regular missional training time. Read relevant materials together. Interact. Develop the people's skills. Create avenues for them to engage. Evaluate what is happening. Choose to go. Celebrate those who do!

> IN ORDER FOR PERMEATION TO SUCCEED,
> LEADERS MUST CREATE WITHIN THEIR CULTURES
> THE BALANCE AND THE WEIGHT-BEARING
> CAPACITY FOR GOSPEL INFLUENCE TO FLOW
> THROUGH LIVES ALL THE WAY OUT INTO THE
> NEIGHBORHOOD, COMMUNITY, AND WORLD.

The third section of this book will illustrate the ways your people can benefit from a mission path. If you are serious about raising up your people to carry the gospel into the world, you must assess what it will require, realistically. *You get what you aim for!*

———

The wise, empowering leader realizes that it is necessary to approach any given problem from multiple points of attack. As you lead, one thing you need to convey often is that *mission does not get dynamic until it gets specific.* People may listen to you. They may pray, in general. But nothing amazing or miraculous will occur until they stop trying to reach the world and start trying to reach someone in their relational circle, until they stop trying to reach their neighborhood and start trying to reach a neighbor. When it gets personal, the learning curve begins. They will try and fail. Don't rob them of this experience. Failure is success. Each engagement is a mirror. It begins their missional formation toward becoming Christ-following disciples.

In the next chapter, we will add another pillar to shape your people's interface with the world. We have talked about the importance of *pattern* and *permeation.* Now, let's add to the culture mix the raw potency of *posture.*

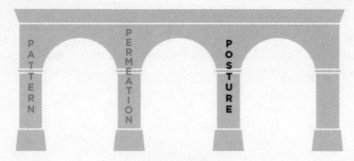

## REFLECTIONS

1.  What do you think of the author's analysis that refraction is occurring in the teaching ministry of the church? Have you ever experienced an instance of this type of refraction?

2.  From your assessment of your own people, what would be sufficient to close the pulpit-to-pew gap in order to shape effective representatives for Christ? Get specific. Make a list.

3.  Do you have a serious training mechanism in place? Along those lines, how effective do you consider your missional training ministry at this juncture? Rate it from 1 to 10, 1 being not at all effective, 10 being completely effective. Be sure you aren't wearing your rose-colored glasses!

## REMISSION TAKEAWAYS

1.  Mission formation occurs within the form of learning, practice, and engagement.

2.  Up-front teaching has limitations that must be recognized and addressed if the church is to realize its missional potential.

3.  A serious training structure must be in place to support your people as they extend their influence all the way out into the community.

4.  It takes *pattern* (emulation) and *permeation* (engagement learning) to achieve *ReMission*.

# —5—

# THE POSTURE

In every block of marble I see a statue as plain as though it stood before me, shaped and perfect in attitude and action. I have only to hew away the rough walls that imprison the lovely apparition to reveal it to the other eyes as mine see it.
—Michelangelo Buonarotti

**W**ho could not but be intrigued by a film with an opening voice-over in which a character states, "I'm forty-two years old. In less than a year, I'll be dead." Every now and then, a movie comes along that has a lot to say or gives us a lot to talk about. The 2000 Oscars Best Picture winner, *American Beauty*, did both. Its R rating means that it's not for everyone. Just consider this sampling of the list of key terms related to its plot:

> Depression, lust, drugs, sex, teen sexuality, adultery, guns, domestic abuse, older man - younger woman, voyeurism, dysfunctional family, fantasy, marital problems, gay sex, self hatred, child abuse, midlife crisis, dissatisfaction, deceit, masturbation, murder, alienation, suburbia, camera, role models, unhappy marriage, family dinner.[54]

The mere fact that a man's midlife crisis has him fantasizing over his daughter's cheerleader friend is enough to qualify this film for the "debauchery" shelf, yet there's a mildly redeeming sliver of hope that threads

---

54. http://www.imdb.com/title/tt0169547/keywords (accessed March 3, 2014).

its way throughout this story. We see the classic dichotomy of successful suburbanites in search of something more. Perhaps you can relate to this yearning of the soul. I know I do. As a backdrop to this sense of stirring, as alluded to in the title of the film, is the idea that beauty exists all around us—if we could only see it.

The theme comes sharply into focus with the character of Ricky, Lester's teenage next-door neighbor, who comes across as a creepy pervert with his incessant videotaping of teenage neighbor Jane through her bedroom window but turns out to be genuinely enamored of Jane's real beauty, not her body. Indeed, high-school-age Ricky videotapes everything, much of his subjects mundane. Yet as he shows Jane what he has captured on film, one has to agree that there is a strange kind of beauty to it. He's particularly proud of some footage of a plastic bag blowing freely in his driveway—"And this bag was just dancing with me. Like a little kid begging me to play with it. For fifteen minutes," he says. "Sometimes there's so much beauty in the world, I feel like I can't take it, and my heart is just going to cave in."[55]

The thread continues with the main character, Lester Burnham. InterVarsity movie critic Pete Luisi-Mills interprets...

> This is a film about how Lester learns what true beauty is: what his marriage was before they lost their way; the happiness of his daughter; making the right decision when the time comes, and doing the right thing regardless of what misguided thoughts he may have entertained in weaker moments. The fact that he loses his life just as he discovers what makes life truly meaningful is sad and ironic, but the important thing is that he learned it at all.[56]

What I am doing here is attempting to engage in a dialogue with *you* about the intersection of mission and culture by selecting a movie's decadent menu to set the conversational table. If you were to reference this movie, which depicts questionable morals, in your next sermon, Facebook

---

55. *American Beauty*. Directed by Sam Mendes, Universal City, CA: DreamWorks Pictures, 1999.
56. Pete Luisi-Mills, review of *American Beauty* by director Sam Mendes, *DreamWorks Pictures* (September 17, 1999).

post, or church newsletter, you would provoke a wide range of respons-es. Not everyone would appreciate the down-and-dirty commentary on contemporary life. Some might even disapprove of your viewing choice. In fact, you might be questioning mine right now.

What does the run-of-the-mill Christian think about *American Beauty*, I wonder? How much righteous angst should we generate toward our lost world and its artful expressions? On a higher note, not wanting to presume, I wonder what God thinks. We know God hates sin. But when he eyes the real soul-searching sinners embellished in this film, what does he see most clearly? Does any of this really matter when it comes to the church fulfilling its mandate?

Therein lies the kernel, a dark seed that deserves a great amount of light.

———

Standing outside the church venue, twenty-year-old Jeremy felt like a fish out of water. "What am I doing here?" he wondered aloud. Fringe friends had encouraged him to come, so he risked a stop-by. When Andrew, on staff, started up a conversation, Jeremy asked if anyone had a cigarette. It just so happened one of the members did, and he offered Jeremy a smoke. As he lit up, Jeremy bantered with a female connection leader, "Your church has a lot of hot girls." Scanning for and then finding the words for a reply, she said, "Yes, we do!" Later, Jeremy spouted off a few expletive-laden thoughts, but it didn't faze Andrew, as they conversed fluidly.

Jeremy felt comfortable with this group, and so, when Andrew invited him over for dinner, he accepted. As everybody sat down to share a meal together, Jeremy reasoned to himself, *This church is not as bad as I thought. I might even come back.* And he did.

Have you ever observed your members engaged in an impromptu mis-sion test such as this one? How did they do? In their neighborhood or the church parking lot, would they eagerly embrace and ably interface with someone like Jeremy? While we were attending a conference, my wife, Robin, had a conversation with a lady who told her she would never attend another public baseball game because of the awful (inebriated) people in the crowd. Then, in the elevator, we watched a woman roll her eyes and heard her snide comment about another woman's "seamy" dress. What type of conference were we attending, you ask? It was a mission conference. The entire event was devoted to the goal of reaching others for the gospel. It just didn't seem that these attendees had any idea what that might require of them. *How do leaders shape a culture that reaches the increasing numbers who view church as a club to which they do not belong?* Seeing churchgoers as morally upright and spit-polished clean already, the witty but skeptical author Samuel Clemens (better known by his pseudonym, Mark Twain) deduced, "Church is a good person talking to good people about being a good person." We laugh. But, from a mission angle, it's no laughing matter. The really twisted thing is how all the "good people" in church are nothing close to being good. To prove my point, most churchgoers can probably identify quite personally with one or more of the aforementioned plot words associated with *American Beauty*. Go back and take a look at them, one by one.

As much as it's not my aim to shame anyone over their sin condition, I want us to stay on this very question: *How do we shape a church body or group that relates well with unsaved people, in and outside its walls?* Can the living water flow freely apart from its people's attitudinal space? For purposes of *ReMission*, I'm asking you to think deeply about the culture you are creating—the end result of your discipleship efforts. As Michelangelo observed each raw slab of marble, envisioning its perfect shape in attitude and action, what kind of Jesus-disciples are you molding? Are they profoundly honest, deeply humble, grace oriented, and missionally focused? How do you even begin to influence and develop a whole culture to fulfill Christ's prime directive?

Church leaders must be discerning here. In *Church Turned Inside Out*, authors Linda Bergquist and Allan Karr ask compellingly, "But what if, despite our good intentions, we are actually propagating church systems that in our day are creating the opposite of what we want?"[57] To lean the discussion practically, let me rephrase the question: *What kind of chipping and hewing will be sufficient to reveal a masterpiece mission culture?* Of course,

---

57. Linda Bergquist and Allan Karr, *Church Turned Inside Out: A Guide for Designers, Refiners, and Re-Aligners* (San Francisco, CA: Jossey-Bass, 2010), 10.

biblical teaching and extensive engagement training (which most churches struggle with) play a vital role, given what we see in today's church with its natural drift toward isolationism and self-righteousness. But those may not be nearly enough.

To course correct, church leadership must take responsibility. You could approach the problem through biblical exhortation, but a much more effective way is to work it from the inside out. Mission must be internalized in order for the greatest possible transformation to occur. Anytime we can get outward shaping happening at the internal level, we will also see more natural results.

## END-IN-MIND DESIGN

When I was a young boy, my sister won a California State Debate championship. I recall listening to her award-winning speech, which referenced the famous Joni Mitchell song "Both Sides, Now." The lyrics speak of having looked at life from two sides. Part of my own story is that I have looked at church from both sides. I grew up in the modern scene, planted some churches, and then served five years at a renowned postmodern church. From those distinct contexts, I formed an opinion on the most effective shapers of missionality.

Matt Brown founded Sandals Church with a vision of authenticity—*being real with ourselves, God, and others*. The rejection he experienced after admitting to a particular sin led him to start a church where people could talk openly about their struggles. The hope was to create a culture where he could wear sandals, and others would accept him, even with his big, ugly, gnarly toes. (Matt, you are beautiful, brother.) Today, 9,000 people call Sandals home because they need daily doses of grace, too. The story is similar to that of Toby Slough from Cross Timbers Church in Texas, who began a church for people with "life issues" like his.[58]

These, and many other real-life churches, hold great appeal in an era when people are dying for truth and grace, do not want to be shunned because of past or present behaviors, and dislike pretentious Christians. It takes guts to lead authenticity-aimed ministries. Where others might

58. Scott Thumma and Dave Travis, *Beyond Megachurch Myths: What We Can Learn from America's Largest Churches* (San Francisco, CA: Jossey-Bass, 2007), 30.

attack or criticize a leader for being so open about his or her personal mess-es, these church families are okay with their falling short. They don't ex-pect their leaders to be perfect or to stand on a pedestal.

> REAL-LIFE CHURCHES, HOLD GREAT APPEAL
> IN AN ERA WHEN PEOPLE ARE DYING FOR TRUTH
> AND GRACE, DO NOT WANT TO BE SHUNNED
> BECAUSE OF PAST OR PRESENT BEHAVIORS, AND
> DISLIKE PRETENTIOUS CHRISTIANS.

In my doctorate program, a colleague researching church-planting pitfalls addressed the class. Seeking examples from church planters, and being aware of my storied journey, he called on me. I responded by sharing about my close call with a nervous breakdown before the launch of my first church, and said that I faced a battle with lust and temptation in my second (I recall reading Proverbs 5 over and over again). I know these disclosures may have shocked a few members of our high-level course; and you may know, from my public story of recovery, that I didn't even tell them every-thing. It's hard for leaders to discuss the sick parts of who we are because we are "supposed to be" above sin—always—at every moment and in every season of life. The message subtly conveyed by most churches is "Shame on you, if you're not!"

Yet idyllic expectations of our leaders, or of ourselves as leaders, do not serve us well. When we try to look better than we really are, our intrinsic spin machine undercuts our efforts at transparency and undermines our righteousness. Although I have not always had the spiritual innards to bare it all, after I made that disclosure during class, a pastor of a growing thou-sand-member church walked over to me, thanked me for my courage, and then said, "The temptation level from women in my church is scary, and what would I do if one pursued me?" We talked in a refreshingly candid way. Afterward, I couldn't help but wonder if I was the only safe person with whom he could share his struggles. I reckoned that by confessing to me, he had cut away the nasty web that had been pulling on him. Honest confession has that kind of power.

> WHEN WE TRY TO LOOK BETTER THAN
> WE REALLY ARE, OUR INTRINSIC SPIN MACHINE
> UNDERCUTS OUR EFFORTS AT TRANSPARENCY
> AND UNDERMINES OUR RIGHTEOUSNESS.

## HARD ASSESSMENT: RESIDUAL TOXICITY

After gathering reflections from church leaders, I developed a chart based upon value prominence. I realize that my analysis may be controversial. Before pelting me with vegetables (or stones), please keep in mind that I am not familiar with your church or group. You can use the chart to assess where you think you and your church would be, and consider whether my observations ring true in any way. They may not in your church. Or you may think they don't apply, only to find out, later on, that they do! I created this grid as an evaluation tool for shaping culture by examining the chain reactions from the two primary focuses: the modern value of righteousness and the postmodern value of authenticity.

Now, I realize that modern-minded believers tend to equate the word "authenticity" with genuine spirituality. That is not the way I am going to use it for the person who is transparent with personal sin. However, please notice how that preferential usage supports my distinction. How you interpret the word "authenticity" will indicate where you stand, value-wise. In general terms, the righteousness church desires for its people to live righteously (practicing right living) before God and others. The authenticity church seeks for its people to live authentically (practicing open confession) before God and others.

Obviously, since both groups teach the whole counsel of God, I am talking about emphasis, not mutual exclusivity. In that vein, let me quickly affirm that righteousness churches do value honest confession, and that authenticity churches do value righteous living. But the difference exists in the emphasis on what ultimately matters, and how that emphasis shapes disciples.

Look at what occurs from a sequential chain-reaction perspective:

| RIGHTEOUSNESS | AUTHENTICITY |
|:---:|:---:|
| Hiding of Sin | Honest with Sin |
| Without Confession<br>*(Less Growth & Righteousness)* | With Confession<br>*(More Growth & Righteousness)* |
| Judgmental Posture | Humble Posture |
| *Not Positioned for Mission* | *Positioned for Mission* |

Again, this progression is anecdotal, not based on hard data. I'll admit that any one of us may have a skewed perspective, but, as a writer, I am striving for objectivity. From my wide-latitudinal observations, I believe the authenticity value better shapes the church toward effective mission. The logic is sequential. If church members honestly own their personal sin issues, there is greater humility, and a corresponding growth in compassion. In addition, with humility, members more naturally embrace a broader range of people, not seeing themselves as superior to those in the culture (I'm not referring to their positional identity and standing in Christ). A deeper awareness of sin enables them to relate to, and connect with, unsaved individuals along many common issues. When it comes to mission, this matters!

That said, just because a church is positioned for mission does not guarantee the fruitfulness of its efforts. Not all authenticity churches are as effective as they could be, because of other key elements we will discuss in the course of this book. Yet the interfacing posture with the Jeremys of our world is significant and should be underscored. The attitudes of your people *will come out* in their convictions and conversations. This, from my vantage point, is where the church is missing it big-time!

Of course, righteousness-focused churches can value humility, too. I read an article in *Leadership Journal* about a church that was going through a process of confession and repentance sparked by the departure of 50 percent of its members. This historically prominent church owned up to four areas of sin, two of which were "arrogance" and "gracelessness." According to the article, these sins found expression in the "pulpit, pew, parking lot, and public square."[59] The article detailed people's unsavory attitudes toward other churches and toward fellow members of their church body. This act of open confession was a beautiful, courageous step on the part of this church, but you don't have to be a sociologist to see that the two noted sins—"arrogance" and "gracelessness"—are righteousness-value by-products. If a church overemphasizes the attainability of righteousness, these residual effects of superiority will undoubtedly ensue.

But how do unbelievers see the church? As you might expect, they commonly express that Christians appear "unchristianly" and judgmental.[60] Why is this perception so widespread? I would argue that it's not because we stand for truth and righteousness, but rather that there's something religiously Pharisaical in the mind-set of churchgoers that affects their interface with the world. In other words, non-Christians are picking up something toxic. Like lead bleeding into the water supply, the toxicity is pervasive. Who, I ask, is going to change or check that toxic flow? And how? If you are not pointing at yourself, you might need a moment with Jesus. My favorite John Maxwell quote is, "The church is where we led it." His words confront us indiscriminately: *Leaders look in the mirror!* You are responsible for your people.

So, in the spirit of *ReMission*, let's carve into church culture with a hewing chisel.

---

59. Doug Tegner, "A Repenting Church: How One Congregation Turned (and Continues to Turn) From Its Sins." *Leadership Journal* (Spring 2010). Available at: http://www.christianitytoday.com/le/2010/spring/repentingchurch.html?paging=off.
60. David Kinnaman and Gabe Lyons, *Unchristian: What a New Generation Really Thinks About Christianity…and Why It Matters* (Grand Rapids, MI: Baker Books, 2007), 28.

## CULTURE SHAPER: CONFESSIONAL PRACTICE

The confessional act of James 5:16 is esteemed in both modern- and postmodern-leaning churches, yet it is scantly practiced. You may have seen the video of a discussion between singer/songwriter Bono and Eugene Peterson on the "brutal honesty" of the Psalms; it spoke volumes to me. Bono, alluding to the disparity between the psalmist's rawness and today's (church) songs, says, "I would love if this conversation would inspire people who are writing these beautiful gospel songs [to] write a song about their bad marriage. Write a song about how they're pissed off at the government. Because that's what God wants from you, the truth. And that truthfulness...will blow things apart." Then Bono makes this jarring aside: "Why I am suspicious of Christians is because of this lack of realism." Eugene Peterson commented that he translated the Psalms in his *Message* Bible with the goal of getting his readers to understand that "praying wasn't being 'nice' before God." He was aiming for honesty, which is "very, very hard in our culture."[61]

Admittedly, it is hard to be transparent. Who doesn't want to look good? One thing is certain: Whatever your chosen focus, whether righteousness (which caters to your looking godly and being complete) or authenticity (which exposes your sinfulness and neediness), there will be corresponding outcomes. In my best, fair assessment, the authenticity value achieves more in shaping the church in the right projection, missionally speaking.

By leading your people into greater honesty/humility with themselves, you will shape them and your church culture. A grace culture positions the church to accept and embrace messy people—*people like us*! By becoming equals (again, not referring to our positional standing in Christ), we elevate our chances of reaching nonbelievers. That's because we can relate! Christians who rid themselves of the toxicity of self-righteousness can more readily disclose aspects of their own sin condition to show nonbelievers how Christ is working in them by his grace and power.

---

61. "Bono and Eugene Peterson: THE PSALMS," YouTube Video, 21:42, discussion about the Psalms' relevance, April 26, 2016, posted by Fuller Studio, August 14, 2016, https://www.youtube.com/watch?v=-l40S5e90KY.

A GRACE CULTURE POSITIONS THE CHURCH TO
ACCEPT AND EMBRACE MESSY PEOPLE—*PEOPLE
LIKE US*! BY BECOMING EQUALS, WE ELEVATE OUR
CHANCES OF REACHING NONBELIEVERS.

This humble posture, after the pattern set by Christ, can be leveraged for major gospel impact. Do your people, like the thirsting Jesus
asking assistance from a Samaritan woman, lead with their need? His
vulnerable query *"Will you give me a drink?"* (John 4:7) launched her
salvation story. And this practice is critical for postmodern influence.
In my first book, I termed it "The Disclosure Window" (which corre-
sponds with Skill #5: Disclosure). One of the ways to provide a clear
window to the spiritual remedy, this is the instance of believers allowing outsiders to glimpse Christ's light from the dark backdrop of their
vulnerably exposed lives. In this age of raw reality, it's a potent way to
share our faith.

In the process of producing a YouTube series on the concepts (also
available on RightNow Media) I share in my book *Soul Whisperer*, I
interviewed two people who had used the method of disclosure to
lead their friends to Christ. While in his hometown of Boston, Scott
Brennan had gotten to know a college-aged man through a series of casual conversations. One day at Starbucks, they got into a deeper dialogue in which the young man shared about his struggle with same-sex
attraction. Scott, in turn, told of the anguish he experienced from the
words and eventual abandonment of his father when he was twelve years
old, and the devastating wound that had wreaked havoc on his soul. In
the video, Scott recounts, "Right after I shared that, he began opening
up, saying, 'You are talking about my life.'" As they weighed in with each
other, Scott said, "Disclosure led to other disclosure. Through that, I
was able to allow him to share—to bring him to the place to come all
the way out, and expose the fears, expose the sense of abandonment
and shame." After this deep connection was made, Scott found it easy
to direct the young man to Christ with these words: "Is there anything

holding you back? This is where God meets us." There were tears. They prayed together.[62]

In another video, a man named Marc opened up at work about his marital breakdown, which caused his nonbelieving friend to reciprocate, disclosing aspects of his own battle with stress: "I feel like the weight of the world is on my shoulders."[63] This open exchange segued naturally to the words of Christ in Matthew 11:28–30: "*Come to me, all you who are weary and burdened, and I will give you rest. Take my yoke upon you and learn from me, for I am gentle and humble in heart, and you will find rest for your souls. For my yoke is easy and my burden is light.*" From this seeded thought, his friend Tom, who had long been disbelieving and uninterested, suddenly went out to purchase a Bible. Months later, Tom began attending church and came to faith soon thereafter.

The benefits of personal disclosure are massive in the mission column: (1) It comes across in the communication naturally, (2) it deepens relational bonds, (3) it draws reciprocal sharing, (4) it shapes the nonbeliever's heart toward humility, setting the need for the cross, and (5) it gives a true picture of the Christian faith. To recapitulate: Christ reaches for every person in his or her weakness, and the skill of disclosure helps others see how he meets people right where they are with his grace and power. Have you thoroughly developed this skill among the people of your church, group, or mission agency? How many of your people have led others to faith by sharing their own need? We could reach so many more by tapping into this skill!

The *ReMission* challenge of leaders, then, is to get the humility-based posture extending through every member of their congregation or group, because they are the ones who will be rubbing shoulders with the Starbucks friend, with the Toms and the Jeremys of the world. They're the ones who must pass the mission test. With the mantle placed on leadership, the first way to synergize the transformation is through modeling. The principle is

---

62. "Real Evangelism: Does Honesty Hurt the Gospel?", YouTube Video, 10:14, Gary Comer interviews Scott Brennan, posted by Soul Whisperer Ministries, April 21, 2015. https://www.youtube.com/watch?v=hqCoW3n9q4s.

63. "Relational Evangelism: Learn How to Draw Hearts to Christ," YouTube Video, 7:30, Gary Comer discussion with Marc Santoro, posted by Soul Whisperer Ministries, April 21, 2015. https://www.youtube.com/watch?v=wDFeJNgfKY8.

this: *If the pastor can't be honest and confess his or her sins and struggles, the people can't do it, either.*

> CHRIST REACHES FOR EVERY PERSON IN HIS OR HER WEAKNESS, AND THE SKILL OF DISCLOSURE HELPS OTHERS SEE HOW HE MEETS PEOPLE RIGHT WHERE THEY ARE WITH HIS GRACE AND POWER.

In one-on-one communication, disclosure does have its limits and boundaries. We do not want to be inappropriate, to dump too much on our listeners, or exceed the level of intimacy of our relationship. But I tend to believe pastor-teachers who are already esteemed by their congregants can be far more impactful by leaning into being vulnerable and transparent. Observing the self-labeled "Chief of Sinners," aka the apostle Paul, pastors, and all believers, can make personal disclosures to their audiences in four ways: (1) their sin, (2) their struggle, (3) their striving, and (4) their story.[64] What made Paul so effective was his specific relatability: talking on the theology of sin in personal terms (see Romans 7); talking about his vulnerable emotional states: he was in *"fear and trembling"* (1 Corinthians 2:3) in Corinth and *"under great pressure, far beyond our ability to endure, so that we despaired of life itself"* (2 Corinthians 1:8) in Asia (sounded almost suicidal); talking about his strivings and unfulfilled dreams (mission blockage, the Corinthian authority-usurping ordeal); talking about his story of how God leveraged divine power by curbing his pride through pain in weakness (*"to keep me from becoming conceited, I was given a thorn in my flesh"* [2 Corinthians 12:7]). Ralph Winter, a film producer with notable credits that include the *X-Men* films, critiqued, "Christians are bad storytellers when they omit the journey that leads to the transformation."[65] But that wasn't Paul. As a communicator, he used disclosure brilliantly to

---

64. Comer, *Soul Whisperer*, 62–66.
65. Ralph Winter, "How the Gospel is Represented in Modern Film" (presentation at California Baptist University, Riverside, California, February 28, 2013).

show the untidy inner conflict, gut-wrenching tension, and difficulty of his Christian life.

| SIN | Sin-Nature Vulnerabilities | Romans 7:14-15 |
|---|---|---|
| **STRUGGLE** | *Life Difficulties* | 2 Corintians 1:8-9<br>1 Corinthians 2:3<br>2 Corinthians 2:4 |
| **STRIVING** | *Limitations to Achieving* | 1 Thessalonians 2:17-18<br>2 Corinthians 1:23-2:2 |
| **STORY** | *Overcoming Obstacles* | 2 Corinthians 12:7-9 |

from the life of the Apostle Paul

Do not Paul's "tellings on himself" sing hope to our souls, letting us know we are not alone in our human experience and the spiritual fight? If you teach up-front, I am just going to say it straight: There is an enormous honesty gap in the church that is hindering the flow of the Spirit. Stop pontificating, and start sharing how it is that your life—fallen, flawed, and frayed as it is—intersects with the holy call to this radically other being we call God. And when you do, just watch what happens. Applying Paul's categories will take your communication to a level of powerful connectivity, and God will honor your integrity by using it! Of course, you can't fake it. It's going to have to be real—you in your own skin—if it's going to resonate with the broad brush of culture.

Disclosure also opens a window to what other people cannot readily see: our daily need for Jesus. I have always loved this prayer of humility: "God, I thank you this day that I haven't gotten impatient or upset with anyone, nor have I acted from selfishness or spite, but in a few moments, Lord, I am going to get out of bed—and when I do, I am going to need your help." How refreshing it is for church members to hear pastors and leaders admit their need for Christ! We should say, for example, "In our household, we have been working through some hard issues lately. If you have struggled in your relationships or your marriage, I want you to know, we need Christ's help, just like you do." Or, "This week, I found myself testing the depths of selfishness. Apologizing to my kids, I thought, *I do not have love in myself; I desperately need Jesus for that, freshly, every day.*" Or, "After the staff meeting, I was so frustrated that if I hadn't gotten a dose of supernatural patience from God, I might have killed someone!" Okay, maybe avoid that last one. But, from time to time, we should tell our people how grateful we are for God's grace that forgives and restores us again and again.

A man who has spent a lot of time with pastors all over the globe, author-speaker Paul Tripp writes the following in his book *Dangerous Calling*:

> I wish I could encourage you with the fact that most pastors are known for their humility and approachability. I wish I could say that most pastors minister out of a deep sense of their own need. Yes, I wish I could say all of these things, but I can't.[66]

In defense of pastors, the way that modern church culture has put them on a pedestal, turning churches into cults of personality, can make honesty virtually impossible. To support authentic leaders, soaring expectations from church boards should return to something more realistic. Idealistic overseers directly prevent the congregation from learning to extend grace because they force the pastor into pretending, and the pastor's fear of being truly known spreads into the body. Everyone remains afraid of being honest and vulnerable. It doesn't even have to be said; the pew picks up on a pastor who *doesn't ever* confess sin, and they conclude that Christian normalcy is sinlessness.

Thus begins the duplicity that stems from the decision, "I will hide my sin from others so that my life looks closer to what I see in my pastor. As long as I keep up that public perception, everything will be okay. If I am really struggling, or if I fall, I know that I will need to find another church where they don't know the truth about me. But, for now, I just need to hang in there. Perhaps, in time, I will become righteous like everybody else."

---

66. Paul Tripp, *Dangerous Calling: Confronting the Unique Challenges of Pastoral Ministry* (Wheaton, IL: Crossway, 2012), 29.

This line of reasoning continues, "As to the world, I will keep my distance from nonbelievers, who could pull me down. The most important thing is my purity. In fact, my pastor told me the reason nonbelievers are not following Christ is because I'm not devoted enough. Damn it! Oops, I shouldn't have said that. Sorry, God. If only I really lived the Christian life. I'll have to work much harder on my righteousness, so that my unsaved friends will look on from afar and, seeing my shining example, come to faith." (At this point, if you are feeling nauseous and need to grab a bucket, please go ahead.)

This false front is sad, especially in that it disables believers from doing anything more than pew-sitting. Dan Crowley, the soul care pastor at Sandals Church, once told me, "The focus on behavior has turned so many away from God and the church." In his ministry, Dan says, the focus is not on behavior but rather on what is going on at the deep soul level. "If we don't get to the deeper formation level," he says, "we have not achieved anything." Sounds like Jesus, doesn't it? I realize that good teaching addresses behavior and action, but if it's true Christianity, it's an inside-out, grace-girded job!

## LEVERAGING LANGUAGE

A powerful tool for sculpting culture is the sin template. Writing on congregational shaping, JR Woodward states, "Language is central to any culture. It is through language that we have a narrative to inhabit."[67] Providing a description of common sin patterns gives your people the language to talk about their own issues. Teaching them how to identify the roots of sin not only shapes your culture but also liberates your people from the bondage of sin. That's because it's one thing to acknowledge that you struggle in an area; it's quite another to discern what drives that struggle.

Besides a vulnerability to lust, my other "signature sin," as I've learned over time, is deceitfulness. I know that makes me sound like a terrible person. Yet by discerning how this tendency plays out in me—*wanting to look better than I really am*, or *in my unhealthy drive for success*, I have gained clarity on what is off in my soul's fallen fabric. In fact, deceitfulness is driven by

---

67. JR Woodward, *Creating a Missional Culture: Equipping the Church for the Sake of the World* (Downers Grove, IL: InterVarsity Press, 2012), 36.

a warped need to succeed. The pattern has plagued my entire life! Exposing this internal propensity has proven enormously healthy, taking me to the foot of the cross when it comes to my worth, or my lack thereof. I am able to pull out my own red flags when deceit tries to emerge. As you may see, this type of ruthless evaluation is immensely productive for personal growth, fostering deep-rooted correction.

My wife and I have had amazing conversations on how our sinful tendencies affect our marriage. Her signature flaw happens to be pride, and it's fascinating to observe its manifestations. Sometimes, behaviors of hers that seem, on the surface, to be perfectly justifiable are really just clever outworkings of her sin pattern. What? You think I'm going to criticize myself and spare my wife? This is the deeper perspective that occurs when you equip your people with terms to talk about their own issues. By the way, if you work through the list of sins I'm about to share with you, and you cannot identify at least one area that particularly applies to you, then we know what your signature sin is: Pride.

If you teach in a thoughtful way on the manifestations of sin, you will set up your people for some helpful epiphanies. I taught a class in which a woman told me she'd always thought her core vulnerability was lust, but then she traced it all the way back to fear. Her deep sense of insecurity was the driving force that prompted her to act out sexually. This insight was a potent realization. She was seeing her life clearly for the first time. It was the beginning of her breaking new ground in personal growth.

IF YOU TEACH IN A THOUGHTFUL WAY ON THE
MANIFESTATIONS OF SIN, YOU WILL SET UP YOUR
PEOPLE FOR SOME HELPFUL EPIPHANIES.

Because God did not choose to wipe away the sin nature from mankind, believers still have the false self with which to reckon. (For anyone who would argue that Paul is talking in Romans 7 of his pre-Christian life, not his present condition, I say: Consider the placement. If that were the case, the content of Romans 7 should have been positioned prior to Romans 6, and we would not have need of Romans 8!). This sometimes mystifying mixture of natures aligns with God's perfect wisdom in making us humble as we daily abide in his power. Just as everyone has strengths, it is also true that each of us has at least one vulnerable area of weakness. Remember, even Superman had his kryptonite. We have found that in putting your finger down and naming your sin, you take a step toward victory. Naming a sin gets it into the open, out of the place of denial, and harnesses the need for accountability. As the Bible reveals, confession is the gateway to healing. (See James 5:16.)

Right now, take a moment to make an introspective review of some common sins.

*Anger*...the need to be perfect.

*Pride*...the need to be needed.

*Deceit*...the need to succeed.

*Envy*...the need to be unique.

*Greed*...the need to possess.

*Fear*...the need for security.

*Gluttony*...the need for pleasure.

*Lust*...the need for power.

*Laziness*...the need to avoid.[68]

Where are you vulnerable? Could you sign your name to any of the above sins? As a leader, don't you think it would be good for you and your people to know where spiritual yielding is critical, and where the enemy will attack?

The journey into greater authenticity will affect your spiritual life and all your relationships. Introducing confessional language into your church services will also deepen levels of community, since intimacy is a natural by-product. Moreover—and most important for our subject—it will be an

---

68. Richard Rohr and Andreas Ebert, *The Enneagram: A Christian Perspective* (New York, NY: The Crossroad Publishing Company, 2004), 49–178. I am grateful for this work, which pushes us to dump what they term "cosmetic piety."

inside-out shaper of your people's posture toward a lost, sin-conditioned world. You will enhance their agility in interfacing, tooling them to speak humbly and openly about their sin and their need for Christ. In turn, the gospel will flow out through them to others in a more sincere and palatable way.

> THE JOURNEY INTO GREATER AUTHENTICITY WILL AFFECT YOUR SPIRITUAL LIFE AND ALL YOUR RELATIONSHIPS. INTRODUCING CONFESSIONAL LANGUAGE INTO YOUR CHURCH SERVICES WILL ALSO DEEPEN LEVELS OF COMMUNITY, SINCE INTIMACY IS A NATURAL BY-PRODUCT.

I know there is a counterargument to authenticity. In an article published by The Gospel Coalition entitled "Has Authenticity Trumped Holiness?" one contributor states, "While we think self-deprecation causes us to be more relatable and empathetic to non-Christians, it's ultimately communicating a sense of disappointment, disillusionment and discontentment."[69] Really? I disagree. Through the years, as I have led numerous people to Christ through my personal disclosures, not once has any nonbeliever judged me or turned away from the gospel because I entrusted him or her with that vulnerable information, or because I had shared a deep insight on what Christ can do for a soul in need.

And I ask: Disappointment for whom? If we are trying to win non-Christian moralists by out-moralizing them, we have adopted the wrong strategy. I've reached moralists. They need to see sin's pervasiveness, which envelops them just as much as everyone else. Not the watered-down "we have made a mistake or two" sham! If we can't talk about and own our sin in a personal way, then there's no need for a Savior. Moralists are

---

69. Brett McCracken, "Has Authenticity Trumped Holiness?", *The Gospel Coalition* (January 26, 2014). Available at: www.thegospelcoalition.org/article/has-authenticity-trumped-holiness-2.

sinners at their self-righteous core, worthy of God's judgment. Propping up the spiritually glamorous façade does not get goody-goodies from *where they are* to *where they need to go*. Sorry.

Again, God, in his wisdom, chose not to make the eradication of the sin nature part of salvation. Even a spiritual giant such as the apostle Paul admitted to having a pull toward such sins as pride (see, for example, 2 Corinthians 12:7) and acknowledged not having yet arrived (see Romans 7; Philippians 3:12–13). In the Psalms he authored, David was intensely transparent about his wayward heart. We should be very careful how we measure holiness. Jesus viewed the super-devout, moralistic Pharisees as being devoid of love. (See, for example, John 5:42.) Tell me, when it comes to being poured out in love like Jesus was every day in his mission for the Father, is anyone even close?

As difficult as it is to emulate, Christ's pattern is clear. He stepped down from his exalted position to take on the human form, thereby identifying with our human weakness. In this act of humiliation, he surrendered his status in order to open the door for our salvation. (See Philippians 2:5–8.) We have the privilege of doing the same—identifying with other people and their weaknesses for their salvation's sake.

> CHRIST'S PATTERN IS CLEAR. HE STEPPED DOWN FROM HIS EXALTED POSITION TO TAKE ON THE HUMAN FORM, THEREBY IDENTIFYING WITH OUR HUMAN WEAKNESS. IN THIS ACT OF HUMILIATION, HE SURRENDERED HIS STATUS IN ORDER TO OPEN THE DOOR FOR OUR SALVATION.

I know there are many stellar churches full of righteous superstars with huge hearts for mission. We can celebrate them and their testimonies. But all churches ought to have one thing: posture, or a spiritual stance that relates, identifies with, embraces, and attracts real sinners. One that's not so far removed that it keeps believers from putting themselves in others' shoes—understanding the messiness of their lives, feeling their pain, and showing them the path to a better way, even as they travel that road themselves. Yes, that's the church culture I believe can reach today's divergent individuals with the good news. And when I'm looking for a church, if the leader doesn't get this concept or appreciate the raw reality of the human plight, I won't be there for long.

## THE SIGNIFICANCE OF THE SCRAWL

Meditating on the story from John 8 of the woman caught in adultery and corralled by a religious, stone-throwing community, I, like so many others, have puzzled over why the writer captured the detail, *"But Jesus bent down and started to write on the ground with his finger"* (John 8:6). Initially, I surmised that it could have been just one of those mindless actions that had no bearing on the story. Obviously, we will never know, this side of heaven, what Jesus wrote.

Yet perhaps the content of his scrawling misses the point. Maybe the Gospel witness recorded the observation because of its visual effect. Just as the well in John 4 is a symbolic picture of the deep needs of the Samaritan woman Jesus met there, so here, too, Jesus' scribbling means something. These kinds of details, when captured in Scripture, are never haphazard. This mention was made not for the purpose of showing Jesus as a mindless doodler. I didn't see it at first, but one day, the idea dawned on me, much to my excitement: *Could it be that Jesus' scribing, like the imprint on a published record, conveyed the permanence of his words?* Such a thought is fitting, considering what he spoke immediately after his first instance of writing: *"Let any one of you who is without sin be the first to throw a stone at her"* (John 8:7). Interpretively, we could synthesize this timeless truth: There will never be a time, this side of heaven, when you or I will be totally without (or invulnerable to) sin. Wow! What a leveler. When the stone-holders heard his penetrating statement, they silenced their gripes and loosened their grips. Jesus' words insulated the adulterous woman from them, not just that day, but forever! Jesus' next statement also had permanence. Confirming that none had remained to condemn her, Jesus again wrote on the ground to reinforce his words, after which he declared, *"Then neither do I condemn* you….*Go now and leave your life of sin*" (John 8:10). Here, he relayed the fact of her full justification, as well as established her new, permanent life projection of following him, along the lines of what Paul wrote in Romans 8:1: "*There is now no condemnation for those who are in Christ Jesus.*" With his authoritative signature, this vulnerably exposed woman walked away covered in divine favor. It would protect her from sin's shame and penalty, not just that day, but for the rest of her life!

I sometimes wonder what kind of church we could be if we appropriated these juxtaposed truths: First, as confessed sinners, we are never in the place to feel superior to, or throw stones at, anyone. Second, Christ's favor covers all our dark, multidimensional sin in full. Because of those two defining truths, we have every reason to carry the message of his stone-dropping grace to the whole world.

If you were to ask me what I love about the Christian faith, there it is… beauty.

———

The fourth and final pillar, *process*, is no less significant than the first three in shaping your culture. Developing process is a make-or-break concept for missional effectiveness. Let's go!

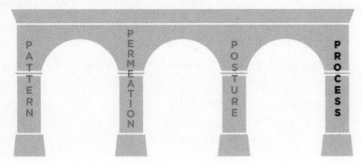

### REFLECTIONS

1.    Do you agree with the assertion that it is the leader's responsibility to shape the posture of the people he or she leads? Why or why not?

2.   Which of these two is the primary emphasis in your body of believers: righteousness or honest confession?

3.   How did you respond to this chapter's analysis that authenticity (honest confession) better facilitates Christian interface with today's culture? Did you feel threatened? Enlightened? Maddened? Empowered?

4.   Take another look, along with your team, at the five benefits of disclosure featured in this chapter. Then, discuss which benefits seem as if they would be the most influential among unsaved people. Finally, brainstorm ways to incorporate the practice of disclosure into your lives on a daily basis.

## REMISSION TAKEAWAYS

1.   Multiple benefits result from using honest disclosure to communicate the gospel.

2.   Pastors must lead the way in shaping their people's open honesty with those outside the faith.

3.   A brilliant communicator, the apostle Paul used four categories to convey personal information on his spiritual journey.

4.   A sin template is a way to give your people the language they need in order to talk about their own issues.

# —6—

# THE PROCESS

If you can't describe what you are doing as a process, you don't
know what you are doing.
—W. Edwards Deming,
American engineer, statistician, and author

**M**erely mention the word "aqueduct," and it will conjure mental
images of tiered arcades bridging valleys and rivers. Yet did you
know that those famed historic structures represented only 8 percent of
the channel? The majority of their length ran along the ground. To protect
their system of transporting water, the Romans erected a brick-concrete
dome over their half-man- to man-and-a-half-sized portals.[70] It illustrates
a point: *Mission flows most abundantly at the base.*

A notable feature of the Romans' groundwater channel was streamlining. The Romans used stone and brick to erect a skeletal housing; next
came a concrete foundation for the gutter bed, and then they applied a
finer cement layer on top. It's what they did next that's really fascinating.
Reckoning that the final layer was not optimal, they polished the cement to
attain a slickened surface. As to scale, this labor of buffing had to occur for
miles on end—kind of like waxing thousands upon thousands of cars! At
the project's end, the workers faced the foreman's touch test. Was it glassy
smooth?

The mirror polish had massive benefits. It enabled the water to transfer
without impediment, ensured steady water flow at even the most miniscule

---

70. Hodge, *Roman Aqueducts & Water Supply*, 93–99.

of grades, prevented sediment buildup, and lessened calcium deposits caused by the lime in the water. Can you appreciate the painstaking efforts of the ancients to maximize the efficiency of their system? Although it must have been tempting to bypass such tedious prep work, they learned that the sweat was every bit worth the payoff.

———

In this finale to our discussion of *ReMission* culture-shaping, we are aiming for a mirror polish. No barriers or restrictions. Steady flow for maximized results. The word that best captures this type of streamlining is *process*. By the time you reach the end of this chapter, I believe you will see some of the detail ahead of you, the type of modeling needed from leaders, and the value of wise, persistent oversight. Someone is going to have to play the role of engineer and foreman, so that what is accomplished is productive instead of counterproductive. Shortcuts will tempt you, as will the tendency to default to former ways. Don't give in! If you avoid cutting corners, it will save you far more in the long run.

Hear it now from a voice crying in the wilderness (better known in our era as "the marketplace"): Prepare the way for the gospel! God goes before you. If you train your people well, you will reach more souls. They, and others, will be blessed as pivotal participants. Let us not forget that God's miracles accompany his ever-extending "good news." *He champions the leader who champions his or her people.*

## HARD ASSESSMENT: PROCESS VOID

Researching *process-centered* designs of corporations went beyond anything I could have predicted. With the divides of secular versus sacred and profit-motive versus Spirit-movement, I am reticent to apply market principles to church matters. But when I studied the evolutionary development of business culture from the 1980s through the present day, I saw that it paralleled the church's current need so closely that it warranted special attention. In this chapter, it will be as a candle to light a darkened corridor.

Comparing the church to the "reengineering" school of thought, we see managers detailing processes at far superior levels than before. To give you a feel for this, if your average business leader were to evaluate the church's mission goals and the processes we have set in place to achieve them, he or she would be dumbfounded—and maybe even a bit miffed. Top-level managers would call us all into a meeting and speak unfiltered words to us. To appreciate how differently business leaders think, let's now consider a brief excerpt from the chapter "The Triumph of Process" in Michael Hammer's groundbreaking book *Beyond Reengineering*:

> Process centering, more than anything else, means that people—all people—in the company recognize and focus on their processes. Process identification requires a new cognitive style, an ability to look horizontally across the whole organization, as if from the outside, rather than from the top down. The company must:
>
> #1 Recognize and name its processes.
>
> #2 Ensure that everyone in the company is aware of these processes and their importance to the company.
>
> #3 Know how well they are performing, and that means having a yardstick.
>
> #4 Continue to focus on its processes so that they stay attuned to the needs of the changing business environment.[71]

Given that we have a prime directive to make disciples, if we were to apply the above ideals, I submit that an expert from the business sector would confront church leaders with a statement along these lines: "Your people are not involved. Most do not know how to execute critical functions. Your processes need to get broken down and clearly defined. You talk too much of ends, not the means or steps. In practice, the people are not doing what they need to do now so that you see the desired results later. You need different and better measurements. Additionally, your approaches are not adaptive enough to reach people *where they are* in the shifting climate." Then they would add the clincher: "The responsibility for these failings falls on your leaders, who are not clear on the necessary training, and who are not evaluating what is actually occurring in the field."

---

71. Michael Hammer, *Beyond Reengineering: How the Process-Centered Organization Is Changing Our Work and Our Lives* (New York, NY: HarperCollins, 1996), 14–16.

Whoa. I know this is only a hypothetical situation, but I believe that such a statement isn't far from what most business leaders would say! When it comes to the outer mission thrust, we are failing in all four of the requirements Hammer identifies. Knowing that our work is empowered on high by the Spirit, from a church organism standpoint, we would benefit greatly from adopting aspects of "process-centered" thought.

Let's transition from the business context to the metaphor of a football team, just to bring things closer to home. Football players are guided by a head coach (pastor) with a clear vision and by associate coaches who preside over each position: quarterbacks, running backs, receivers, linemen, and so on. Yet everyone knows that having those people and positions/ structures in place does not guarantee a winning team. Strong football programs assume that vision and structure matter only if they translate into effective execution on the field. Sports entities measure themselves by their performance in games. If they are not winning, they have to examine why.

Shooting for game-time success, coaches dig into the details. "The wide receiver is not pushing deep enough in his pattern to create separation from the defensive back," they might say. "The quarterback must throw the ball before the receiver makes his break and place it on his receiver's back shoulder." "We need to double the end with a running back to give our quarterback time." "Watch it all the way in…and catch the darn ball!" In order to up their team's chances of winning, coaches pay attention to what is occurring on the field, down to the smallest detail; and they make adjustments, as needed, to ensure their best shot at victory.

In the church, the essential process links for mission success are missing. We have plenty of vision, and some structure, but we are not good at executing in the field. We need well-defined processes that promote real-life success. In our enterprise, mobilizing our members to influence people outside the church and to make disciples requires much more detailed development. Strategic process development drives *ReMission*, because if you don't have it working for you, you'll quickly discover that the desired results can't be achieved.

## SEEING THROUGH THE HAZE

Process gives leaders functional insight. Any mission endeavor stands to be enhanced by better guidance and the application of a few simple principles. To better see the significance of process, let's now consider what occurs when process is absent.

I have observed many compassion ministries that have reached next to nobody in their communities. Let me say, I advocate Christians being God's hands and feet—meeting the practical, tangible needs of food, clothing, and shelter in their neighborhoods and cities. But let's not be shy in constructively critiquing any kingdom work, especially if we can do it better. Too many mission arms of the church look like this. They show up once in a blue moon to show God's love, feel good momentarily, and then leave. Fully vested compassion workers have coined a derogatory name for these people: "do-gooders." Granted, doing a little good is better than doing nothing, and one would hope it is a first step toward something more substantive. However, without ongoing dedication from participants, the results of such efforts will be minimal and temporary. It doesn't take long for the people helping, as well as the people being helped, to recognize a half-hearted effort. When a ministry gains a reputation for surface-level relationships and conversations, a lack of formation impact, and no vital connection to the Lord, it becomes a losing team. Something has to be done about that!

WHEN A MINISTRY GAINS A REPUTATION FOR SURFACE-LEVEL RELATIONSHIPS AND CONVERSATIONS, A LACK OF FORMATION IMPACT, AND NO VITAL CONNECTION TO THE LORD, IT BECOMES A LOSING TEAM.

The assessment is this: *Many (perhaps most) ministries don't know what the heck they're doing.* They lack the understanding of process and its value.

The crucial steps of execution remain undefined for their participants. No one is looking over the whole plan to point out any adjustments that may need to be made midcourse. Just labeling something a "missional group" does not make it truly missional or even fruitful. Christians love to believe that they are the "light of the world," even if they have the illuminating capacity of a cell phone running out of battery power. Who is watching and coaching the Good News team?

Mission drift occurs in even the most mission-intensive projects. Shockingly, church plants are often nothing more than a reshuffling of the deck. We get all excited: A new church is born, seventy new people in the kingdom. The truth is, in many cases, few are reached. The planter did a great job of gathering displaced or disgruntled Christians. Ironically, some of our most successful church plants are the smaller ones. Though people perceive them as being less "successful," the opposite is true in God's eyes. When the planter has gotten it right, the thrust of planting is about reaching unsaved people, and the plant actually expands the kingdom. What a novel concept.

This process, by the way, fits the biblical vision of church planting, as seen in the efforts of the apostle Paul. He would travel to a new region and evangelize it over a period of time. He spent a year and a half working as a tent-maker in Corinth (see Acts 18:11) and approximately three years in Ephesus (see Acts 20:31). Then, as a result of new believers popping up, the apostle started a church.[72] Today, we do it backward: We plant a church and then say, "Now let's begin evangelizing." Critical outward-emphasis DNA is lost, as is the synergistic impact of starting a church from the outer relational rings of unsaved people and their friends.

Satellite launches can be the same. I had an intimate talk with a video-venue campus pastor of an esteemed megachurch who told me on record that they had regathered a number of believers who had previously attended church, but, so far, they had not reached anyone new to the faith. By the way, their numbers were good. Their new site constituted an extension of the body but not an extension of the kingdom.

72. Ed Stetzer, *Planting New Churches in the Postmodern Age* (Nashville, TN: Broadman & Holman), 32.

I recently ran across this tagline on Twitter: "Fulfilling the Great Commission one tweet at a time." I laughed, but it made me wonder: *How many Christians believe that social media is an adequate replacement of relational influence?* I know that "God can use anything," but I find that answer to be a cop-out. Tweeting alone will not fulfill the Great Commission! Though I am a big advocate of the arts, Christian movies will not meet our challenge, either. Their place is to interject values into our culture and spur meaningful conversations among individuals, but art will never replace incarnational conveyance. Michael's Frost's book *Incarnate: The Body of Christ in a World of Disengagement* is a timely wake-up call to the reality that we are losing real relationship.[73]

Let's cut to the chase. If your church or ministry does not have a steady stream of living, breathing new believers coming into the faith, growing as disciples, and reaching ever-extending networks of people, you have veered off course. In business speak, you are "in the red." In football terms, you are losing. In the church, you are stagnant—and stagnation is a movement-killer. We need to see what is actually occurring at the contact points with our community. We may not have a profit margin or a scoreboard, but someone needs to watch closely and point out any critical adjustments that must be made.

## THREE KEYS TO BEING MORE PROCESS CENTERED

So, how can you make your church or ministry more process centered? Here are three keys, which I will expound upon in the pages that follow: (1) provide evaluative tools, (2) provide detailed training, and (3) provide opportunities for collaboration.

### #1: PROVIDE EVALUATIVE TOOLS

The ancient Romans who engineered the aqueducts accepted that a routine inspection of their water system was mandatory. Historian A. Trevor Hodge writes, "Maintenance of the water system was a continuous task, and the Romans assigned a Curator Aquarum to oversee this

---

73. Michael Frost, *Incarnate: The Body of Christ in a World of Disengagement* (Downers Grove, IL: InterVarsity Press, 2014), 35.

undertaking."[74] They built manholes where inspectors could descend a shaft using crossbar ladders for close-up, real-time viewing. Once inside, the inspectors were able to identify and deal with needed repairs, cleaning, and alterations.

It is here that our grand metaphor both helps and hobbles. It helps by illustrating the need for on-site evaluation, yet it hobbles in the sense that mission insight comes at a rare premium these days. In other words, it's possible, and even likely, for a seminary-educated pastor to visit a compassion ministry, a neighborhood community group, or a core gathering of a church plant, and not have the necessary tools to discern critical correctives that would make the mission more effective. It requires asking the right questions by someone with the equivalent of a Roman Curator Aquarum's seasoned eye. So, without further ado, allow me to pass along a usable diagnostic tool that you would do well to read, adopt, and impart to other leaders.

Spearheading a homeless ministry, Ricardo takes his team on weekly ventures into the riverbed where an entire homeless population routinely congregates. On Saturday mornings, the group arrives with tables, chairs, E-Z UP Instant Shelters, and food. They lay out a spread worthy of kings. For a year, they have not missed even one Saturday, saying, "The homeless don't get a weekend off, so why should we?" The local roof-deprived souls have learned to count on this meal and gather communally. At many such gatherings, someone from Ricardo's team shares a personal testimony or a biblical message.

After serving with his team for a couple of weeks, I met with Ricardo over coffee. Following some latte-induced chit-chat, I introduced an evaluating tool that I frequently use with compassion ministries. Expositing Matthew 9:35–36, we discussed the various levels of human need as referenced by Jesus—making the distinction between "harassed and helpless" and "sheep without a shepherd," the former referring to their general life condition, the latter invoking their spiritual need. For the purpose of critiquing a mission, I expand these categories to three distinct need-levels common to all people:

74. Hodge, *Roman Aqueducts & Water Supply*, 102.

Level 1:     Life-Condition Needs

Level 2:     Relational Needs

Level 3:     Spiritual-Formation Needs

Then, to compliment Ricardo's leadership skills, I affirmed how his group was already doing many things right. As you probably know, it's easier to point out the negative than to highlight the positive; yet people are far more receptive to what you have to say after you have praised their efforts in some way. There was plenty for which to praise Ricardo. You see, much mission activity never exceeds level 1, managing to merely meet people's *life-condition needs*. However, Ricardo's group was meeting needs so consistently that I affirmed they were in position for meeting relational and spiritual-formation needs.

What happened next really impressed me. Ricardo leaned back, shook his head in a show of dawning acuity, and said, "The truth is, we are only scratching the surface with number two, and have not even gotten to number three." In that moment, he saw his whole mission in a new light. This epiphany turned into an enormously rich conversation about how to take their mission to the homeless to increasingly deeper levels as a true vessel of transformation.

PROCESS ENGAGEMENT ALWAYS INVOLVES EVALUATING WHAT IS MISSING FOR GOSPEL TRANSFORMATION TO TAKE PLACE. IT IS THE LEADER'S ROLE TO ENSURE THAT THE PROPER STEPS IN THE ENGAGEMENT ARE DEFINED.

The next time that he and his team ministered to the homeless, they got focused in their conversations, asking probing questions designed to discern where these people were, spiritually speaking. They discovered that the majority of those they were serving either had roots in a nominally Catholic upbringing or held a very superficial view of God and Jesus. Based on this new understanding, the team began to dial in on how to more effectively evangelize and disciple, according to the holistic vision of Christ. As a side note, none of their public proclamations and testimonial messages ever got to effecting the faith formation that they desired to see in people's lives. It only came through sit-down dialogue.

As a result of this conversation, Ricardo's team improved their relief efforts (to meet life-condition needs) as they began to track those whom they had helped *out* of the riverbed. The latest count, according to team member Ethan, was eight individuals! Process engagement always involves evaluating what is missing for gospel transformation to take place. It is the leader's role to ensure that the proper steps in the engagement are defined. Leaders equipped with this evaluative tool will be able to assess their own efforts, and their mission will sharpen qualitatively through rigorous inspection and evaluation.

———

In the healing ministry at Sandals, a man named Eric came to faith during a breakout conversation. The group leader, Adam, and another group member led him to Christ. Afterward, Eric was lit with joy! Adam later admitted that evangelism had been low on his list of priorities. He confided in me that his main focus had been living the gospel before people. To address his truncated thinking, I chimed in with some words about the verbal value and power of the gospel, saying, "This salvation was not just for Eric; it was a sign from God to you. God wants to bring salvation to many in your healing-recovery ministry!" Adam pointed to his arm, showing me his goose bumps. I added, "You need to raise this part of your game so God can touch and transform hearts." Adam sensed the Lord in this calling, and we have seen miracle after miracle occur in his healing ministry—a ministry that always introduces people to *the* Healer. Again, hands-on observational training will focus your church. Who has a close enough proximity to the ministers to see the needed adjustments and provide the requisite wisdom and encouragement for them to reach the next level?

It's one thing to charge your leaders with a mission; it's another thing to give them tools to sharpen themselves. Believe me when I say that it's easy for people to spin their wheels and simply go through the motions.

Without the means to hone our efforts, we are apt to fail the vision. By providing a mechanism for evaluation, we enable leaders to see and measure their actual impact. And the corresponding course corrections always equate to a harvest of greater fruit.

## #2: PROVIDE DETAILED TRAINING

In this same vein of empowerment, process-centered thought involves picturing and parsing the engagement so that, in the end, we see God's work flourish. We have to paint a full, compelling portrait for the whole process of reaching and discipling people. In training sessions, we should ask our team members to envision just how the accomplishment of kingdom impact will look, thereby tapping the power of visualization.

Ask: If we are going to succeed in discipling people in our neighborhoods—at our shelters, in our book clubs, in our marketplaces, at City Hall, in our public schools, at the ball field, at community socials, at our local recovery center/support group or yoga class, or at our local mosque—chances are, it's going to look something like this…(and get specific). As an example, if we are going to succeed in reaching our Muslim neighbors, then it is going to require our exhibiting love, being part of their lives as friends, and developing the ability to respond to Islam and its tenets in a kind, compassionate manner. So, we must get ready in heart and mind. Here, we are not playing the role of the Holy Spirit. God can do whatever he wants in whatever timing he chooses. What we are doing is helping people to crystalize a picture in their minds for execution. It's important for them to see it first, because the results will be whatever they're aiming for! It also helps them to "count the costs" for undertaking the gospel call. (See Luke 14:25–35.)

As to specifics, one of the most important things is for Christians to see influence happening within a relational process (a detailed breakdown of which I will share in the upcoming chapter "Pinpointing the Flow"). Though it is greatly ignored by the church, the Bible recognizes process with a multiplicity of verses, such as Paul's reasoning with the synagogue over successive Sabbaths (see Acts 13:42; 17:2) or the Athenians' words: *"We want to hear you again on this subject"* (Acts 17:32). When you instill the idea of getting alongside someone outside the church, you quickly discover the importance of process. From the place of relationship, I teach Christians how to discern a sequence that occurs in the hearts and minds of nonbelievers (Skill #7: Progression Steps). God revealed this insight to me during my own relational journeys with an atheist and a theistic skeptic. After both individuals came to faith over a long series of meetings, I dissected what had occurred, noting that each one had gone through four progressions.

The layered breakdown pictured below shows the kind of processing that people need, and it also shows your people where to focus their conversations. If I hadn't helped my skeptic friends through these steps, they would not have come to faith. Like a stairway to heaven, each step was vital for the one that followed. By offering this training to our people, we take something that is difficult and make it doable. Consider the following chart:

| STEPS | "THE HANG UP" | HELP WITH... |
|---|---|---|
| **OPEN TO** | *Interest* | Asking |
| **ABLE TO** | *Reason* | Answers |
| **WANT TO** | *Motivation* | Appeal |
| **CHOOSE TO** | *Response* | Application |

The formation of faith follows a logical sequence: openness to explore, ability to discern truth, desire to follow, choice to believe, and finally the journey toward being a disciple. Thus, we see that disciplemaking begins not with our offering a full explanation of our beliefs but with our attracting others' interest to explore and learn. If that can be achieved, then one step will lead to the next. They will be led to discover, then to discern, then to desire, then to decide, and, finally, to follow.

Discovery --> Discernment --> Desire --> Decision --> Disciple

For this progression to work, the believer must observe and sometimes draw out where their friend is, spiritually. That process, in itself, produces a sharpening. The believer starts to see more acutely what the person needs or where he or she is hung up. Of course, what I desire to see happen with all those I disciple is for them to engage with unsaved people and work the process all the way through. For leaders, it begs the question "Can our people do it—can they make new disciples?"

One day, I told my son that we were going to change the oil in the car. He shot back, "I know how to do that, Dad. You already explained it." "Okay, then; do it," I replied. Could he? No! He didn't know the proper technique for loosening the bolt and ended up hurting his hand.

When proper training has occurred, the trainees can work all the steps themselves. They understand what they are trying to do because they have engaged in real terms; they have done it. Having worked the process themselves, they benefit from these two great teachers: failure and success. Of course, when they gain experience and insights, they develop conviction on how to influence others, which gives them something valuable to pass along. (See 2 Timothy 2:2.) This creation of real "know-how" is the crux of multiplication. It applies to many missional endeavors, such as when leaders train group members to launch their own missional groups.

> WHEN PROPER TRAINING HAS OCCURRED, THE TRAINEES CAN WORK ALL THE STEPS THEMSELVES. THEY UNDERSTAND WHAT THEY ARE TRYING TO DO BECAUSE THEY HAVE ENGAGED IN REAL TERMS; THEY HAVE DONE IT.

Getting into the nitty-gritty specifics creates definition for a learning curve. Thinking through what makes discipleship exciting also has merit. Michael Gerber, in his bestseller *The E-Myth Revisited: Why Most Small Businesses Don't Work and What to Do About It*, describes how process-centered thought reignited the passion of a woman named Sarah for her pie-making business. She started with the inner fire, but once the routine set in, her vision and passion got lost in the daily grind of making it happen. Gerber made the following appeal to Sarah:

> Wasn't there a specific way your aunt taught you to cut the fruit? A specific way to hold it? A specific way to prepare it? Wasn't there a specific way to do everything your aunt taught you to do? And wasn't the creativity, the continuous stream of surprises, a result not just of the specific work you were doing but of your continuous and exhilarating experience of improving as you learned how to do those very specific tasks better and better, until you could do them almost as well as your aunt?

> Wasn't that where the joy came from? That if you were resigned to doing one thing, one way, forever, without ever improving, there would be no joy—there would only be the same deadening routine? And isn't that what your aunt taught you as she taught you to bake pies—the mystery that change can bring?[75]

Do you get flashes of Paul out on the road with Barnabas, Silas, Timothy, or Titus, talking on the wonderment of making the gospel's mystery known to people in various regions? Or can you imagine the early Christians' groundswell of excitement when they had to distill, on the fly, so to speak, how to adapt the gospel message to the wider Gentile audience?[76] Same gospel, different delivery. Imagine yourself participating in the conversation of how to tailor the gospel to the widely religious Roman culture, shifting the Jewish "Jesus is the Messiah" to the Gentile-oriented "Jesus is Lord" (Romans 10:9). The slight but significant alteration of the message exalted a crucified man over Rome's legions of lords! Talk about getting on message.

This same thrilling idea burst can occur with your people. Notice that the process follows a one-two progression. When I train a group on tailoring a message, I tell them: There's a key to the cross. The key is a resonant message that connects the life situation of their audience to what Christ can do.

75. Michael E. Gerber, *The E-Myth Revisited: Why Most Small Businesses Don't Work and What to Do About It* (New York, NY: HarperCollins, 2007), 45.
76. Green, *Evangelism in the Early Church*, 116.

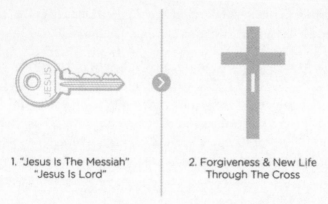

1. "Jesus Is The Messiah"          2. Forgiveness & New Life
   "Jesus Is Lord"                     Through The Cross

Later on, I will break down how to teach this skill used by Jesus and the early church. For now, just know that when we teach our people how to present the gospel in a way that resonates with their audience, we defy tedium by giving them the possibility of mastery. They can become "approved workmen" for God in the missional sense. (See 2 Timothy 2:15.) With personal character and honed skills sharpening their engagements, you and those you lead will see a much greater harvest of fruit.

## #3: PROVIDE OPPORTUNITIES FOR COLLABORATION

In his book, *Creativity, Inc.: Overcoming the Unseen Forces That Stand in the Way of True Inspiration*, Pixar's president, Edwin Catmull, tells the story of his company. Like most of us who have learned best from the school of hard knocks, Pixar went through its own developmental journey. What is insightful about their passage into becoming a world-renowned animation studio is how they managed to quantify the culture essential for success in the innovation industry. You may not have been privy to the fact that the film *Toy Story 2* was a disaster in the making. Pixar had to take drastic measures to pull a wayward script back into the realm of believability. But, through it all, they crystalized the precepts that began to drive them as an organization.

The first axiom to surface from the near-debacle was that having the right team is more important than having the right idea. As Catmull articulates in his book, "Find, develop, and support good people, and they in turn will find, develop, and own good ideas."[77] The right team, in the

---

77. Ed Catmull and Amy Wallace, *Creativity, Inc.: Overcoming the Unseen Forces That Stand in the Way of True Inspiration* (New York: Random House, 2014), 42.

company's view, consisted of individuals who could relate well to and complement each other, and who could stay focused on how the team was performing, not on the talents of specific individuals. As process managers, they paid close attention to environmental factors, how meeting rooms were set, and anything that seemed to help release the team's contributions. They also studied companies in Japan that were gaining market share by implementing the theories of American engineer W. Edwards Deming, such as making a chord or "stop button" available to every worker in the assembly line to involve the workforce in improving production.[78] Can you imagine if every church member's mind was engaged in improving what the church was doing for and in its community?

On the coattails of these ideas came what was, I think, an overlooked catalyst. Pixar figured out that what they primarily needed was to extricate the most valuable kind of collaboration: honesty. They did this by cultivating a culture where candor was highly valued. In short, they needed to get true opinions of their work so they could reach the highest levels of excellence.[79] Can you see the potential power of this emphasis within your own team? No yes-men, no spins. Tell us what you really think!

When pastors trust elite programmers to shape their church services, outward mission has the capacity to engage the whole body in speaking into an ever-moving mix: entering the unknown, exploring new relationships, reading people and situations, strategizing and implementing steps, building mobilization structures, cultivating gospel receptivity, developing effective communication patterns, and creating cultural transformation. Yet the typical church puts disproportionate focus on its weekend services (get that fog machine oiled) and invests minimal imaginative thought and team building toward what is happening outside its walls during the week. Compounding this trend, there's little to no allowance for candid input or feedback. The unspoken rule in churches is, "Shut up. Don't ever question your spiritual authorities."

Although the concept of submission to authority is biblical, I fear that its exclusivity often buries God-given talents and squanders some of the best ideas. The church needs to open avenues for its people to become

---

78. Ibid.
79. Ibid., 67.

actual players, creators of movement. This does not only apply to the millennials who are desperate for a seat at the table. If you don't give your people a chance to speak into the process, don't be surprised when they feel undervalued—they are! Researcher Josh Packard writes, "The dechurched are leaving to do more, not less. The church isn't asking too much of people; it's asking the wrong things of them."[80] Not enough kingdom work. Not enough effectual training. Not enough exciting opportunity. Not enough vital contribution. Not enough real engagement. Can you see it? The lines begin to blur. Is church about the pastor's ego? Or is it about Jesus' vision for what he wills to do through his people for the world?

> ## IF YOU DON'T GIVE YOUR PEOPLE A CHANCE TO SPEAK INTO THE PROCESS, DON'T BE SURPRISED WHEN THEY FEEL UNDERVALUED—THEY ARE!

Now, I know that a council of numbskulls may do more harm than good. You need some quality control in place. Not everyone should sit in the director's seat. So, get the right people in the room. Set it up as a brainstorming session. Give them a voice and some education on how to discern ideas that are realistic to implement, with a dose of Christ's humility! Not all ideas are worth doing. Yet I would rather risk the possibility of a little friction than miss tapping the insightful thoughts of my people. Believe in their ability to contribute, and when they land on something good, seize it! The payoff can be huge for the mission, the body, and themselves. Again, to many, the church seems inaccessible, with only top guns at every directional table. Sometimes, it's only the senior pastor. Widen the circle. (Of course, churches partnering together is another form of collaboration that can advance the kingdom cause in our communities.)

In order to produce optimum impact, mission must have the right "angle of attack"—a phrase coined by the Wright brothers to qualify how the plane wings hit the air. In other words, we must keep asking ourselves,

---

80. Packard and Hope, *Church Refugees*, 133.

"How can our people engage in a way so the greatest kingdom impact will be made?"

This type of question spurred some fantastic collaboration at a round-table discussion with the director of an anti-human-trafficking organization. Team members were banging their heads, and banging on heaven's doors, to summon fresh ideas to implement. Eventually, one of the leaders voiced the idea to incorporate a home to shelter and disciple rescued individuals. Thus, Rebirth Homes was born. And the rest is history!

## GOING TO THE HEIGHTS

Eliciting collaboration and creating buy-in are so important, they should make your daily calendar. Returning to the example of the aqueducts, as the cities populated, Roman "water-diviners" returned to the surrounding mountains in search of new aquifers (permeable rocks able to contain or transmit groundwater). Though they did tap water from lakes and dams, they preferred rechanneling the pure springs. In the spiritual realm, the leader must go to the mountains—pure missional vision comes from on high! This could be a new churchwide effort, new channels feeding into the line, or revamped training. Leader teams are always a step ahead of their people. Wisely, they know their churches are always only a step away from stagnation.

Adapting Ken Priddy's Lifecycle, consider the subtle difference in these church orientations.[81]

|  | *Mission* | *Maintenance* | *Malaise* |
|---|---|---|---|
| Faith: | Future, Innovation | Present, Routine | Past, Protective |
| Focus: | Outward, Community | Inward, Congregation | Backward, Core |
| Flow: | High, Conversion | Steady, Transfer | Trickling, None |

Did you notice how the middle column reflects solid ministry? Like a silent killer, the "maintenance mode" lurks stealthily. We must fight this

81. Kenneth E. Priddy and J. Patrick Brag Jr., "G.O.1.X.: Building Your Church's Great Commission Matrix" (2014), 28.

formidable foe. The only way to counter mission drift is to get back to the mission column. You must discover that which God alone can give: fresh faith for reaching more, which, when properly cast before your people, reinvigorates the flow.

As a coaching director of church planters, I've rubbed shoulders with some older mentors who have seen it all. One of our legendary vets, Jay Letey, shared his story of coming into a church that carried a massive debt, turning it around with a renewed vision for the future, and then enjoying a tremendous season of growth and expansion through church plants. Years removed from his lead position, he saw how the church had drifted into the center column, having gone seven years without planting a new church. Let's acknowledge how covert the maintenance shift can be. We may not even see what is occurring.

Therefore, it is vital to observe the practice of returning to the "mountains" to rediscover God's heart for the lost and to recalibrate our vision for mission. Expanding into the body, each ministry and mission team must do the same, spurring their participants to dream missionally all over again as they ask, "Lord, what do you want to do now? What new training conduits and engagement channels should we tap? Show us the way!"

———

Pattern. Permeation. Posture. Process. These four pillars uphold missional flow. As the leader of a church, mission, or group, you are tasked with taking what you and your team have gleaned thus far and working them into your culture. Don't do what so many do during weekend church services, which is to listen and then leave, unchanged. You have received knowledge you must put to use. Each of the four pillars of *ReMission* can make a definitive difference in the outflow of lives. But you have to work it in if you expect to get it flowing out! You have to begin, adjust, and see what God has uniquely in mind for your people and his mission!

The next segment of this book will deal directly with the channel of influence. It's the nitty-gritty section where I will develop two highly practical concepts: tipping and pinpointing. The next two chapters address how to directly increase the empowerment of your people.

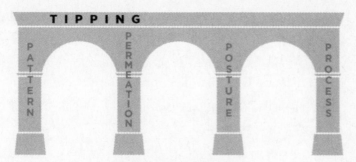

## REFLECTIONS

1.  When you look at your mission as a whole, what areas stand out as needing much more "mirror polish"?

2.  Where do you need to rethink and redesign your processes to enhance the body's impact?

3.  Which of the four aspects of process-centered thought— (1) Recognize and name its processes; (2) Ensure that everyone in the company is aware of these processes and their importance to the church or organization; (3) Know how well they are performing (and that means having a yardstick); and (4) Continue to focus on its processes so that they stay attuned to the needs of the changing environment—stands out to you as being most deficient in the church? What about within your church or ministry group?

4.  Who, in your church or agency, is most qualified to play the overseer's role (the "Curator Aquarum") of making critical mission adjustments? Whom can you train to fulfill this task? Jot down some specific names of people to pray over and possibly approach.

## REMISSION TAKEAWAYS

1.  Providing your leaders with diagnostic tools allows them to unleash their true mission impact.

2.  It is vital that leaders cast a picture of the whole mission process.

3. You create a learning curve for your people by naming the skills and giving specifics on what mission execution entails.

4. Your people must learn to work according to the step progressions that non-Christians make in coming to faith.

5. Maximizing collaboration is essential for releasing the missional imagination of the body.

# —PART II—
## CHANNEL:
## EMPOWERING THEIR INFLUENCE

# —7—

# TIPPING THE TOWER

It doesn't matter the number of followers you have.
Hitler had millions and Jesus had 12.
—Twitter user #LoverOfJesus

**W**hat the outspoken atheistic author Ayn Rand uncorks in her character-driven classic *The Fountainhead* shines a lot of light on the subject of design. It goes to show that you can sometimes find truth in the strangest of places.

On the surface, her relationally indifferent lead character, architect Howard Roark, could not be farther from a biblical saint. But who can argue that there's something remarkable in any man who has clarity on why he does what he does? Roark, in Rand's objectivist view, is the ultimate human being. How many of us stand with unyielding stature regarding the principles that guide our work? Do we have such conviction regarding our ministry constructions that we remain undaunted in the face of compromise, mediocrity, and opposition? In one thematic episode, Rand lays bare her theme:

"What is it that I like so much about the house you're building for me, Howard?"

"A house can have integrity, just like a person," said Roark, "and just as seldom."

"In what way?"

"Well, look at it. Every piece of it is there because the house needs it—and for no other reason. You see it from here as it is inside. The rooms in which you'll live made the shape....But you've seen buildings with columns that support nothing, with purposeless cornices, with pilasters, moldings, false arches, false windows....Do you understand the difference? Your house is made by its own needs. Those others are made by the need to impress. The determining motive of your house is in the house. The determining motive of the others is in the audience."

"Do you know that that's what I've felt in a way? I've felt that when I move into this house, I'll have a new sort of existence, and even my simple daily routine will have a kind of honesty or dignity that I can't quite define. Don't be astonished if I tell you that I feel as if I'll have to live up to that house."

"I intended that," said Roark.[82]

Design integrity—we long for it. It's what we aspire toward, as people, leaders, parents, and spouses. We want "marriage-first" families because that's God's design. Slip into the kids-first mode, and watch out! We want church members to deploy the full range of their gifting, because God intended for them to do so. But to what degree do we desire the integrity of the whole structure? In this chapter, I pose these questions: How clear are you on God's blueprint? Whose ideas compel your vision? How committed are you to seeing it through?

## HARD ASSESSMENT: MISSING INTEGRITY

As the sun was setting on 2011, the sudden death of Steve Jobs after a battle with pancreatic cancer shocked us all. During his thirty-year, intermittent reign at Apple, the world underwent a technical gadgetry revolution. From iPods to iPads, iPhones to smaller, lighter computers—there's hardly a soul who hasn't been touched by Jobs's genius. Marketing/blogger provocateur Seth Godin synthesized the narrative this way: "A slogan might be evidence that you have a story, but it isn't a story. A story is something you live and connect with and come back [to] again and again and again....Apple has had various slogans through the years, but in every successful iteration of the company, the story has been remarkably consistent:

---

82. Ayn Rand, *The Fountainhead* (New York, NY: Signet, Penguin Group, 1952), 136.

Apple's story is that they are idiosyncratic artisans producing beautiful products for smart people."[83]

In the wake of Jobs's passing, the degree of Apple's pervasiveness is yet to be seen. Was this great Apple-run the brilliance of a single iconic, driven man, or is it the flourishing vision of a whole company? Anticipating Apple's future series of groundbreaking products, we'll keep our eyes open. Nothing adds more luster to a leader's legacy than to see followers blazing the visionary's trail and taking innovation to a new, successful level.

## AN ORGANIZATION WITH "STORY INTEGRITY" IS WHERE A MISSION STATEMENT IS MORE THAN EMPTY RHETORIC, BECAUSE IT LIVES IN THE SOUL AND LIVES OF ITS PEOPLE.

An organization with "story integrity" is where a mission statement is more than empty rhetoric, because it lives in the souls and lives of its people. Scouring the business scape, there are other firms that could pass this test. Ironically—and I write this in the big-picture sense—I would argue that the biggest discrepancy between a mission slogan (statement) and its actual story is not found in the marketplace but in the church. This gap is quite pronounced, I daresay. Does it seem as odd to you as it does to me that the institution known for sharing the truth with the world has a story that is, in real terms, untrue? You may be mounting a counterargument in your mind—certainly, not all churches or all Christians can be lumped into this camp. Yet I have cause in what I am saying, so please hear me out.

What churches claim, and what they do in living expression, are often two divergent streams. Most congregations sign on for the Great Commission, but only small percentages of their people regularly and effectively engage in the associated activity. The statistical support has been well documented. If the vast membership is not about the business of

83. Seth Godin, "What if your slogan is true?" (blog), August 19, 2012. http://sethgodin.typepad.com/seths_blog/2012/08/what-if-your-slogan-is-true.html.

making new disciples, then the church's stated purpose is not the story. This instance of incongruity boils down to this: We're claiming to be something we're not.

> EVERY CHURCH I HAVE ATTENDED HAS PLACED
> MAJOR FOCUS ON WORSHIP; IN CONTRAST, THE
> IDEA OF EMULATING CHRIST'S MISSION MANNER
> DOES NOT EVEN MAKE THE RADAR IN THE MAJORITY
> OF CHURCH BODIES.

When I use the phrase "Tipping the Tower," I am asserting that the vertical church culture that has dominated this century has helped to create this disparity. It must now tip over, like an opened soda bottle tipped on its side, pouring outward. Weak mission orientation is our missing link. Every church I have attended has placed major focus on worship; in contrast, the idea of emulating Christ's mission manner does not even make the radar in the majority of church bodies. We must go horizontal. For you as a leader, what I call "tipping" will be a meter of your true influence. It is something that Christian leaders can pursue in almost every interaction they have with their people. I am prone to believe that the fruit of such empowerment can increase substantially. It will change the way you view yourself and your ministry—the way you assess your real impact. I would even go as far to say this is a centerpiece of your own quest for greater Christlikeness.

## LEADING DOWN AND OUT

Drawing from Frost and Hirsch's *The Shaping of Things to Come*,[84] British author JR Woodward zeroes in on the top five equipping gifts: Apostle, Prophet, Evangelist, Shepherd, and Teacher (known by APEST), contending that polycentric leadership is God's biblical prescription for

---

84. Michael Frost and Alan Hirsch, *The Shaping of Things to Come: Innovation and Mission for the 21st-Century Church* (Grand Rapids, MI: Baker Books, 2003, 2013), 169.

the body's effectual health,[85] spurring the outcry "Where are the APEs?"[86] Woodward's template crisscrosses our traditions, and different churches and denominations may define the top five equipping gifts differently. However, no matter your tradition or affiliation, we all can recognize that pastor-teacher gifts dominate in today's church. Woodward argues that this imbalance, along with our hierarchical corporate model, only coddles consumeristic disciples and makes church life lopsided. According to his critique, top leaders should go back to kindergarten; they need to learn to share.

Though I am not a fan of everything that happens in the cutthroat corporate world, I did like the sequence that unfolded with Apple's *Think Different* campaign, when, after seeking to land one of the biggest voices in entertainment (first Robin Williams, then Tom Hanks, and finally Richard Dreyfuss), they got the idea of using Jobs himself for an incognito voice-over. The team thought it would be powerful when people eventually realized that the voice belonged to Jobs. After sleeping on the decision, Jobs decided the next day to go with Dreyfuss, reasoning, "If we use my voice, when they find it is my voice, they will think it's about me ... It's not. It's about Apple."[87]

Regardless of what you think of Jobs and his now-legendary Alpha personality (which was not always a good thing), I found the sentiment of those words to be sound and strangely antithetical to the "I am the brand" verbiage that has been voiced in our modern church.[88] It's not shocking to see rogue dominators in the business sector; it is shocking to see such things in the institution founded by Christ. The issue of dominance that I am raising is not reserved for only the famous. It can happen in any setting, regardless of size, and it strikes at the spiritual center of our leadership. I am not trying to diminish the renowned in the top spots of Christendom,

85. Woodward, *Creating a Missional Culture*, 58–59.
86. Beau Crosetto, "Interpreting Ephesians 4: The Five-Fold Giftings" *Release the Ape* (September 11, 2012), http://www.releasetheape.com/ephesians-4/#.V4QbOTkrJsO (accessed February, 9, 2014).
87. Walter Isaacson, *Steve Jobs* (New York: Simon & Schuster, 2011), 331.
88. Warren Throckmorton, "More Mars Hill Church Grievances: Former Member Calls for Evacuation" *Patheos* (March 20, 2014). Available at: http://www.patheos.com/blogs/warrenthrockmorton/2014/03/20/more-mars-hill-church-grievances-former-member-calls-for-evacuation.

who can be God's pacesetters for the whole movement; but what we see from today's leaders is often a far cry from the example of Jesus, who emptied himself of his positional glory. Is this what servant leadership and the church should be? Note to self: When I begin making "I am" statements, that means *I am* in trouble!

Though polycentric experiments thrive in certain areas, I predict that the hierarchical mainstay will not change very much, for various reasons: some traditional, some practical, and some carnal. As much as I favor the restructuring that Woodward and other top missional guns are calling for, and as much as I would love to see churches harness the healthy use of these divine gifts (offering a seat at the table for others, which would include someone like me!), the *tipping* I seek is not married to those concepts in a mutually exclusive sense. I'm looking at something much bigger. But you're not off the hook! We should all wrestle with the idea of releasing God's full gift-set for the good of his people.

Let me briefly chime in to say that I'm not advocating for wimpier pastors. Strong leaders with excellent preaching skills are gifted assets. I only coach pastors to get better at *drawing* nonbelievers onto the spiritual path and to get smarter about implementation. Since church members need hearts that burn for God, I do not suggest deemphasizing the worship experience. Neither do my chosen terms "vertical" and "horizontal" correlate with the concepts of "attractional" or "missional." If only it were that simple. To be clear, I am not categorically opposed to churches aiming for attraction. Churches with high attractional focus can develop horizontal strength. In contrast, churches with high missional focus can be horizontally weak. Most churches would claim to espouse both focuses, but few, from my perspective, are exceptionally horizontal.

So, if tipping is not tied to worship type or target audience, church model or philosophy, then where is it tethered? It is all about the perceptions of leaders and their people on how mission works and where it extends in the world.

## WHAT OMISSION SAID

A preaching series I attended on the subject of honor, was a good one. Pastors, denominational heads, ministry leaders, coaches, community icons, parents, mentors, teachers, public authorities—all of these positions were spotlighted. Yet, as the series headed to its close, I could not help but notice a glaring omission. Can you think of someone important who was not honored on that list?

Week after week, I had been waiting for the time when the pastor would bring up several members to highlight their influence in the community and describe how they were touching lives with the gospel. I imagined the excitement of congregants hearing reports of how God had used them. I envisioned them relaying the loving acts and compelling talks they'd had with unbelieving neighbors, including those fearful, awkward moments of doubt or resistance followed by long-sought-after breakthroughs. I anticipated fires of inspiration being stoked within the hearts of the listeners as they relived stories of the gospel's drawing power and life-intercepting miracles. Then, I envisioned the moment when a special bestowing of honor would be made for them—the carriers of the gospel—in line with the historic torchbearers of Bible fame. That honor, by the way, would have applied to the whole auditorium. It would have been an awesome moment! I kept waiting for it. But it never came.

> IN OUR HIERARCHICAL CULTURE, THERE'S SO MUCH FOCUS ON WHO'S AT THE TOP—THE NARCISSISTIC GROOM, PER SE—THAT, IN MANY CASES, WE'VE LOST SIGHT OF THE BEAUTIFUL, HUMBLE BRIDE.

When the series ended abruptly, I felt that the omission told its own story. Perhaps I was the only one in the room who noticed, which would be telling! To me, it reflected something amiss—a striking absence. The vertical church exalts its higher-ups, while the commoners ("Average Joes and Janes") fight it out in the trenches, getting negligible press and little honor.

Was the omission biblical? No doubt, God calls people to honor and submit to their leaders, (See, for example, Hebrews 13; 1 Peter 4.) But does subservience imply that the role of the people is somehow less important or less honorable? Of course not. Yet I'm afraid that in our hierarchical culture, there's so much focus on who's at the top—the narcissistic groom, per se—that, in many cases, we've lost sight of the beautiful, humble bride. Why did this pastor of a major church forget the people? It's easy to point fingers. However, no one is immune from making such an oversight.

Ephesians 4:11–13 clearly indicates that God's design is for church members, not top leaders, to compose his prime workforce. We get the same gist from Jesus' decision to raise up 12 unlearned everyman-types to lead his world-changing movement. How interesting to note that Jesus didn't care as much about gathering crowds as he did about developing them. It's staggering to see the enormous "gospel" vision he had for the ragtag bunch of no-name misfits he summoned as his disciples. Yet, despite these examples and many other reinforcing passages of Scripture, this pastor did not explicitly honor God's rank and file.

I didn't leave the church feeling upset or compelled to send a nasty note. Nor did I think less of the teacher; he had done a decent job with the series. I just wished that the people had been given a time to stand and have the church leaders lay or wave hands over all them, recognizing their role as the primary agents of spreading the gospel.

Though some might consider this omission to be an immaterial oversight, I see it as an indication of warped ecclesiology. In fact, not only is the spotlight's aim off, but, from a leadership perspective, the kind of honor given in the church is off, as well. This error falls directly in line with the title of this book. *ReMission* is about infusing fresh mission into the lifeblood of the church, but it also seeks to restore health to hardened arteries with disease-like symptoms. Honor must shift.

In the 2012 London Summer Olympic Games, U.S. gymnast Aly Raisman shined by winning two gold medals and one bronze. The camera captured an intimate glimpse of Aly giving some pre-performance encouragement to teammate Gabby Douglas before she took the beam. The broadcast announcer noted, "Aly, the leader." Then, after the team won the gold, Aly took off her medal, walked over to her coach, and put it around his neck. In this rare, unanticipated gesture, she showed deference to her coach's vital contribution to the team's victory. This is the type of honor we need in the church: The people achieving the dream, then appreciating the pastor or leader who helped them to achieve it. Such an act would reflect horizontal leadership. Instead, we usually see everyone heralding the pastor, who appears to be doing everything right, while, in the missional sense, the people are performing poorly.

Omission exposes the ingrained nature of our "untippedness." We're more vertical than horizontal. The pastor's role is vertical—too much focus on preaching performance, not enough focus on the people's ability to share the gospel message. The teaching structure is vertical—too much focus on learning the Bible, not enough on living it out. The mission structure is vertical—too much focus on class instruction, not enough on actual engagement and skill development. The attraction model is vertical—too much focus on the church service, too little celebration of what God does through his body during the week. Even the process of hiring within the church is vertical—too many posts inside the walls, too few positioned at the outer engagement points.

> ## WHAT MAKES THE NEW TESTAMENT CHURCH MOST DISTINCT FROM THE OLDER COVENANTAL SYSTEM IS THAT THE SPIRIT WAS NO LONGER CONCENTRATED IN THE TOP LEADERS BUT RATHER DISSEMINATED THROUGH EVERY MEMBER.

What makes the New Testament church most distinct from the older covenantal system is that the Spirit was no longer concentrated in the top leaders but rather disseminated through every member. (See, for example, Acts 1:8.) The story of the church is not primarily about a gathering of people but rather the outward movement of God through the messaging of his people to reach the world. Like the mobilized church of Acts, which was poured out, bold and lucid in action, we ought to have more Christians who are filled with the Spirit for mission. Instead, we've got mostly sidelined spectators.

# HORIZONTAL LEADERSHIP

How do we transition from the vertical paradigm of passivity-producing pew-sitters into a thriving outside-the-church-walls movement? Pastors and church planters, may I invade your psyches with a simple query? Do you want to *have* a great church? Or do you want to *be* a great church? Those are two different things that require distinctly different things from you.

When I first studied Disciple-Making Movements (DMM) in India, the lead trainer's greatest fear was to see one of his newly launched mission groups turn into a cul-de-sac. Reproducing ever-extending networks was their passionate quest. His biggest pet peeve—the thing he was constantly on the lookout for and would call out in an instant—was the emergence of hierarchy. If he saw someone even remotely resembling the physical posture of a "holy man," standing barefoot in front of the group or seeming to exercise exclusive authority, he'd attack it like the plague. He considered such arrangements to be unqualified movement-killers. One of the men generated a sizable following, and he was quickly confronted with the critique, "That is not what we want!"

Though regional strategies diverge quite radically from the Mississippi to the Nile, from the Tiber to the Jordan to the Ganges, all church leaders stand to benefit from answering the same urgent questions of my astute DMM friend: "Are we bottling the movement?" "Does the spotlight on us hinder the movement through them [the people]?" In a candid moment with a professor who oversees seminary curriculum, mentioning the gap between the professional and the pew, he commented, "We're part of the problem, aren't we?" It's not that we don't need to raise professionals; it's that we need to reequip them to be movement-makers.

I remember vividly, on a visit to Italy, standing along the cobblestoned section of the Appian Way. The ancient adage "All roads lead to Rome" reflected another strength of the Roman Empire. Roads increased mobility for community and commerce, also enabling the swift movement of military forces. Along with a common tongue (Koine Greek, from Alexander's world conquest), and the Pax Romana (an extended time of peace), the roads played a vital role in the gospel's first-century expansion.[89] Our

---

89. Green, *Evangelism in the Early Church*, 13–19.

challenge: How can we pave the way for people to move from impotence to powerful mission impetus?

In order for that to happen, the church's top leaders are going to have to take a page from John the Baptist, who demonstrated this principle in his mission: *Horizontal leaders become less so that the church can become more.*

Behold, the true test of spiritual leadership. Again, let me be quick to qualify that I'm not saying pastors and ministry heads should have less influence; on the contrary, they should have greater influence—the kind that lifts their people to places of prominence. So, there you have it. The vertically oriented church tends to rely on the unparalleled strengths of the pastor, to the neglect of the people's calling and capacity. At face value, of course, most pastors and ministry leaders would deny outright that the terms "pastor-centric" or "leader-centric" describe their group. But how would they know the difference? How would you?

Since it might be difficult to discern where you stand, I will now present four mission-related axioms for you to use in sizing up your own style of leadership. Every leader falls somewhere along the spectrum of 1 to 10, 1 being highly vertical, 10 being highly horizontal. Some of the principles I'm about to share will undoubtedly encourage and affirm your leadership. Whether you would identify yourself as a 1 or a 9, you will find that you have room to grow. Regardless of the church model you have adopted, these precepts, when put to practice, will matter. So, as you rate yourself, make sure you select a number indicative of strength to exceed or weakness to shore up.

Please consider the following four defining principles of horizontal projection:

### 1. HORIZONTAL LEADERS MEASURE THEMSELVES BY THEIR PEOPLE'S PROWESS

With all the disruptive feelings of crisis, pastor David Mills described his philosophic nosedive. Epitomizing the larger-than-life pastoral persona, his preaching tallied 1,400 conversions in his first ten years. But staring back at him all-too-glaringly was the breach between this number and the "disciples" who remained. Weekly service attendance at his church was 400, on average. Facing the weak discipleship angle, David had to admit the means were not producing the desired ends. It was also difficult for him to accept that after all his years of delivering inspired sermons, he was still leading an unequipped, disengaged church body. The tipping point to his leadership had begun. With it, the real influence potential of his church would rise.

When I interviewed him sometime later, he commented on how, from time to time, he would spar with his colleagues, "How many of your people actively engage in evangelism?" Most would retort, "Maybe five percent." And that was his initial answer, as well. Yet, when he moved to an evange-listically focused group model, he clocked new measurements:

50 percent were engaged in sharing the gospel.

70 percent were making efforts to befriend people outside the faith.

90 percent were praying weekly for friends to come to Christ.[90]

Periodically invited to preach at his church, I was able to observe it closely. With their minds activated on reaching others, the members were asking the right questions. They realized, from the early efforts of their "connect groups," that it was not easy to draw the interest of or win over nonbelievers. Yet, as they continued in their mission pursuit, God began to reshape their horizontal projection. Though the fruits of conversion were not as sexy or record-setting as their previous numbers, they came from the people, and because of the relational angle, they remained. True church growth was happening. As a body, they were on the path to God's design.

One day, Sandals Church Executive Pastor Dan Zimbardi asked me what I thought of the church's new corporate goals. Sizing up the list, I said, "Those are attractional bars." He looked back at me quizzically. I ex-plained, "It's entirely possible that a church can grow numerically but not mirror the growth that God desires. Transfer growth is one example, but it's more than that." I continued, "Instead of aiming for attendance, bap-tisms, and giving levels, what if we shifted measurements in the mission

90. David H. Mills, "Integrating Unbelievers into Small Groups" (D.Min. Dissertation, Golden Gate Baptist Theological Seminary, 2012). Available at: http://www.worldcat.org/title/integrating-unbelievers-into-small-groups/oclc/815971516.

direction? (That's what *Re-Missioners* do, after all!) What if the goal was 1,000 people engaged in ongoing relationships with nonbelievers?" I was not implying that other growth measurements were unimportant, only that missional goals provided a truer lens of vitality and were closer to the heart of God. We could then meter passion for the lost, as well as "on mission" practices.

Here is the crux of the matter: If you are to be missionally dynamic, your metrics must be different. Your church or group will begin to change when you change what you value and measure. Is your people's mission prowess your ministry's measurement? Rate yourself on a scale of 1 to 10. Don't fudge.

## 2. HORIZONTAL LEADERS BRIDGE TEACHING WITH ENGAGEMENT

Leaving refracted thinking behind, *ReMission* leaders equip Christians to be gospel influencers, knowing that teaching alone will not suffice.

In my younger years, after clawing my way up the depth chart to second-string status and the nickel spot, I blew out a knee in a spring football game. It wasn't the worst kind of knee injury (medial collateral ligament), but it did require surgery, followed by a long rehabilitation process. To speed recovery, they sawed a rectangular window atop my cast in order to electro-shock my now-dormant quad muscles with atrophy-countering therapy. Feeling the muscle twitch, I supposed it was working. But on the day the cast came off, I sat looking at a muscle-less limb. No exaggeration—my leg had been reduced to skin and bone. I learned a valuable lesson that day: *You can't fake exercise!*

Electro-stimulation, like wearing a vibrating belt around your stomach in an effort to drop pounds, is a gimmick that propagates a lie: "You don't have to work it; just sit back, and we'll do it for you." When I did nothing, atrophy was inevitable.

Can you see the church parallel? *All our high-powered electro-shock treatment messages cannot create the kind of muscle-skill development that can come only from use!* Too many congregants sit, soak, and settle. They haven't even begun to exercise in a missional manner. They don't know what it's like to come alongside people in full character, intention, knowledge, and mission skills. The horizontal leader properly estimates their developmental need and then puts the necessary training-engagement pieces in place.

How are you doing with this one? Rate yourself on a scale of 1 to 10. Don't be too easy or too hard on yourself.

### 3. HORIZONTAL LEADERS RELEASE THE REINS OF CONTROL

Those who lead real movement increase flow by releasing control. The gospel is meant to be fluid and free. Giving your people the reins to run with their ideas and to experiment with missional endeavors will produce learning experiences that God can build on. When the people you lead are empowered to think and dream for themselves, they will even keep you on track.

> GIVING YOUR PEOPLE THE REINS TO RUN
> WITH THEIR IDEAS AND TO EXPERIMENT WITH
> MISSIONAL ENDEAVORS WILL PRODUCE LEARNING
> EXPERIENCES THAT GOD CAN BUILD ON.

Sandals Church got some notoriety for a home-makeover project that went semi-viral. The story behind the vision is worth telling. It all began with the righteous anger of a longtime member over how "her church" was doing "nothing" for those with extreme needs. "I love our church, but we can do better!" she exhorted her pastor. The vision did not come from the members of the pastoral team; it occurred in spite of them. Owning it, Pastor Matt Brown relayed the true inspiration. The initiative was all hers. What she synergized—the outpouring of love from mass numbers of the membership laboring and contributing their time, goods, and expertise to a beautiful home makeover for a single mom and her kids—was incredible. It touched a needy family and the entire surrounding neighborhood, as well. (Watch the reaction at #ourrealfamily Mother's Day Story – YouTube[91]).

---

91. "#ourrealfamily Mother's Day Story," YouTube Video, 59:32, (church blesses family with home renovation), posted by Sandals Church, May 12, 2014, https://www.youtube.com/watch?v=eGjAHD-pxBE.

I predict that the control issue in churches will take center stage in the decades ahead, and here's why. Meet Leone. Her life mission is to reach Muslims. Do you want to hear her qualms with the church? "Churches are not good at giving up control," she says. Describing the hindrance to planting Muslim-peopled churches, she adds, "Converts from Islam are not going to become the church's Muslim ministry." Her point is well-made. After all, who is better qualified to know what the new church plant needs to be: those from the Muslim culture, or Westernized church leaders? If we are going to launch legitimate missions to Muslims, we will be required to let go of control.

Once, when a ministry director sought input on training, envisioning spontaneous moments when his team would encounter fertile ground to share Christ, I quipped, "The Holy Spirit does not wait for our programming." Neither does the Spirit subjugate himself to our models, timing, or thinking. Like a river's tributaries that are continually breaking to new regions, God is always working, and we must surrender control and go with him. (See, for example, John 5:17; Isaiah 43:18–19.) Being led by the Spirit keeps us on our spiritual toes, as we stay ready, willing, and able to step into divine opportunities and, when needed, adapt. How much are you following and releasing others under God's flow? Give yourself a rating from 1 to 10.

### 4. HORIZONTAL LEADERS CAPTURE THEIR PEOPLE'S MISSIONAL STORIES

As much as I can, I try to get churches to re-envision story capture. Do you know the difference between an *attractional story* and a *missional story*? From this real account, try to discern which is the more prominent narrative.

One Sunday morning, having reached the end of his rope, Mick walked to the road's end, not aware of the close proximity of a church. Skirting past the building, he stopped to talk with someone before heading into the surrounding hills. Getting news of his "loaded" condition, the executive pastor, Dan Zimbardi, and a church member made their way from the building up a dirt pathway in search of Mick. Spotting a man seated, they approached him, not knowing that he had a razor blade cupped in his hand, as he prepared to take his own life.

They introduced themselves, and a life-saving conversation ensued. The next Sunday, Mick came back to church all by himself. Coherent, and clean for seven days, he shared what had really occurred on the hill: As the dialogue progressed, "Z" led him to Christ. Soon he was baptized. With tears welling up in his eyes, Mick hugged his newfound friends. And he has never looked back. A beloved member of our church family, he is now a faithful disciple.

So, tell me, would this story be considered "attractional" or "missional"? At first glance, it might appear attractional, since the man came by the church on a Sunday morning. Upon closer review, however, one realizes that this story has every marking of being missional. The executive pastor got out of his office to *go* get this young man. Influence happened *outside* the main service, and through the people, *not* the senior pastor. Yes, this is a missional story.

When Sandals Church filmed Mick's testimony sometime later, they highlighted his transformation at the church (exciting to hear!) but, typical of most churches, excluded the engagement aspects. Yet the details of how his conversion unfolded are rich! Don't you want to know how this guy—at the end of his rope—found hope? Don't you wonder what enabled the impending tragedy to tip? We want more of this kind of testimony, don't we?

As we saw in the finer telling, the executive pastor did something we can all go to school on. Discerning Mick's despair, he spoke with utter confidence, painting a picture of a whole new life that Mick could have with Christ (and invoking Skill #8: Projecting). How many church members know how to do this? It began by asking Mick a simple yet pointed question: "Are you thirsty?" Then the pastor repeated the question, leaning into the deeper meaning: "Are you thirsty—*at the soul level?*"

Mick, trying to comprehend the question, picked up something hopeful in the pastor's earnest tenor, and replied, "Yes." "Then let's go down to the church and get you some food and drink, and we'll talk more about that," Dan directed him. En route to the church, they discussed a new course for his life—a new course involving the church's support, of course. That week, the body sprang into action, following up with him, and offering help as they were able, such as rides to church.

When you capture the story of reaching others, using personal interviews and videos, you help others see what missional engagement entails. Your people learn from the examples, and the gospel movement gets celebrated. Think of the synergistic impact of telling a story such as this one. The hearts of your people will be burning for Jesus and the gospel! Don't squander the opportunity.

This is why "on-mission" Christians should be included in the ritual of baptism. We're moving away from being pastor-centric, right? Involving other church members in this sacrament honors these people for their work of reaching and discipling their friends. Don't forget the old adage "What gets recognized, gets done." So, recognize your missional champions. By celebrating the story of God's movement through your people, no doubt others will be motivated to get in the game!

How do you rank in this category? When was the last time your church told a missional story for all to hear?

## THE SIGN AT THE STAGE

Standing on the stage beside our pastor, I waited, but the gathering of a thousand-plus people didn't budge. Just like the fortnight service, the message call hadn't quite done it. Tension filled the room like a thick fog—blockage—as if demons had barricaded the aisles. We soon learned there was a reason, and that God wasn't done. A believer named Julie, seated twenty rows back, arrived that morning with no idea of the crucial part she would play. As everyone hung in what seemed like suspended animation, suddenly, she arose. After taking a moment to organize her tubes, air tank, and walker, she began a trek to the front.

I watched as she came forward, not knowing her predicament, the courage, or the cost. Only later did we learn Julie's backstory. Following a bout of pneumonia, she had contracted a rare lung disease—"idiopathic pulmonary fibrosis," they called it. It's when scarring wraps itself around the lungs, limiting air from getting out, and making every new breath harder than the last. Julie's condition was terminal. During the past months, God had become exceedingly real to her, and it was with inexplicable joy that she awaited her promotion to heaven to be with Jesus.

Still active, she was able to be at worship that morning. Commenting later, she simply said, "I just thought, if I went first, others would follow." Like a dam breaking, her move released the flow. I remember it as if it happened yesterday. One by one, they came. And it didn't stop until fifty-six people lined the front of the stage. Julie died a month later, but her legacy lives on.

The visual impact of what happened that day stays with me to this day, stamped on my psyche like a tattoo. I saw God's power released by a regular church member. I witnessed her being the pivotal piece, the barrier-breaker, pushing us up and over. On that morning, something else occurred—another indelible inking. Having gone with the group to the collecting room, she, being saved already, returned to the service. When she walked into the sanctuary, the whole place, having witnessed her catalytic role in the altar call, stood up and applauded! Without any premeditated plan or any orders from the leadership, the church body honored the contribution it had seen her make.

Looking back, there is no doubt in my mind that it was God who orchestrated the buildup. He brought us all out onto a limb, where a woman, an obscure church member drawing her final breaths, would be the star.

## WHAT IS MISSING IN TODAY'S CHURCH? IT'S THE INERTIA-BREAKING ROLE OF ITS MEMBERS.

What is missing in today's church? It's the inertia-breaking role of its members. Perhaps, all of us should repent: the pew-sitters, for idolizing their pastors and assuming those leaders should do the work that is rightly the body's; and the leaders, for expecting too little from God's front line. Let's stop gauging our spiritual lives by the feelings we get from a message or a song, and start focusing on our feet. I believe that as we head into what will be the biggest, most dynamic epochs of church history—when the largest population ever recorded will be outside the joining circle—what the church desperately needs is a return to the acts of its people. Hold on!

Stories of the gospel are yet to be written. Let's release their full potential, for such a time as this!

———

Next, we will take the tipped projection and add a key empowerment feature that I call *pinpointing*. Perhaps no other singular concept in this book will do more for the influence of your people.

## REFLECTIONS

1.  How does the lack of missional integrity make you feel about today's church? What emotions does it evoke?

2.  Do you think we need to tap the other equipping gifts (apostles, prophets, evangelists) to better realize the movement? If so, what would be the best way of doing that?

3.  How vertical is the general church, in your estimation? How horizontal is your church at this juncture, 1 to 10?

## REMISSION TAKEAWAYS

1.  The spotlight plays a major role in what happens through the church.

2.  The measure of the pastor is the messaging prowess of the people.

3.  The Christlike leader steps down in order to raise others to prominence.

4.  Horizontal leadership is marked by four empowerment principles.

# —8—

# PINPOINTING THE FLOW

It's interesting how little the New Testament talks about church growth, and how often it talks about "gospel growth."
—Colin Marshall and Tony Payne, *The Trellis and the Vine*

Coming into the stadium, jacketed conference officials joined the crowd, ready to crown their champion. At a pivotal fourth-quarter, fourth-down time-out, signal caller Dave Curry called me to his side to give some very precise instructions. Have you ever wondered what a coach tells his player before a big moment? This is what he said: "If the corner is positioned outside the receiver, punt. But if he is playing straight up, the fake is on." Note the directive of a Division 1 head coach, when Long Beach State faced one-day NFL Hall of Famer Randall Cunningham's UNLV (University of Nevada, Las Vegas) squad for the PCAA championship.

Running to midfield, I posted myself between the center and punter, then focused my gaze on the left side of the defense. Catching eyes with the corner, I could tell he had scouted the trick play that we had run against San Jose State. But it didn't matter. Their coach had failed to make the adjustment. Seeing him playing straight up, I called out the audible "Down" instead of "Set," which relayed to my team that the fake was on! The center snapped it short to me. I bobbled the ball in the air (crazy!), finally gathered it in, and then threw a strike to the receiver, fading the ball just inside the chalked line. First down! Heading to the sideline, I got several whacks upside my helmet (a kind of love language). Our offense stormed back onto the field and then drove for a touchdown. With our "D" making the stop, our "O" got the ball back and marched for a field goal in the closing minute to win the game!

A guy told me afterward, "That play was the turning point; you won it for us." His comment wasn't entirely true—it was just one play in a bigger sequence—but it was a big play, and I felt great about having contributed to our victory.

What did my coach do? He sent me out onto the field to *make a read*. In a shifting, highly energized climate, *making a read* is a million times more effective than *predetermining a call*. It's why master game-calling NFL quarterbacks such as Peyton Manning and Tom Brady are deadly against their opponents' defenses. Top football coaches get this. It's too bad church leaders don't.

## HARD ASSESSMENT: STATIC TELLING

Across the wide spectrum of the church, pastors exhort their flocks to go *tell* the gospel. Parishioners pour forth as faithful heralds (tellers), even though the vast bloc has little comprehension of *what* this significant endeavor requires. Well-meaning church members are so uninformed that, after fumbling along in futility a time or two, many of them go mute, dropping the ball entirely. We are so unlike the broad, impactful movement of early Christianity.

How can we turn the tide and flip the confidence vacuum on its head? We need to *stop telling believers to "tell," and start teaching them to make a read*. We should not underestimate how catalytic this change could be, or how much it is warranted. Do you send your children into the world bereft of navigational training? Of course not; for then, how would they prepare to make good choices? Without proper training, they won't be able to handle that which unfolds before their eyes. As my coach did with that critically timed call, we can equip decision-makers with *dynamic* skill sets that enable them to work with what they see in live action, and that will become second nature to them. No more canned, memorized presentations, but a natural/supernatural approach that blends unique personality with the power of the Holy Spirit, makes believers sensitive to the cares and needs of others, and enables them to respond with love and truth. When you send your people to their "fields" of friends, neighbors, colleagues, and whole new cultures, their ability to *make a read* will mean big plays for God's kingdom!

This *ReMission* focus shift, as you might guess, is a radical revision. It is a theme I go after in my training: Reverse the epicenter for evangelism. Being that influence flows from relationship, we do not start with telling anyone anything; the conversation begins with them, not us. From the pattern of Jesus, we should:

+ Start where they are.

+ Read what they need.

+ Know where to take them.[92]

In lieu of dropping a conversation transition out of the blue or trying to explain too much too soon, conversations should begin more naturally with our friend's situation. In real-life relationships, changing the starting point changes everything. It leads Christians to enter into dialogues that will zero in on the relevancy of faith for a unique individual. Like the Samaritan woman whose heart jumped when she heard Jesus' offer of "living water," those in our mission field can hear words pinpointed to their lives. Whether we realize it or not, no one is drawn to faith unless he or she first sees the related benefits.

This is where Jesus began his conversations with people. Have you ever met anyone who was not gripped by words dialed in to address his or her personal longings and desires? Aren't you drawn in when someone speaks compassionately and compellingly to the situation you yourself are dealing with? What is your most pressing obstacle right now? How might God, and faith in Him, be of remedy or resource? If only I was present with you to dig that insight out—then perhaps I'd be able to whisper potent words that could have come from the very lips of Jesus!

Think of your friends outside the church. Ever get close enough to them to make a read? Why wouldn't you want your people to develop the necessary skills to *disclose* or *describe* the spiritual life as the answer? This *picturing* skill takes practice. It involves listening, reading, and interpreting a message. Not merely telling, but interpreting what others are saying, and

---

92. Comer, *Soul Whisperer*, 3.

then speaking to it, meaningfully. It's not the prototypical say-the-same-thing-to-every-soul evangelistic pitch. Rather, it's deep, dialed in, personal, and powerful! I call it *soul whispering*. It's what Jesus did.

Now, I need to qualify something. The Greek New Testament language used different clusters of words to describe gospel messaging. Two ideas stand out: (1) *Kerusso*: "To proclaim like a herald," and (2) *Martureo*: "To bear witness of facts and truths to be vouched for."[93] An important and helpful distinction that I make—and one which, I realize, others do not make—is that the church must employ two types of training that align with these biblical meanings:

1.  For pastors/church planters from the pulpit: Proclamation (preaching, presentation before groups)

2.  For people during their everyday lives: Process (personal, dialogical with friends)

As with beer and wine, you shouldn't mix the two!

Churches that apply the Antioch principle create their own training environment to raise apostles and prophets. (See Acts 13:1–3.) This incubator for top leaders will fuel your church-planting expansion. To support your equipping, I would encourage you to get hooked up with a church-planting network, as well. I will present a concept for raising powerful presenters in the forthcoming chapter "Step On." Because you already have many tools for achieving number 1 on the above list from the up-front church platform, I will focus this chapter on your people's empowerment (number 2), in their neighborhoods and in the marketplace.

When it comes to the church body, process training is the way to help your members be fruitful. Thus, I do not favor the word "proclamation," because it implies the idea of making a speech or a presentation. Rid that preachy image from their minds, and the gospel may even have a chance! Learning to embrace a "bearing-witness" process is a better way in every way.

## OPENING NEW VALVES

To *ReMission* flow through the body of Christ, we must open the arteries, so to speak. Like a stent inserted in the heart patient, the word I

93. Green, *Evangelism in the Early Church*, 48–70.

have chosen to mark this change isn't cardiac-related, necessarily, but it's accurate: "pinpointing." *Horizontal* is the influence projection of the channel. *Pinpointing* is where that projection pays off. Pinpointing means teaching our people how to dial in to the person they're speaking to, with that person's particular storyline. For your gospel training purposes, consider the following tactics as your main valve openers:

### OPENER #1: FRAME A RELATIONAL PROCESS

Unlike the telling motif, with its tight range of influence, the relational approach works far better in our pluralized society. It shifts the focus from a single "telling" task to a heart-"drawing" sequence, from a proclamation point to a relationally driven process. Get the whole church making this shift, and we could become mission viable once again.

Though there will be ripened souls coming toward us whom we must faithfully lead to Christ, from an outreach perspective, the thinking that we can make disciples through a onetime gospel pitch to a stranger is fundamentally flawed. Such methods often breach relational trust, a key for truly effective disciplemaking. You must therefore help your people see evangelism in a new way. I break the engagement process into three phases. Pay attention here, because the church needs help in executing each one, and you're just the person to do it!

**TORCH**          **TRAIL**          **TRACTION**

It begins with framing a spiritual conversation (Torch Lighting), proceeds in an ongoing relationship and dialogue (Trail), and eventually leads to the crossover into faith (Traction). This sequence happens between individuals, as well as within a group context. And it can include invitation and inclusion to the large group gathering. One highly teachable biblical image that is valuable for use in training is where Philip gets positioned beside the eunuch's chariot, then climbs up into the chariot beside the eunuch as a passenger. Somewhere down the road, they pull over, and Philip baptizes the eunuch. Can you see how illustrative this image is? If your people don't get *positioned* alongside others in an ongoing, journeying way, their friends won't find Jesus! What would have happened to the eunuch, had Philip refused to step up and engage in conversation with him? Let it not be missed that it was his obedience to *go* and "stay near," and then to get seated beside him, that led to the eunuch's coming to faith. (See Acts 8:29–31.) The result was not only this man's salvation, but also his taking the gospel to the African continent. This is what happens when we empower gospel mobility. The movement takes off!

If we break down this Spirit-led encounter, the *torch* was getting positioned for a conversation to begin, the *trail* was the journey alongside him, and the *traction* was gaining ground for a faith-commitment decision. Working these three stages typically requires specific skill training in advance, as well as an appropriate amount of time.

*Torch.* In one of my training seminars, a lightbulb moment occurred with a woman who said, "Oh, you want it to be ongoing." Yes! What did she do? She started meeting her neighbor to exercise every week. Another woman in my course shared that her work associate had begun spouting off some wild beliefs, and though she was at first tempted to correct her, she replied instead, "Janey, I would like to hear more of what you think about all that. How would you like to get together next week for coffee?" Another trainee told me how he led his friend to Christ by framing. Dumping what I call "one-hit-wonder thinking," he showed interest and initiated another time with his counterpart by saying, "This was a great conversation with you today, my friend. Let's hook back up to talk more next week." Every question and objection expressed by a disbelieving friend is an opportunity to frame a continuing dialogue, where relational love and real influence can blossom.

Have you imparted this biblical skill to all your people? It's vital!

*Trail.* Once framing occurs, the Trail aspects of reading a person's receptivity, creating safety to explore, and gauging pace become very important. You do not want to frighten or overwhelm, but rather to bring the person along. In my book *Soul Whisperer*, I explain how to avoid sinkholes that can take others down before they get to a place of having spiritual impact.

It is here that your people are learning how to maintain momentum and be truly committed to a lost soul who is precious to God.

This training has huge implications for church growth. In my second year of leading a church plant, I had a conversation with a core member during which I inquired if he was bringing anyone to our pancake breakfast. Dissenting, he explained, "We already invited all our neighbors." By the shriveling numbers at the event, we figured that what was true of him was true of most. We had hit the "inviting wall," a wall we hadn't even known existed until that moment! It explains what happens when the church fails to invest in new relationships outwardly: Opportunity is exhausted, and the flow trickles. Teaching your people to engage missionally is what you need to do to keep expanding your range.

## TEACHING YOUR PEOPLE TO ENGAGE MISSIONALLY IS WHAT YOU NEED TO DO TO KEEP EXPANDING YOUR RANGE.

*Traction.* Not only do we need to teach framing (how to get alongside) and how to journey with others; we also need to give our people the skills to achieve breakthrough. In sit-down talks with Joshua Stock, director of Snowboarders & Skiers for Christ, and Gavin Linderman, planter of Axiom Church in Peoria, Arizona, I listened as both men identified the same barrier. Committed to mission penetration, Josh leads 30-plus SFC chapters to reach the slopes of America and the world, and Gavin is planting a church in urban Phoenix. Hearing echoes of frustration from these men, I helped them diagnose the problem their mostly millennial-aged constituents were facing. Their people had intuited that relationship with their unsaved friends was essential, yet they struggled to get it moving into the right direction of tapping into the interests, desires, and motivations of their friends in order to develop faith formation.

This gap is precisely what I attempted to bridge in my book *Soul Whisperer.* Your people can engage relationally, but if they don't understand how to draw others through "attraction building" (the gut-level why-to-follow-Jesus impetus), their effort gets stymied. The ability to envision how faith intersects with lives is a training concept I have termed the *gospel key*. It is the skill of connecting the dots between their friends' needs/situations/storylines with Christ's life-giving offer.

In many ways, *Soul Whisperer* precedes *ReMission* with its horizontal focus. I purposed to recover evangelism from the insensitive, overly aggressive, and intimidating image in our culture (partly realistic, and partly distorted by the media) that had been built up, as well as to infuse the sharers of the good news with a new set of fluid skills. True to form, Joshua Stock said, "The one thing the younger crowd would not receive was anything that sounded like a pitch." Dumping canned approaches that are not conducive in today's authenticity-based climate, faith-sharing is better received when it flows naturally. In fact, sometimes it is not received at all unless the flow is natural. From the leader's view, this relating factor also greatly affects church members' willingness to express the gospel. After observing mute Christians over the last three decades, I came up with the adage, "It's natural or nothing."

This is why personal disclosure is so important. What could be more natural than talking about your present-day struggles and the resource you have found in God? When you add honest vulnerability into the mix, your unsaved friends may actually listen to what faith means to you, and may consider what it could mean for them. A paradoxical truth I teach is that the more a Christian grows in holiness, the more darkness he can see in himself. This is true of anyone getting closer to the Lord, the Light of life. Disclosure is the way to become a window to the need for Christ. I want Christians to leverage their own lives for the gospel, saying, "If they never see your darkness, they may never see his light," and "When you open up, you open a window to Christ."

Influence training gets the whole church back in the game. From my journeys with unbelievers, I have defined specific skills for each phase: (1) Torch: How to initiate dialogues from three lines: story, learning, and question; (2) Trail: How to manage dialogues with pace, safety, honor, friction, and patience; and (3) Traction: How to leverage dialogues with breakthrough techniques (anticipation of belief, alignment with reason, contrasting faith and doubt, going experiential with God, questioning the hang-up). Honing these vital engagement skills will bolster spiritual growth and improve your team's ability to reach others. It is in *Soul Whisperer* that I develop and illustrate those skills over many chapters.

At this juncture, I have chosen to reveal the paradigm and to teach one quintessential skill.

### OPENER #2: TAKE FAITH-SHARING DEEPER

Named for the pattern set by Christ, "soul whispering" is an influence paradigm. It teaches believers *how* to relate lovingly with unsaved people and to share their faith resonantly. It does not abuse, run over, or create non-gospel-related offense, all of which are common outcomes from the telling paradigm. Do we really need more "in your face with the truth," megaphone-wielding Christians turning waves of people away from our faith? People say it doesn't matter how you do evangelism. That's a lie. It matters. Others are always coming behind us, because it is God who is seeking to bring people to himself in every way possible over time. Consequently, we must steward our methods to avoid creating baggage and causing a backlash of counterproductive proportions. We want to, at the very least, move each person once step closer to Christ through our interactions, not drive anyone farther away from the faith.

I fully realize that there are those who don't like Christians. I realize that the gospel can sometimes offend. But there are times, in relationships, when we are called to be passionate and strong, like Jesus with his blunt words to Nicodemus (see John 3:1–21) and to the young rich ruler (see Mark 10:17–27). Both of these exchanges were disturbing to the men involved, but they were also perfectly placed, and they exemplify Jesus' ability to influence. Spiritual giant Nicodemus heard what he most needed to hear: *All his great religiosity meant nothing!* Boom. He needed to be "born again." The rich young ruler heard what he most needed to hear: *Radical surgery was required on his idolatrous soul!* But in every one of Jesus' intimate conveyances of truth, he wasn't a jerk. He loved Nicodemus (who later followed him [see John 19:39]), and he loved the young ruler (see Mark 10:21). He spoke truth and grace to the crowds. (See Matthew 5–8.) Therefore, the approach I am offering you reflects how Jesus engaged the pre-saved;

it is decidedly character-driven. When you are like Christ to someone in the full pattern of your life, the message you carry and offer him or her will reflect Christ's compassion and love.

As you have gathered, I champion dynamic process over presentation. I am pragmatic, never wanting to make sharing or receiving harder than it should be. If someone is hungering or asking, you should explain what Christ has done on his or her behalf, then lead him or her to faith. The simplistic telling approach is insufficient, however, for those whose hearts are not yet there—and that category encompasses most of the people in our post-Christian culture. As stated previously, they choose not to believe. Establishing relationships (soil preparation) and creating open, safe conversations that pique spiritual interest (seed planting) must happen first. Again, the traditional telling paradigm has no regard for receptivity and pace; it has a job to do, and its goal is to dispense truth, whether the person listening is ready or not. Nine times out of ten, that approach is a huge turn-off to most thinking nonbelievers.

THE TRADITIONAL TELLING PARADIGM HAS NO REGARD FOR RECEPTIVITY AND PACE; IT HAS A JOB TO DO, AND ITS GOAL IS TO DISPENSE TRUTH, WHETHER THE PERSON LISTENING IS READY OR NOT. NINE TIMES OUT OF 10, THAT APPROACH IS A HUGE TURN-OFF TO MOST THINKING NONBELIEVERS.

Teaching people how to come alongside relationally, read people, and tailor their communication accordingly is a dynamic approach. As such, this approach has the precision to evoke interest—to touch and even strum another's heartstrings.

The newer paradigm keeps evangelism in the learning curve. Investing relationally, the Christian must first draw out specific thoughts and feelings from his or her friend. It takes effort, patience, and sensitivity to the

Holy Spirit's leading. Often, it is necessary to utilize second- and third-tier follow-up questions, such as "What did you mean by that?" and "So that I might understand you better, can you explain more of your thoughts/feelings?" You have to train your people to do this. It takes poise to shut up and go deeper in a relationship and in understanding before speaking. God knows what each person needs to hear. Alter the way your members interact on spiritual matters, and they will become more sensitive to the Spirit's leadings as they seek his revelations.

Yes, evangelism starts with discovery! Like digging for treasure, it makes the whole endeavor exciting. It is the insight that Jesus had with people that explains why he didn't give the same message to everyone. Jesus was an influencer, not a teller. Following his deft manner will change the way you think with every non-Christian you meet. By reading others deeply, at their soul level, Jesus was able to speak words that were spot-on.

Contemplate the chart below, focusing on the categories of "Need" and "Story."

| PEOPLE | NEED | SYMBOL | STORY |
| --- | --- | --- | --- |
| Nicodemus JOHN 3 | INCEPTION | Birth | *Religious teacher learns he must begin all over again by God's Spirit.* |
| Samaritan Woman JOHN 4 | INFILLING | Well | *Soul thirsting woman hears about experiencing "living water."* |
| Adulterous Captive JOHN 8 | INSULATION | Scrawl | *An expose' question protects a guilty woman from self-righteous accusers & shame.* |
| Canaanite Inquirer MATTHEW 15 | INSTIGATION | Dogs | *Derogatory words stir up a foreigner's exceptional faith.* |
| Zacchaeus LUKE 19 | INCLUSION | Home | *Jewish tax-collecting outcast receives an inclusive invitation.* |
| Rich Young Ruler MARK 10 | INCISION | Release | *The command to release riches seeks to scalpel an idolatrous heart.* |
| Hemorrhaging Woman MARK 5 | INSTILLING | Knees | *A call out from the crowd cements her newfound faith.* |

A pastor once said my ideas were ahead of their time, noting that European Christians and other more "closed" international climates would benefit more than Western culture would. I strongly disagreed, for two reasons. First, the principles stem from our Bible. Second, from my perspective, a shift to teaching *influence skills* is long overdue. Consider the average churchgoer's ineptitude in the evangelistic arena, and you can clearly see that something must change to make the "good news" palatable for both the sharer and the receiver.

The following real-life scenario will give you ideas on how to begin to collaboratively train those in your midst.

Sitting in with a team that ministers to those rescued from human trafficking, Monique discussed her last trip to the safehouse, where she met a sixteen-year old girl who'd had to run away because her parents were enabling her uncle to molest her sexually. (Talk about ripping your heart out!) We began, as a team, to discuss how to sensitively communicate the gospel to her in a meaningful way in light of her unique, dark predicament. She was a victim.

I had the team members take turns sharing their thoughts on what this sixteen-year-old might be feeling and thinking. Granted, in faith sharing, the only way to truly know how someone thinks and feels is to hear the person express it firsthand, but this hypothetical guessing game created a teaching lesson full of compassion. One group member lamented, "Shame." "Dirtied," said another. "Distortion of her true identity and worth"; "Anger and mistrust," others chimed in.

Then we talked about what the gospel might be for her. The team began to brainstorm how she might hear "good news." Can you see it? Is it on the tip of your tongue? Do you know what the pinpointed message should be for her? In other words, if you were Jesus, what words would you speak directly to what was pounding so painfully in her heart, every moment of every day? Think about it. Write down your ideas in the margin of this page or on a separate piece of paper. Imagine your team doing this exercise, as well.

Several team members weighed in on what they thought Jesus would offer this young woman.

"Expiation," one said. Well, that's a nice five-dollar theological word plucked from a church membership class. It's one that we should never use in conversation, though it is rich in concept. But his sentiment was actually in the right vein. What words might assuage her pain? What kind of expression would sing hope and healing to her soul? Are you thinking, "Tell her she's a sinner who needs to repent"? I hope you're not going there. I can't see Jesus doing that. Would you want to be treated that way when you were in the depths of pain and confusion?

Next, I wanted to practice imparting a message in a tone that felt natural and honoring to the relationship. How would it sound? I've mentioned that this is a learned skill. Reading a person's true need, interpreting the gospel's meaning to that person's life, and then discerning how to communicate that idea are essential skills for every Christian. If you think that your congregants or group members do this automatically, you're wrong! Someone will have to help them develop this ability so that they may be more fruitful with the gospel.

> READING A PERSON'S TRUE NEED, INTERPRETING THE GOSPEL'S MEANING TO THAT PERSON'S LIFE, AND THEN DISCERNING HOW TO COMMUNICATE THAT IDEA ARE ESSENTIAL SKILLS FOR EVERY CHRISTIAN.

As we continued, my group wrestled with finding the words. So, we got specific by suggesting possible phrasing that would feel right in the conversation and also express the right content in the right spirit to this beautiful, young victimized girl. Acknowledging there would be an appropriate time within the developing relationship to express this, we zeroed in on these words: "Jenny, if you were to come to know God in a personal way, your relationship with him, and his love for you, would overshadow what you have gone through, and bring healing to your heart. God can do what no one else can." One member of the group said, "I can totally see myself saying that!"

We sat around brainstorming some more on how important that communication could be to someone like her. Not only could it bring "good news" to her; it would open doors for a future dialogue about what it means to know and follow God, and what he did for her on the cross.

For perspective, this example of an abused person is not an easy read. My initial experience in leading someone to Christ using this key was with a person suffering the abandonment of her spouse. Can you see the interpretative key and guess what my approach was with her? My appeal—that Christ would always be there for her and walk with her into the future—was powerful. A week later, my skeptical friend gave her life to Jesus. Afterward, I diagrammed on my whiteboard what had occurred with this woman, then taught the concept in a large class setting, and watched Christians get excited about having a tool to use with their friends. Two weeks into the class, one gal, Janel, grabbed me at church to say that she had just led her militarily outbound cousin to Christ using the key I'd taught her. Another was seeking my input on the right message for her perfectionistic friend. I cannot count how many times people have said to me, "Did you hear *the key* when they said this?" Or "I think that might be *their key*." Though it is a more sophisticated method in that it studies a human soul in order to dial in to a resonant message, even new believers have caught on to it. Laurie reported, "I did what you told us to do, I listened to them first, and then I shared something about faith that related to what they were going through."

Some believers have become rather prolific with the skill. One of our mission trainees met a Japanese woman whose American husband confessed to having been unfaithful with 100 women. As she listened to this woman unload, she kept asking herself over and over, *What is her need?* Sensing that the woman was feeling overwhelmed and utterly shocked, she pointed to a massive planter close to their table, and said, "Maiko, you were not made to carry that planter. And you cannot carry this burden." She then talked with the woman about Jesus, the only One who could carry her burden. Like the metaphor of "living water" that Jesus used when speaking with the Samaritan woman (see John 4:1–42), the planter metaphor became the communication piece that led Maiko to faith. A week later, she met again with Maiko, who cried out in prayer and embraced her mighty Savior with tears streaming down her face.

For a training-technique takeaway, your people must be able to fill in the blank of this statement for anyone they are trying to bring into the fold of Christianity: "If you were to become a Christian, I see _____ happening in your life." By envisioning the spiritual result of the gospel for their friend, they learn to "connect the dots" between the person's storyline and what the person will hear as good news. Note: World-class disciple-makers use compelling descriptions or metaphors to cast a picture of what it will mean to have a relationship with Christ. Can you begin to picture the many kinds of examples? "If you were to follow Christ, your trust in him would deliver you from the anxiety you are facing right now." "He would give you the inner power to overcome those desires." "He would re-deem what you have done by using it for his highest purposes." "He would shower you with the truth of your undeniable worth." "He would trans-form your marriage by changing you from inside out." "He would deal a deathblow to your apathy by giving you something big and far greater to live for." (For a full treatment of this technique, see chapter 6, "The Gospel Key," in my book *Soul Whisperer*). With those in the experiential fray, the key might be easier to decipher; with others, it will not be found on the sur-face. You must draw it out and dig for it! If your members cannot answer the question above, they haven't done the work of discovery. Sometimes, in training sessions, we have to stop and say, "You're not getting it. You must focus on *drawing out* so that you can gain insight on their need."

Thus, all the skills work together: Framing, creating safety, drawing the other's thoughts, reading and interpreting, and then delivering God's message.

Listening ❯ Discovery ❯ Interpretation ❯ Communication

Back to our training story: The key points to the cross. The young victimized girl would learn the full message of the gospel through a deep-er interchange about what Christ had done, about her sin, and about his salvation. I told the abolitionist group, "At the safehouse this week, as you connect relationally, asking questions and listening to hearts, contemplate possible communication angles for your return visit." This was just the start of their training. They would need to develop the life skill with a "live" non-believer. Working it, they would have to see success in creating spiritual dialogue that sparks desire. By choosing to walk alongside a person, they'd have the positioning to prepare hearts for faith, and also to walk forward with those people in discipleship. It's a process that all Christ-followers can learn. If they complete that exciting endeavor, they will build confidence in their ability to make new disciples.

If you want to create horizontal projection, then you, or your assigned leaders, must walk your people into disciplemaking. Equipping happens through a combination of training and engagement over an extended period of time. It takes time and patience. This process isn't a quick-fix, one-and-done training session. In no way ashamed of the gospel, your people will tell, in their own words, Christ's intervention story on their friends' behalf; and they can use a presentation mechanism, like the classic "bridge" illustration, to explain the legal saving power of Jesus Christ. Though you can sprinkle in the gospel message as you go, usually, the big discussion about their commitment to Christ occurs later in the journey, when they are ready to hear and respond. As the fruit comes and then extends to others, you will be catalyzing a movement of God.

Jesus' drawing paradigm works in all scenarios, whether local or global, greasing the skids for our wide-ranging mission. The engagement aspect of coming alongside others, not surprisingly, can be formidable. The person beginning farther from a Christian worldview will require more time and, undoubtedly, supernatural breakthroughs. As I graphed in my first book, in certain cases, belief platforms must get built (#8 Skill: Platform building).

Just as I am now meeting regularly with a local imam, I met weekly with my formerly atheistic friend for nine months. There are no shortcuts. When we first started, I thought my chances of reaching him were about the same as the chances of my getting a call to play for the Los Angeles Chargers! I truly didn't know where to take it, but God eventually lit the way. An insightful note: You reach an atheist by moving him into agnosticism, and then using multiple angles for generating belief in God (I identify nine proofs in Soul Whisperer).[94] Coming at it from the science angle alone can be a big mistake. The inventive C. S. Lewis, in Mere Christianity, bypasses the scientific method for a deeper, more philosophic argument: the inlay of human conscience.[95] Being analytically oriented, skeptics must

---

94. Comer, Soul Whisperer, 267–77.
95. C. S. Lewis, Mere Christianity (New York: Macmillan Publishing, 1952), 17–39.

be given reasons to believe. I called it "platform building" because, eventually, they will have to have something solid to stand upon. Know this: My atheist friend would never have come to faith outside a lengthy process.

Reaching people farther out revolutionized the way I viewed evangelism. It exposed where skills and knowledge were needed. It's why *Soul Whisperer* became a 300-pager—because the processes of "making reads" and "knowing where to take them" involved mapping. It requires some work to build enough trust to get inside a person's head and heart. I wanted my readers to see particularized paths of reaching common types of people: God accusers, cultural Christians, pleasure seekers, moralists (goody-goodies), progressives, theistic skeptics, atheists, and those from other faiths.[96] The basic breakdown of Jesus' soul-whisperer paradigm works for all.

The second part of the paradigm, *read what they need*, encompasses two levels: a messaging read and a processing read. From the person's true starting point, we must ask:

1. What gospel-related message will resonate with his or her life situation?

2. What kind of processing journey is needed to reach him or her?

We are always dealing with the head and the heart, couched inside a spiritual battle. Welcome to the frontline!

A word to pastors: Oversimplified clichés do not help. At a local gathering, one person remarked, "We just need to show our Muslim neighbors love." I respectfully countered, "You won't reach any Muslim by 'just' showing love. We will have to answer Islam with a compelling rationale for our faith." Those who are already locked into a belief system that is different from Christianity will need to be loved *and* persuaded. In the addendum to this book, I have included four major apologetic lines to reach Muslims. In the forthcoming pages, I will also share the conversation I had with a Muslim from Lebanon. But you should know this truth: Merely telling the gospel does nothing. You have to journey together with someone to get to the place where that person can *hear* it. Can you see the difference? Establishing common ground is a great way to lay the groundwork

96. Comer, *Soul Whisperer*, 246–98.

for an open and honorable conversation, but you eventually have to reach the place of persuasion.

> ## MERELY TELLING THE GOSPEL DOES NOTHING. YOU HAVE TO JOURNEY TOGETHER WITH SOMEONE TO GET TO THE PLACE WHERE THAT PERSON CAN *HEAR* IT.

Just so you can see what we're talking about, here is an overview of my four apologetic lines for reaching Muslims: (1) the Qur'an's view of biblical authority, (2) the tests for divine revelation, (3) the cross of Christ versus Islam's dismissal of history, and (4) the infinite Trinity meets finite minds. Again, if you don't challenge the belief system of those who are outside Christianity, you shouldn't expect to see kingdom results.

Lest we forget, the reason influence is not simple is because it's so significant. Eternities hang in the balance as we implore others to make the transition from the kingdom of darkness to the kingdom of light. Satan will not easily give up what is his. Teaching your people how to engage conversationally puts them smack-dab in the middle of the fight! Bear in mind that they'll need to be ready for the spiritual warfare that inevitably comes with these endeavors. Don't shield them from this. Better they feel the heat of battle than remain innocuous to the enemy.

### OPENER #3: DIVERSIFY YOUR VEHICLES

Once you have gotten a clear vision and have developed the engagement skills to teach, then you must thread mission training throughout all your ministries. One of Michael Green's contributions was to show how the early church penetrated the culture through a multiplicity of means.[97] At Sandals, we implemented my *Steps to Faith* course, an Alpha-like evangelistic class to reach the wider questioning pre-Christian; trained new believers to reach their networks; launched Discovery circles outside the

97. Green, *Evangelism in the Early Church*, 194–235.

church; mobilized ministries to meet needs in the city; offered a class that taught faith-sharing skills; and trained our community groups in holistic disciplemaking. Other leaders built mission teams, training their members through projects and peer-learning groups. Please know that we were only scratching the surface in our quest to train those within the church and reach those outside it. The work is never done!

A great avenue for mission training is small groups. Of course, a shift of aim will undoubtedly raise a flag, because small groups in the church tend to center on Christian needs, being fellowship- or affinity-focused. This presents yet another challenge to the leadership: How do you deprogram your groups from an affinity focus so that mission can have a chance? Many leaders will drop the ball right there, saying there's no way they are going to disrupt the worlds of their core members. How about envisioning something greater? Isn't it time to push the limits of your leadership moxie?

You have two options. One is gradual, the other is radical. Pick your poison. If you go the gradual route, you will transition new groups into being community groups. Here, you *phase in* the missional focus. The radical approach, in contrast, is when you meet with all your group leaders. Working the process, you take time to honor them for all that they have done. Only after they feel totally loved and appreciated do you introduce a fresh vision that God has given you to reach the neighborhood and city through community-based groups. The groups will continue to learn and fellowship together, but they will be "on-mission" together. Inform their leaders that every facilitating leader will be assigned to key staff for training.

Next, communicate that if this vision is to be realized, the groups must be reorganized based upon region, not affinity, so that efforts can serve and include common neighbors. Additionally, regionally located groups can better partner together on outreach projects and block parties. Finally, announce that the groups will be baptizing new disciples in common community pools, where church pastors will oversee, but those who have actually reached the people will perform their baptisms. A visual such as this may help them picture it.

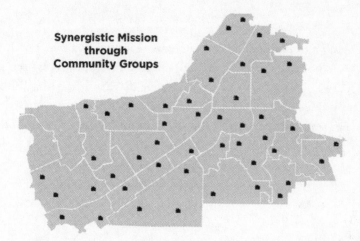

**Synergistic Mission through Community Groups**

Whichever option you choose, or if you just want to provide "mission training" to your group, I have written a curriculum for community group engagement called *Launch Point: Moving Small Groups into Mission*. Having completed the eight-week course and the corresponding extension activity, one leader reviewed it as follows:

> This book walks you step-by-step on how to listen well and understand where people are coming from, and then imagine with them what their faith journey might look like. It helps people who love Jesus overcome barriers and misconceptions that keep us from doing what we want and should do: sharing that relationship with others. Everyone in my community group learned and grew in this process. And even better, we have new relationships outside the group as a result. And that has breathed new life into our group.[98]

When we did the series at Sandals, the engagement creativity was amazing. Groups quickly learned the power of serial activity. One group did consecutive Bunco parties to reach the gals in their neighborhood. Another group planned a quarterly movie night. One group met the ongoing needs of a single mom. Releasing people to have ownership will unleash their neighborhood influence. With the right angle, the fruit will grow exponentially.

98. Irene McDowell, "It's Easy to Follow and Doesn't Take Much Preparation," review of Gary Comer, *Launch Point: Moving Small Groups into Mission* (*Wipf & Stock*) (July 1, 2014). Accessed February 6, 2015, https://www.amazon.com/Launch-Point-Community-Missional-Engagement/dp/1620328291.

———

Tipping and pinpointing are vitalizing concepts for the church body. To support both culture-shaping and empowerment, the final section of this book will look at how to develop your discipleship path. Too many churches do not have this area working for them. What you do here will have major reverberations in the lives of your people, and has the potential to blow down doors for the kingdom of God!

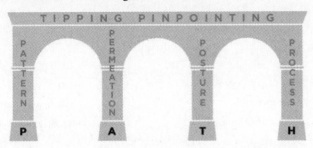

## *REFLECTIONS*

1.  Do you agree or disagree with the author's assessment that we need a dynamic approach to meet the shifting climate of a pluralized society? Why or why not?

2.  At what level are your people engaged in relational evangelism? Be honest. Ask this question of a few people in your ministry, and see if their assessments match yours.

3.  How dynamic is your current training? In what specific ways can this chapter help you increase the effectiveness of your people? What are you going to do to make the necessary changes?

## *REMISSION TAKEAWAYS*

1.  New paradigm: Start where they are, read what they need, know where to take them.

2.  Making a read on a resonant gospel message is a skill that develops through practice.

3.  We open the floodgates by giving our people a relational process approach, dynamic working skills, and vehicles for engagement.

# —PART III—
## COURSE:
## CHARTING THEIR INSTRUCTION

# —9—

## YOUR PATH DESIGN

I think there is always going to be inspired music and there are
always going to be inspired listeners and there is always going to
be an inspired method of getting it from A to B.
—Anthony Kiedis, singer-songwriter

Relating the highlights of his recent trip to the Grand Canyon, a pastor friend described the stirring moment when he and his wife had experienced a new attraction called the Grand Canyon Skywalk. Perhaps you have heard of this protruding glass-floored platform that extends seventy-five feet over the edge, enabling people to walk out above the canyon as if walking on air. Manny confessed to having felt scared, and related to me how he clung to the side rail to help alleviate his vertigo-like sensation. But he added that it was a "super-cool" visual!

Once Manny and his wife were back on solid ground, Manny noticed another man nearby photographing his own wife as she stood on the platform. In a lighthearted tone, Manny asked whether he was going to join his wife. The man answered emphatically, "Absolutely not! I will never go out there." Manny ruminated on this encounter, and when he and his wife returned to their hotel, he told his wife, with a sense of brokenness, that the mind-set of that man paralleled the perspective of so many people in his church. Something exciting and wonderful was extended before them, yet they were willing to go only so far. They seemed to lack the basic courage to step into the adventure-call of God, which could color their lives with invigorating vision. Manny's heart was breaking. He knew they were missing it, just like that gentleman at the Skywalk.

181

How can we alter this sad picture that fits so many people in today's church? A common hiccup—the first barrier that I count on coming against when I consult with church leaders—is the all-consuming complacency of church members. When people are fearful, busy, distracted, untrained, dysfunctional, half-hearted, and misled, leaders face a particularly daunting challenge to move them into mission. It is in this vacuum where God's leaders must step in and stand strong, believing for people in the midst of their unbelief in themselves.

As stewards of the Great Commission, we must begin by having what every leader should have, and what church members often lack—and that's clarity. By our simple act of designing a path, increasing numbers of people will have the courage to get out there. You can't force them onto the glass, but you can offer a dynamic training progression that will encourage their steps forward. If you point the way forward and give them ample support, if every step is ultimately preparing them for the prime mission, you will see much greater results and real movement. Don't doubt it!

———

A true privilege and blessing of leadership is overseeing the whole picture. Whether you lead a church, a mission entity, a ministry, or a group, you get the honor of setting a strategic course—of directing the flowchart. At the height of the Roman Empire, that vista would have seen eleven major aqueducts flowing into reservoirs supplying over two hundred Roman cities.[99] Your planning will be no less significant. The path of eternal life, and its outward conduits, will emanate from this vision. To set the table for what is a top-level discussion, we must ascend the acropolis to get a panoramic view of the master plan.

## HARD ASSESSMENT: TOO LINEAR

Sitting down for lunch with Sandals' Senior Pastor Matt Brown, I shared one of my whiteboard "brain bursts" I had scrawled with Sharpie on a piece of thick cardstock. He opened the folded drawing, glanced at it, and said, "This looks really good." Previously, Matt had shared a three-step

---

99. Hodge, *Roman Aqueducts & Water Supply*, 9–11.

sequence that his team was contemplating. I had morphed it into a hub design where the key values of the church would be central.

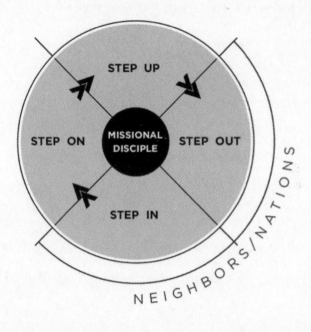

When Sandals' Executive Pastor Dan Zimbardi probed my thoughts on Saddleback's famed baseball-diamond church-life structure, with all due respect to this legendary church and the substantial fruit it has borne, I told him that I didn't like how linear it was. Growth in any single spiritual value happens progressively in life, typically needing layers of repetition and reinforcement over time. Thus, a linear path, which zeroes in on a theme and then tries to achieve the development in one class or stage, is not a sound design for the desired formation. For this reason, I find "linear" to be insufficient.

Take the mission value as an example. Becoming gospel "influencers" for Christ does not culminate through a singular course or series. I am a trainer, first and foremost. When I train, there are some who take the concepts and run forward like gangbusters. Others, however, have difficulty getting to the place where the concepts enter their real lives. But when you are able to circle back with them so that the value gets a second hearing, and you keep working at it through further instruction, while also increasing expectation and structure for their engagement, eventually, the experiential formation you're seeking will occur. Notice the graphic below, and how each of your key values gets triple treatment.

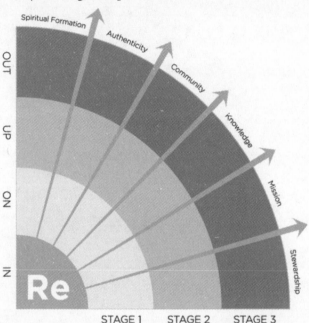

**RE-MISSION MODEL**

A detailed description of all six values of the path model may be found in the addendum to this book. For now, let's keep to the big-picture view. The linear nature of training in most churches today explains at least partly why we have failed to raise mission prowess in the body of Christ. The proof of mission formation is in the fruit. If there is no tangible evangelistic disciplemaking fruit to speak of among a good proportion of core members, your path is failing somewhere. Like a non-bearing tree, it reveals unhealthiness. At some point, you will have to course-correct.

To achieve success, you must heed certain laws. One such law, which I have already introduced, is *Form must match formation*. Simply stated, you can't produce the formation of a value if the format doesn't practice that value. Another law familiar among church leaders is, *Begin with the end in mind*.[100] Though the specific wording can vary, I put authentic "missional

---

100. Stephen Covey, *7 Habits of Highly Effective People: Powerful Lessons in Personal Change* (New York, NY: Simon & Schuster, 1989), 97–100.

disciples" at the hub of all training. That term should work for most church-es. If mission isn't the hub, there's something wrong, because it is mission that expands the glory and love of God by making worshipers. Any end goal should touch all parts of your church, its path, and its ministries. Your particular mission call will have its own qualifying distinctives, no doubt. Answer this question: To be a disciple at your church, *what is God calling you to emphasize, uniquely?*

Saying that the missional value is the hub is a lot easier than making that statement a reality. The challenge is getting the *broad swath of people* integrally engaged. It's easy to feel like you are doing it when you're not. Thus, a mission path provides a measurable track. In the rhythmic activity of busy lives, you want to see the gospel flowing at the highest possible rate from the greatest percentage of people. They will be reaching lives and bringing threads of restoration to society's fallen fabric. Like the challenge for the Roman engineers, achieving this movement requires exceptional detail, oversight, and execution.

Chomping on my CPK (California Pizza Kitchen) gourmet pear pizza (far better than it probably sounds), I explained to Pastor Brown the simple yet substantive fourfold progression of the path: (1) Step in, (2) Step on, (3) Step up, and (4) Step out. Every church should define its path for disci-pleship. Because we're here to complete the work that Jesus Christ began, mission should be the epicenter occurring within all phases. The sequence, then, outlines a road map for a person to come into the church, embrace its values, receive practical training, and then be sent into the mission field. It prepares your people for local and global engagement to reach their Jerusalem, Judea, and so on.

In this section, I am going to address how to maximize the potential of each quadrant. For now, though, I will introduce the concepts from a designer's perspective.

## IN – ON – UP – OUT

Walking into my local Target store, I noticed two single words on the doors. One door said, "In," the other, "Out." At the entry point, nothing else was needed. In the marketplace, as well as in churches, the higher the con-centration of people flowing in and out, the more important simplicity of direction becomes. I like simple. But don't be fooled. Walk into Target, and there's a massive store to explore. In the same way, there's a whole lot to un-pack behind these four short words "In," "On," "Up," and "Out." The people in your church are in one of these four positions right now. Every time you stand before them, these four types sit before you. How well do you see them? This is no irrelevant exercise. Spiritually speaking, these are your people! The four stages represent the journeys of precious human souls, and the quadrants are a way to hone your focus to meet your people right where they are.

## EXECUTION IS EVERYTHING

In this section, I will address certain features that undergird the mission Christ has passed along to us. As a caveat, I cannot cover all that is involved in the training. But the structure I am giving you is valuable if you can see its simplicity and power. Within the model, you will have room to introduce your own ideas and make the training your own. I care about mission efficacy, and so, zeroing in on the developmental process, we'll highlight and illustrate what is uniquely opportunistic for your outreach efforts within each phase. Whatever curriculum you use, design asks the question, How do we intentionally chart our people's growth in the mission pattern of Christ? Throughout this discussion, we will look continually to God's revelatory Word.

As we bound forward, it's not a bad time to inject some humility. Mission success is no given. Not today. Anytime we undertake to implement something of kingdom significance, it will be opposed, and man's designs often fail. Stephen King once wrote, "Remember…someone *really did* design the *Titanic* and then label it unsinkable."[101] Imagine yourself sitting poolside at a beautiful hotel, sipping iced tea, when, suddenly, you smell something burning, then feel an intense sensation on your head. This was the recurring problem at the luxurious new Vdara Hotel in Las Vegas, where the concave exterior glass of the building created a magnifying effect that had guests getting singed![102] How would you like to have that one on

101. Stephen King, *On Writing: A Memoir of the Craft* (New York, NY: Simon & Schuster, 2000), 214.
102. Scott Mayerowitz, "Vegas Hotel Pool 'Death Ray' Burns Tourists," *ABC News* (September 28, 2010). Available at: http://abcnews.go.com/Travel/las-vegas-hotel-pool-sunlight-swimming-tourists/story?id=11739234.

your architectural resume? Flawed designs have consequences, and someone usually gets burned, whether literally or figuratively.

In the church, the problem is that people just get left out. Unreached. Unengaged. Underutilized. Underdeveloped. Good design and development will bless your people, but it's much more than that. Countering selfish or consumeristic desires, your "path" will move aspiring disciples in needed directions, breathing spiritual health and life into their lungs. It will prompt their growth. It will offer them undeniable purpose. In lieu of the occasional optional class or seminar that a few people may elect to attend, following a workable "path" creates a broad channel for developing everyone in critical areas.

> IN LIEU OF THE OCCASIONAL OPTIONAL CLASS OR SEMINAR THAT A FEW PEOPLE MAY ELECT TO ATTEND, FOLLOWING A WORKABLE "PATH" CREATES A BROAD CHANNEL FOR DEVELOPING EVERYONE IN CRITICAL AREAS.

Granted, there are some viable options for tackling the discipling challenge. Allow me the liberty of putting two such options before you. One is to work the materials through your small groups (or whatever you may call them). Some churches will take this route, infusing their groups with select curriculum. If you go this course, the time you spend developing the facilitating leaders will be critical, as will be the task of monitoring their actual engagement with the groups. Another way is to offer a *series of classes*, with overseeing teachers to work out the values and engagement pieces. Churches that follow this route are what we call "three-legged-stool churches": they make use of (1) church services, (2) small groups, and (3) training apparatuses.

Of the two, you already know that I favor the latter. Here's the ammunition for my preference.

+ Not all people decide to join a small group. A note on assimilation: You will have more success getting new people into a class with a set time frame and no expectation of the intimacy often associated with home groups.

+ Not all groups succeed in kingdom functions, let alone at staying together. Critical training can be lost.

+ Not all group leaders will facilitate the materials and engagements effectively. Imbuing skills to influence unsaved people is not typically a strength of small-group leaders. This is why I like to appoint trainers over classes that work in concert with the group system. It adds strands of strength into the church fabric.

Further, I favor using successive stages, as reinforcement helps the values stick. I also sanction the practice of quality control by tapping and utilizing gifted teachers within the body (preferably not the senior pastor, so that the movement is horizontal rather than vertical). The teaching-style format must be interactive, group oriented, practice angled (involving both role-playing and in-the-field work), and relationally based. As stated, the church needs skill development.

Either way, whether you decide to work through groups alone or through classes alongside groups, small groups are key places to introduce and instill values.

In a nutshell, here's a quick glance at the four stages we're talking about.

1) Step IN

God's gracious community receives all people, regardless of background and of past or present behavior. In this stage, we explore how to widen the net by meeting people on the outside where they begin.

2) Step ON

Every church needs a discipling vehicle for newcomers, especially newer believers. Churches that are not assimilating and developing new believers are failing in the mandate to make disciples. Do not assume that discipling is occurring adequately from people merely attending your services.

3) Step UP

All churches, including church plants, must raise maturity levels and develop leaders—game-changing players who will become the solidifying skeleton to your vision.

4) Step OUT

Christ's church exists to equip and send its people out to create gospel impact. Not just a few, but everyone! By design, we aim to engage all members in reaching communities, cities, and countries.

> CHRIST'S CHURCH EXISTS TO EQUIP AND SEND ITS PEOPLE OUT TO CREATE GOSPEL IMPACT. NOT JUST A FEW, BUT EVERYONE!

That is what the path helps you do. It maps how to go about raising your people into mission prominence. All members must take on a new mind-set about what it means to follow Christ and his pattern, and what it will take to reach the world. It is the church leader's responsibility to cast such a vision and to equip the people accordingly.

*Training enables people to go to higher levels.* When I was recruited to play at Long Beach State, I was coming from a junior college in San Diego. Both programs involved weight training, but there was a difference. At the J.C., we did mostly repetition training, maxing out only periodically. At Long Beach State, every time we lifted, we "maxed." UCLA was waiting in the wings as our opening opponent. The goal was to get bigger and stronger, and the only way to do that was to lift heavier weights. I suddenly found myself in a distinctly more effective training environment. Everyone yelled and screamed at each other to go higher! By the end of the summer, I went from bench-pressing 225 to 310 pounds. No kidding. I got bigger. Everyone noticed, not only my girlfriend! What transformed this scrawny pencil-neck DB into a buffed human specimen? It was being a part of a Division 1 program.

When they asked me to design a path at Sandals Church, I responded, "A Division-1 church needs a Division-1 program." What does that mean? Bottom line, if you are not seeing high percentages of equipped disciples reaching others for Christ and impacting their cities and world, then your program is not Division 1. Think of how intentional this must be. Now, someone may insert the notion of wanting to be more "organic." Let me quickly say, a good program will always take advantage of influence where it naturally exists or can be easily cultivated. The two are not mutually exclusive. But what we are talking about here, on a grand scale, will not just happen organically. Sorry.

Can you imagine the Long Beach State coaches saying in the spring, "We'll see you all at the Rose Bowl in September; we're going to let the team develop organically this year"? No way! They prepare. They push the team to new levels in critical areas. They do those things because when fall comes, and football season starts, they expect to win.

———

*ReMission* will produce other benefits for your church. When I present the Path vision to church staffs, I highlight six bulleted by-products: (1) Trained Disciples, (2) Tracking Mechanism, (3) Close the Back Door, (4) Mission Mobilization, (5) Stewardship Growth, and (6) Infrastructural Development. In the chapters ahead, I will touch on all six of these. Right now, let me say a few words about what I mean by "Tracking Mechanism." A path gives you a chance to observe your people over finite periods of time. Because your aim is to raise their prowess, you will be tracking their progress. What this affords you is the relationship and the opportunity to give your people what they most need, and that's feedback!

Your trainers—the group leaders and engagement leaders—will be positioned to speak with vital mirroring into the lives of the people going through this equipping process. With a loving tone, they may say, for example:

+ "When I see your expression, I often wonder if you dislike everyone. You need to warm up and smile a lot more."

+ "We are not just hearers but doers of the Word. Start putting these mission tools into practice. Yeah, this week!"

+ "You need to dial down your intensity to give your friends the space to express themselves and hear what you have to say."

+ "You might not realize how prideful you come across regarding what you know. Show Christ's humility. Know this: They won't care what you know until they see how much you care."

+ "If you want to become a leader in this church, you need to raise your game and show us fruit in what you are doing in the community."

+ "Being with you is like a slice of heaven. But God will not be able to use you for his gospel if you do not invite unsaved friends into your circle."

+ "This pattern is hindering your witness. What do you need to do to make a change, and how can we support you in the process?"

+ "Sometimes I get a feeling of disinterest or indifference when I talk with you. How do you think that will affect those to whom you are reaching out?"

+ "Hey, brother, suck on a breath mint once in a while!"

Can you see the power of this tactic? If your church cares enough to train up its people and address the character defects or leanings that threaten to undermine their influence, you might just become a powerhouse!

IF YOUR CHURCH CARES ENOUGH TO TRAIN UP ITS PEOPLE AND ADDRESS THE CHARACTER DEFECTS OR LEANINGS THAT THREATEN TO UNDERMINE THEIR INFLUENCE, YOU MIGHT JUST BECOME A POWERHOUSE!

*Each quadrant is customizable* and *expandable*. At the outset, you may start with one or two training vehicles in each sector. My discipleship/missional engagement books are content rich and proven. Yet, as you develop, you will add various resources to your training apparatus. As you stir the passion for making a difference in your city and world, you erect infrastructure by getting overseeing mission leaders in place.

## THE POWER OF YOUR BELIEF

When basketball coach and Shakespearian sage Paul Westhead took over the reins at Loyola Marymount University, he introduced what he called "The System." By pushing the pace and having his team members shoot within five seconds of each possession, he aimed to win by attrition. At some point in the game, he preached that the other team would eventually break under his team's up-tempo style. It was outside the box, innovative, and crazy, with a rationale to back it up.

That season, little guy LMU leaped into the national spotlight by posting a twenty-five-game winning streak, averaging an unthinkable 122 points per game! Alas, we will never know what that team could have done, because, as if part of the script of a Shakespearian tragedy, toward the end of the season, superstar Hank Gathers dropped suddenly to the floor and died from heart failure.

During the proceeding NCAA tournament game, in tribute to his fallen friend's lefty approach, right-handed co-star teammate Bo Kimble stepped up to shoot a free throw left-handed. When people watched that ball loft upward and then sink into the net, it created one of the most moving moments in sports history—a bucket was made to memorialize a person who'd been lost. The ovation would not stop that night, and many grown men blubbered like babies.

LMU's system did end. Sadly, the coach resigned due to the lawsuits that spun out from the tragedy. Westhead struggled to find the right chemistry in other towns, becoming a journeyman coach with little result—until he was sought to coach the WBA team Phoenix Mercury, where he once again implemented his "system" and fashioned another champion![103]

103. "Guru of Go," DVD, directed by Bill Couturié (USA: ESPN Films: 30 for 30, 2010). Available at: http://www.espn.com/30for30/film?page=guru-of-go.

In terms of church mission philosophy, I don't know what you believe. But no matter what, you need a vision that you are totally convinced of—one that you know will achieve the ultimate end. We are not talking about winning games, but rather winning hearts to the person and mission of Jesus Christ. You need a system to raise people from the bottom up to effectively engage for the gospel's sake. You may choose not to adopt my path, but let me be clear: You need one that achieves the same things. I did not design my path haphazardly!

+ You must create room for everyone at the limitless level of the cross.

+ You must make new disciples who are grounded and geared to reach this world.

+ You must raise up members and leaders for greater capacities.

+ You must send people out to reach this lost world.

The question is, How good will you become with your system? Will your church produce legitimate Christ-patterned champions? Will you be the epicenter of gospel expansion? Do you believe so deeply in what you are doing that God will see it done?

Perhaps, at this point, you've realized something. Maybe it's become evident just how much you must elevate your own game. Stop to take it in. Breathe the esteem that God has placed over you in leading the charge. Now, get your team following behind you. Go on a walk through your own colonnades to put together something that will be powerful for your people!

————

To firm your leadership mettle and resolve, let me be straightforward in saying that not everyone will be thrilled with your initiative. The naysayers will have their say. You might find resistance on your elder board and even among the members of your pastoral staff. Change isn't always pretty. Perhaps some of your fellow leaders should move on. Your church isn't a country club, after all.

I believe that if a church is functioning properly, it will achieve four things at high levels. The next chapters will address those challenges directly. Sharing conclusions I've drawn based on successes and failures alike, I will raise some hard questions. We will begin with addressing the all-important non-believing people who are stepping IN. For the gospel, come forward!

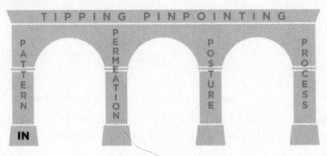

## REFLECTIONS

1. Discuss the difference you see between a linear design and the multi-staged design the author has put forth.

2. What is your current discipleship design, and how could you implement (or integrate) a more holistic approach?

3. The author identified six benefits to implementing a full-scale *Re-Mission* discipleship path. Discuss with your team how you could envision these benefits playing out in the lives of your people.

4. Identify several actual individuals within your relational reach or your existing body that fit each of the four stage designations: IN, ON, UP, and OUT.

## REMISSION TAKEAWAYS

1. It is necessary to reinforce and refine values to achieve the end formation goal.

2. Your path is a way to steer and raise the entire church body.

3. A multiplicity of benefits comes out of a missional discipleship program.

4. You must believe in your path in order for it to become a pervasive and powerful training vehicle.

# —10—

## STEP IN

I read about how you touched them, and they were healed.
Or even if someone just touched your cloak, they were forever
changed. You let a broken woman bathe your feet in her tears.
And you washed your best friend's feet. I'm just wondering
though, did you ever just hug people? I know it's a silly question
and all. I'm sure you would have. But it's one of those things that
was never mentioned. And it got me thinking about it. And how
whenever there was a touch from you, sins were forgiven and
sickness fell. I think I'm caught up with my sins, and last time I
checked all my body parts are working. Nothing special here.
I'm just a kid with a heavy heart these passing sunrises and
sunsets. I don't think our encounter would have ended up in your
Gospels or anything. Because all I really need is a hug.
That's okay for me to imagine, right? That's not conflicting with
any sort of theology, is it? Okay good. Then hug me.
—Bradley Hathaway
"The Hug Poem," *All the Hits So Far (But Don't Expect Too Much)*

A brutal off-a-bridge crash kills the driver, while the passenger, the
wealthy heir of a business mogul, merely sustains injuries to his arm
and face. Following initial reconstructive surgery, one of the man's eyes remains half shut, and his mouth droops rightward, aligning with a scar that
runs across and over his jaw. His state causes him to slur his speech on
occasion. But, other than that, he is the same person. Or is he?

From this tragedy forward, this man faces the reality of his changed
face. He is desperate for facial restoration, but his doctors explain that due

to the pins in his head, they can't perform such a procedure. They offer to repair his arm instead, at which point he screams out, "Who cares about my (expletive) arm?" His face is what he wakes to every morning. It's what everyone notices, and it's how he connects with other human beings. In his reality, it is what he is thinking about all the time. His face.

Sensitive to his trauma, the doctors design a custom mask for him to wear. He goes to meet some friends at a nightclub, and shows up with his new facial "prosthesis." Seeing this version of him for the first time, his friends recoil. His best buddy calls him on it, saying, "Remove the mask, you're freaking us out." Slinging the mask around to the back of his head, he goes to the bar to order a drink, only to have the bartender avert his eyes to avoid face-to-face contact. Angrily, he explodes, "Look at me, b-tch!"[104]

The movie *Vanilla Sky* allegorizes the course of life with the face representing the soul. Everything begins fair-weathered, but then life deals its gale-force blows. Something slams us hard, creating disfigurement. Little did we know how it would affect everything: how we look before others, how we feel about ourselves, how we relate to other people, and how we think of God. These are the faces of those who live in our neighborhoods, who work alongside us, who train with us at the health club, who lie in our beds, and who show up at our church doors. It's the person you just met. It might be you. It's definitely me.

I know what it was like to suddenly have a disfigured face. In my first book, I went public with my midlife drifting debacle: an impulsive, drinking-lust-shoplifting sin and the loss of a job. The acting out was anomalous for me, but the struggle was true to my pleasure-seeking core. (Now you know me at my worst depths!) It marked the beginning of my journey to recovery, during which I learned much more about what was going on inside me. In the aftermath, I penned an entire chapter of *Soul Whisperer* describing the experience of being newly broken—one I never wanted to write! I recall being devastated, lying around in anger and mourning for a month with my dog as my only friend. Eventually, you get up, get help, and start to live forward again. Returning to church hand in hand with my beautiful wife, and with a heart hopeful for healing, it was strange to feel

---

104. *Vanilla Sky*, DVD, Directed by Cameron Crowe (USA: Paramount Pictures, 2001).

so much fear. For nonbelievers, church can be a scary place. I learned, then, that the same can be true for believers.

I remember as if it were yesterday just how conscious I was of a church's generic acceptance. I knew my disfigurement, but they didn't. Getting treated with kindness on the fringe felt good at first. Each morning I'd wake up, look in the mirror at the "disfigured" (yet unseen) lines on my face, and put on the mask. Donning it week after week, though, quickly wore thin. It just didn't feel like me.

Sometime later, at a denominational gathering where I was included on a panel, there was an interchange when a "holier-than-thou" pretense began to stink up the joint, and I just couldn't keep the mask on. So, off the cuff, I pulled it to the side, offering others a slight glimpse of my disfigurement. It seemed okay, but who knows? None in that leadership group was marred like I was—at least, not to my knowledge. Being the aberration made me feel like an outsider. I wasn't really sure what to do with that feeling. I couldn't do anything about it right then.

Over time, though, more and more people saw my disfigurement. I didn't wear the mask quite as often as before, and when the moment seemed appropriate, I allowed others to see my true face (grotesque though it was). Though some cringed, most did not. My true friends even liked me better with the mask off. Then, something unexpected occurred. One morning, I got up, glanced in the mirror, and saw that my face was beginning to heal! I pushed the metaphorical mask to the back of my head and went out with an even brisker stride. The scars, and an occasional slurring of my speech, remain as reminders of what I am capable of and where I have been. But I am so glad that I chose to allow some people to get a true view of me. Without having done that, I might never have truly healed.

As the plot of the movie *Vanilla Sky* unfolds, doctors perform the necessary procedures to restore the character's face, yet traumatic nightmares still haunt him. Struggling to grasp who he really is, he searches for ways to cope. Everything seems affected; his relational pursuits, his professional aspirations, and his sexual desires all become increasingly excessive.

I'm sure you get the point. These are the kind of people who are coming toward you. Fearful of what they've done in their past, and even of what has not occurred in their lives, they try to escape the pain, and end up drifting into a dream world of their own making. Who will rescue them? Who will love them out of the nightmare? Who will look them in the face?

## HARD ASSESSMENT: LIMITED SPACE

The ministry or group you lead should be the premier place where people feel welcome to take off their masks, discover their true identity, be accepted and loved, find healing at profound levels, and be equipped for the greatest cause ever to hit this world. Wow! That's enough to get anyone out of bed in the morning.

Since God has *"set eternity in the human heart"* (Ecclesiastes 3:11), we can trust that each person possesses a divinely placed homing beacon—a pointer to heaven. The strategic question is, How does the church gathered intersect with that soul hunger at the wider edges of the culture? The "Step IN" stage addresses and informs our readiness to invite people in to a place where they will connect and eventually find satisfaction of their deepest longings.

### IN – ON – UP – OUT

Effective churches know that many people need help making the God connection. Managing the entry segues with wisdom and care means meeting people where they are, so that we don't quickly lose them out the front door. In order to ensure that we are reaching the outer rings, we must make space for: (1) the hurting, (2) the searching, and (3) the dreaming.

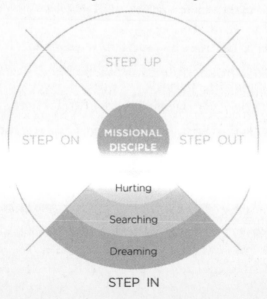

## SPACE FOR THE HURTING

In downtown Phoenix, I dined with a family—a husband, wife, and three kids—on the verge of joining one of our network's church plants. Later in the evening, when the kids had gone elsewhere, the conversation became refreshingly candid when the husband opened up about the guilt haunting him. To reciprocate, I shared my own journey in and out of shame. It became a meaningful conversation in that my own story showed me the horizontal orientation of shame. Because shame stems from our horizontal relationships with other people and our culture, our vertical position in Christ cannot easily rectify it. Anyone living with the emotional residue of shame or past trauma knows this paradox. Where the person dealing with trauma is continually reliving what occurred, the person in shame has been stamped by it.

SHAME KEEPS PEOPLE DISTANCED FROM GOD AND CHURCH. IT MAKES THEM AFRAID OF THE GAZE OF OTHERS. IT KEEPS PEOPLE STUCK IN THE CYCLE OF SIN, HOOKED TO ITS COPING ANESTHESIA. IT KEEPS PEOPLE HANDCUFFED FROM HEALING, AND HINDERED FROM EXPERIENCING HONEST COMMUNITY.

It's why, when the Ashley Madison hacking story broke, I could empathize with the pastor on the list who left a note for his family and then took his own life. Anticipating the onslaught of shame, suicide seemed a no-brainer.[105] Shame enters what I call the "I am-ness of the soul" (I am… stupid, bad, a loser, ugly, perverted, useless, evil, unworthy…insert the shaming word of your choice), and it is virulently noxious. It keeps people distanced from God and church. It makes them afraid of the gaze of others. It keeps people stuck in the cycle of sin, hooked to its coping anesthesia.

---

105. Laurie Segall, "Pastor Outed on Ashley Madison Commits Suicide," CNN (September 8, 2015). Available at: http://money.cnn.com/2015/09/08/technology/ashley-madison-suicide/.

It keeps people handcuffed from healing, and hindered from experiencing honest community. As to the tragic news of the aforementioned pastor, I applaud this comment that was posted on Facebook: "I wish he had a chance to hear from us first." That is exactly what he needed. He needed to have others look at him with eyes full of truth and grace—eyes of someone with the ability to see his enormous worth in spite of his egregious sin, as Jesus looked at the adulterous woman in John 8. When you get to heaven, please don't go looking for "the adulterous woman." You won't find her. Her name, given by Jesus, is Adorae: The Adored One.

Processing the underlying shame in my own life, I backed into a fuller view of the cross of Christ. According to the great story, Jesus made a walk. It was a walk of shame, in every sense of the term, as mocking crowds looked upon criminals stripped naked as the scum of the earth. One day, it came over me, in a moment of clarity and simultaneous wonder, how closely Jesus could identify with my shame. In his walk to the cross, he covered my mile-wide aura of shame in the path of his dripping blood! No matter how long or sordid sin's trail is for a person, Jesus' sacrifice extends to all its poisoning effects. He is the Lock-Cutter to shame's shackles. It is that wider passion picture to which I kept returning. After I had spent years living in a poisoned well, Jesus lifted me to a freedom from which I have never turned away. Building toward shame's release, one day, I even said, "I am born again, again."

I also learned how healing occurs through communal confession and connection. Many of the people who step through your church doors need to feel human favor mirroring God's justification. One Christian man spoke of forgiveness, saying, "I know it in my head but don't feel it in my heart." It is for that reason that I pulled the man aside that night, looked him in the eyes, and leaned hard into sound theology. I wanted him to get Christ's love in the words and eyes of another human being. My James 5:16 paraphrase goes as follows: "Confess your sins *before the accepting eyes of another* so that you will be healed."

What do unchurched people pick up in our eyes? Can we look them in the face? Or do we turn aside to find someone more "suitable"? Teach your church greeters to see souls. If somebody new comes across a bit off-kilter, not quite fitting the mold, train your connectors to compensate. It just may be that a person will decide, on his first trip to church, that it's the home he's always longed for! Of course, to reach and minister to a broken world, you will need to get your hands dirty in the messiness of others' lives. Are you and your people ready and willing? Really? Honestly?

Have you noticed the contemporariness of the man from the Gerasenes who cuts himself with stones? (See Mark 5:1–20.) In one of our healing groups, a man shared about his cutting routine. I listened, marveling at the myriad forms of pain diversion. As to the biblical detail, how fitting was it that his demonic presence was "legion"? The creativity of human escapism knows no bounds. Yet it is for this possessed guy that Jesus interrupted his ministry and took his disciples on a field trip to "the other side." Entering the badlands of the Decapolis (the ten cities founded by pagan nations following the fall of Jericho), Jesus went and brought one man into right-mindedness.[106] Remarkably, it is this demoniac who became God's chosen voice to the ten cities, the forerunning equivalent of John the Baptist to the eastern side of the Sea of Galilee. (See Mark 5:10.) The result is that when Jesus returned, massive crowds awaited him with readied hearts, saying, "He's come back. It's true; he cares for us!" There's a principle here: *When you reach someone in great darkness, you have lit a great light.*

As the disciples did that day on the Galilean seashore, we must follow Jesus into darkness. Whether it's across your street, into the city's red-light district, over the border, or out to a new region or nation, Jesus is "the God of the other side." His invitation beckons, still. Here's how one church appealed with a Facebook promotion:

> Real Healing at Sandals Church is a safe community of healing and recovery for those who are wounded and hurting. We are a community that seeks to create a safe place for people to be real with themselves, God and others. We are on a journey to freedom from the things that can so easily imprison us and keep us from the lives we are intended to live, things like addictions, divorce, abuse, broken relationships, and losing loved ones, to name a few.
>
> Perhaps the greatest barrier to experiencing freedom is this common misconception about God: "Until we get ourselves to-

106. John Ortberg, *Who Is This Man?: The Unpredictable Impact of the Inescapable Jesus* (Grand Rapids, MI: Zondervan, 2012), 67.

gether, God wants nothing to do with us." Nothing could be further from the truth. Do you wash up before getting in the shower? No. In the same way, the cross of Jesus Christ shows us that God does not shy away from our darkest hours or our deepest pains. In fact, these are the places where we first find God, in the center of the dirty messes and brokenness of our lives.

Real Healing is not a place to provide the missing answers, fix problems, or give professional help, but it is a place where we believe the healing power of the name of Jesus Christ can be experienced. We have various groups that meet you where you are. Some go through workbooks, and others operate as a support group. Wherever you are, know that you are welcomed and that we are on this journey to freedom with you.

+ men's and women's drug and alcohol dependence

+ eating disorders

+ post-abortion recovery

+ men's sexual purity

+ women's co-dependency groups

+ women's sexual purity

+ men's same-sex sexual purity

+ anger and anxiety

+ men's codependence

Within the scope of your church's healing ministry, make sure you offer a general healing group for people who are hurting but aren't sure where they should be. I've led one such generalized, catch-all group. It's definitely a bit more difficult to manage, with the wide range of issues it must address, but it gathers those taking initial steps of honesty and courage. Academic Brené Brown explains, "You either walk inside your story and own it or you stand outside your story and hustle for your worthiness."[107] Those early steps mean everything in the healing process.

---

107. Kristen Chase, "25 of the Best Brené Brown Quotes" (May 9, 2012). Available at: http://thepioneerwoman.com/homeschooling/25-of-the-best-bren-brown-quotes/.

Many people won't heal unless they're able to get real within a loving community.

The general group will attract nonbelievers. Since it's not close to being a perfect-imaged crowd, the unrestrained honesty that you'll see is refreshing. Effective and safe healing and recovery ministries allow masks to be thrown aside, and it's awesome! In time, as relationships form, opportunities will fall at your feet for influence with those who feel like they finally belong somewhere. At just the second gathering of our general group, two members, after a lot of deep conversation, very naturally introduced Sean to the Healer! He found healing and a home in Jesus. Of course, we also help them "step ON" to the discipleship path, which is custom fit to their development as new believers.

> EFFECTIVE AND SAFE HEALING AND RECOVERY MINISTRIES ALLOW MASKS TO BE THROWN ASIDE, AND IT'S AWESOME! IN TIME, AS RELATIONSHIPS FORM, OPPORTUNITIES WILL FALL AT YOUR FEET FOR INFLUENCE WITH THOSE WHO FEEL LIKE THEY FINALLY BELONG SOMEWHERE.

For expanding outreach, churches do well to "hire brokenness." This is likely a novel thought for you. Hiring brokenness indicates that a church staff is an okay place to be broken—a place for employing "wounded healers," as Henri Nouwen labeled them.[108] I surmise that such job requirements as "sin" and "failure" are not topping the qualification lists for new church hires. I once had a conversation with a church member who had noticed that the church did not have anyone on staff with a notable redemption story. I was already familiar with the church, and after I weighed his observation, I realized how on-target it was. The church's staff roster was squeaky-clean. Of course, churches want to hire staff who are role

108. Henri J. M. Nouwen, *The Wounded Healer: Ministry in Contemporary Society* (New York, NY: Doubleday, 1972), 2.

models of the abundant life that Christ offers. Yet, when it comes to doing mission in a postmodern world, I couldn't help but notice limitations with that church's existing team because it wasn't at all reflective of the types of people they were seeking to reach.

Counselor Dave Ferreira captured this idea when he said, "God picks pain to minister his Spirit." From his vast professional observations, he has noted how people who have gone through pain have keen insights; once they are healed (so that perspective is not distorted), they have the ability to see things that others miss.[109] I synthesized the silver lining this way: *With the limp came a lens,*[110] and *Loss is a looking glass.* My own redemption story opened my eyes to so many different layers of human feeling and connectivity. With that newfound empathy and ability to relate came waves of new ministry and mission with people whose lives were spiritually sidelined, spoiled, sin-addicted, stuck, shamed, shell-shocked, or shattered. The prophet Isaiah revealed that his writing assignment from the sovereign Lord was *"the word that sustains the weary"* (Isaiah 50:4). Are you hearing the crescendo of Isaiah 40: *"They will soar on wings like eagles; they will run and not grow weary; they will walk and not be faint"* (verse 31)? What a gift Isaiah received from God!

As to afflictions, rest assured that, whether pain is self-induced or circumstantial, the Master Artist wastes not one of his perfectly placed brushstrokes. C. S. Lewis said, "God allows us to experience low points of life in order to teach us lessons we could learn in no other way." Those low points can become invaluable vision-propping pieces that awaken us to a world we haven't seen before—one that needs the brand of compassion God wants to offer through us. I've lived it. One truth I hold dear is this: It took a broken lens to make a writer. If you have wrestled with your own brokenness, look to what God wills to do. His ways are mysterious and wonderful. When you see him take your worst to summon your best, or take your weakness to display his awesome strength, it will make you even more of a worshipper!

Philip Yancey poignantly describes the mission impact that arose out of the personal suffering of author Feodor Dostoevsky:

109. Comer, *Soul Whisperer*, 112.
110. Ibid., 113.

Prison offered Dostoevsky a unique opportunity, which at first seemed a curse: it forced him to live at close quarters with thieves, murderers, and drunken peasants....His shared life with these prisoners later led to unmatched characterizations in his novels, such as that of the murderer Raskolnikov in *Crime and Punishment.*

Dostoevsky's liberal view of the inherent goodness in humanity could not account for the pure evil he found in his cell mates, and his theology had to adjust to this new reality. Over time, though, he also glimpsed the image of God in the lowest of these prisoners. Like Tolstoy, he discovered that remnants of traditional Christianity survived in the peasants, which he began to see as their only hope for a new beginning. He came to believe that only through being loved is a person made capable of love. Dostoevsky saw part of his task as "raising up the lowly." In the brilliant and complex novels he would go on to write, he did just that, redeeming in the eyes of educated Russians a class of peasants and criminal outcasts.[111]

The apostle Paul speaks in 2 Corinthians 1:4 of Jesus, *"who comforts us in all our troubles, so that we can comfort those in any trouble with the comfort we ourselves receive from God."* This principle lives in those who know what it's like to be in someone else's shoes. In God's redemptive upturn, compassion-shaped servants become uniquely qualified to minister to others. In a world where sin and brokenness pervade, someone must be able to speak the language that will swing wide the door for rich evangelistic conversations. So, that guy or gal who's been tossed aside by the modern church, deemed as "disqualified," and labeled "never to be used of God again" might be precisely the person you need! I know it rubs against the grain of our moralism; we are the older brother in the story of the prodigal son (see Luke 15:11–32), or one of the workers who spent all day in the field (see Matthew 20:1–16). I am continually amazed at the wisdom that God instills via other people's failures and recoveries, and how he wishes to use the wreckage and the other side of the healing process to transform us.

111. Philip Yancey, *Soul Survivor: How Thirteen Unlikely Mentors Helped My Faith Survive the Church* (New York, NY: Doubleday, 2001), 137–38.

> IN GOD'S REDEMPTIVE UPTURN, COMPASSION-
> SHAPED SERVANTS BECOME UNIQUELY QUALIFIED
> TO MINISTER TO OTHERS.

Another major slice of the hurting sector relates to marriage. Broken dreams often open hearts to spiritual solutions. When I was at Sandals Church, the marriage minister led countless couples to Christ. They came looking for hope, and he offered Jesus' help. No one can do more for rebuilding and restoring marriages than he. Two other healing ministries were hugely significant. Beauty for Ashes helps women deal with past sexual abuse. The statistics on this issue should not be ignored. And Deep Healing focuses on the dimension of spiritual warfare and deliverance from demons. It's intense! But right now, what is most important is for you and your team to assess what you can offer to the hurting.

## SPACE FOR THE SEARCHING

The Samaritan woman spoke words to Jesus that I have deemed prophetic: *"You have nothing to draw with and the well is deep"* (John 4:11). In her 2,000-year-old comment, she sized up the church's twenty-first-century issue—the challenge of distance. Too bad more churches don't get it like she did. To reach those farther out, you need vehicles that are built for range. Walking through your church doors and bumping up against your congregants in the community are increasing numbers of skeptical, wandering souls who have no idea about Christianity or spirituality, or who are holding on to differing ideas bridled with confusion and lots of doubt, or who may be devoid of any spiritual interest whatsoever. Wise churches position themselves to reach the widening circles by providing an exploratory process with a big, friendly entrance.

At a fund-raising dinner, I sat next to a woman who was part of our church's ministry called Marriage Mismatch—a support group for Christian wives whose husbands are nonbelievers. As we exchanged stories, I alluded briefly to my journeys with skeptic friends. I later offered to reach out to her husband. From the sparkle in her eyes, I could tell that the idea piqued her heart; but, in the end, she did not take me up on my offer. It was sad. This is my read of her: Because her husband had visited church and heard sermons before, to no avail, his wife lacked the faith that anyone could reach him. She had developed a view of the Christian gospel as impotent.

My view? Every skeptical husband, wife, and single person can be won to Christ! However, outside of God beaming a light from above, it takes one or more highly skilled evangelistic specialists to patiently guide a disbelieving spouse to salvation. Did this woman doubt my ability to relate to or build rapport with her secular-minded hubby? I know those shoes. Did she think she was the first spouse I had met who was dumbfounded by her analytically locked-up partner? One wife broke into tears the day her husband, long entrenched in atheism, gave himself to Jesus after I had invested a long time in my relationship with him. In this woman's preconditioned mind, she couldn't fathom the power of a faith-formational journey. When you understand the power of process, you come to believe the following of my favorite adages: "What won't happen today can happen tomorrow," and "Look at anything long enough, and the truth rises to the top."

## TEACH YOUR PEOPLE TO ENGAGE IN CONVERSATIONS THAT ESTABLISH SAFETY, HONOR, AND DIGNITY, WHILE MAINTAINING A PACE TO BUILD, NOT UNDERMINE, SPIRITUAL MOMENTUM.

Just because someone is far from God does not mean he or she can't be reached. But it will take someone who understands his or her unique entrapment and who also sees the way out of it. With God, all are reachable. When dealing with those who are farther out from the faith, you have to work the progressions. It's a law of missions. Teach your people to engage in conversations that establish safety, honor, and dignity, while maintaining a pace to build, not undermine, spiritual momentum. I never would have reached my atheist friend if he had not realized how much I respected his intellect (#9 Skill: Honor). Using the skill of honor means never winning the point if it means losing the person. He was smart. I esteemed his mind to eventually win his heart.

Range is where churches fail. Catering too often to those who already believe, we offer nothing for the irreligious "nones": skeptics, God-accusers, and adherents to various other faiths. We don't know how to come alongside in a productive way. Simplistic telling will not do the trick. Nor will "take it or leave it" proclamation. Nor will simply showing love. Running past or over them, we lose the opportunity. They needed to search, process, question, connect, and learn to hunger spiritually; we gave them a sermon and perhaps an ultimatum, and that's it.

Sensitive to the needs of non-Christians, one man commented insightfully, "They ask different questions." Unrelenting is the mission principle that we must *start where they are*. We must zero in on where they are so that we can lead them to who God is, and where he wants them to be. You can't skip a step or fast-forward to the end of the process prematurely!

A critical element to the design of the Roman aqueducts was mathematics. The ancients had to calculate accurately the descent from the hills all the way down into the valleys. Surveyors employed three instruments—the *chorobates*, the *dioptra*, and the *groma*—to chart incremental slope.[112] Good design takes into account the algorithmic nature of all things. *Oxford English Dictionary* defines *algorithm* this way: "A process or set of rules to be followed in calculations or other problem-solving operations." Not too dissimilar, high-level evangelistic churches garner algorithmic insights. They understand that getting people from point A to point B requires a particular path. The one-message-fits-all oversimplification accomplishes nothing and fails to recognize the varied issues inherent to unique starting points (#10 Skill: Paths).

Harnessing this wisdom, we enter the spiritual realm, where Satan, our cunning adversary, snags people with false pretensions. (See 2 Corinthians 10:5.) Without the demolition of fallacies and the construction of truth, we will not reach anyone. Learning to move people from point A to point B includes intellectual, sociological, and affective dimensions that account

---

112. Hodge, *Roman Aqueducts & Water Supply*, 204.

for the whole person.[113] Part three of my book *Soul Whisperer* offers eight evangelistic maps with diagrams and stories to shed insight on reaching the hard-to-reach categories of unbelievers. If you and your people are willing to go hard and long after distant hearts, you will chalk up legendary stories of how the Lord used you in natural and supernatural ways. People everywhere will be talking about your impact for the gospel!

Again, preaching alone is insufficient for many people in the outer rings, where relational dialogue is needed. One of the masters in church history, John Wesley, once concluded, "We have accomplished more in one-to-one discourse than in ten months of preaching."[114] Back-and-forth dialogue enables your people to get to the heart, eliminating misconceptions and dialing in on what will move others forward.

Nick, an agnostic, hangs around church every week but has never gone into a service. Covering himself, he says, "I know what they are saying in church doesn't make sense, and the evolution crap they are teaching in the schools isn't right, either." He remains on the outside, trapped in his self-protective cage. If Nick is to be won, he must be drawn into an ongoing conversation where there is no expectation that he will change his views, and where there is a lot of exploratory latitude to dialogue. Eventually, Nick must be freed to come out from hiding, to have the truth and the love of God break the fear that binds him. Such an outcome will require one believer or more to establish safety with him first, and then be committed enough to work through the entire process with him.

Other times, it's just faith construction that needs to take place. Hugo tags along with his girlfriend to the baptism class. Afterward, she presses to get him baptized (love her zeal!), but he's far from making that decision. He attends our *exploring* class, and within a month of processing not just what we believe but also the rationale for why, he gives his whole heart to Jesus.

You must tell your leaders and workers not to be surprised by where people start. Do not permit the dropping of jaws, even if, as happened at our group, a young gal visits your church and describes herself as "pansexual"

113. Paul G. Hiebert, *Transforming Worldviews: An Anthropological Understanding of How People Change* (Grand Rapids, MI: Baker Academic, 2008), 85.
114. John Wesley, "Minutes of Several Conversations," in *Works*, 8:303.

(a term elevated by Miley Cyrus' *Paper* magazine interview in 2015).[115] In a First Steps class, during a one-on-one breakout discussion, I learned that the livelihood of one of our regular attendees was selling illegal drugs. He had taken some spiritual steps in coming with his wife to the class every week. I didn't judge him. I encouraged him to keep seeking, and seeded the idea that God would provide for his needs as he followed him. Another man's history with violence would terrify many. It did conjure in us occasional feelings of fright. Yet we accepted him and watched as God miraculously transformed him. He called me one day to share a story that proved how much he had changed, and it made me want to cry.

When I wrote the materials for the Steps to Faith class, my goal was to create the structure for wider conversations to take place. Consider how the book invites an exploratory journey:

> Since the spiritual life is measured in the heart, the initial step must be the open-willingness to explore spiritual truth. Sadly, many people never take a serious look at what faith offers. They are like window shoppers who quickly glance but do not enter. Because of reluctance, they never truly open their hearts to what God has in store for them.
>
> Perhaps, you are different! Are you willing to take a good look at the incredible claims of the Christian faith? If you are, then you have taken a huge step already! May God fulfill his promise that "Those who seek will find!" You just may uncover answers your heart has longed for all your life.[116]

The material in this class also created a conduit to raise up members for mission engagement. I will never forget the class when I veered beyond the script to pull out my big apologetic guns in an attempt to get through to one of our analytically locked searchers. Later, I had a discussion with the team during which I told them that it would be a prolonged effort to reach this guy. However, just a couple weeks later, Stephen became a believer!

115. Emanuella Grinberg, "Know Your Identity Terms," CNN, August 1, 2017. Available at: www.cnn.com/2016/10/10/health/pansexual-feat/index.html.
116. Gary Comer, *Steps to Faith: Where Inquiring Friends Become Solid Disciples* (Eugene, OR: Wipf & Stock, 2014), 3–4.

The team had corralled him, spent hours working through his mental objections, and finally led him to Christ. Needless to say, I was overjoyed to hear about what had happened. My team was in the kingdom-building business!

## SPACE FOR THE DREAMING

The movie my family has dubbed the "man-opera," *Friday Night Lights*, is most famous for the locker-room line "Clear eyes, full hearts, can't lose." But when Landry reads Tyra's college entrance essay and mirrors back, "It's just not you," she sets out to write something that is equally potent. Ditching her stale, phony, predicable, blah-blah-blah first take on why she aspires for a college education, Tyra, at Landry's prodding, finds her voice:

Two years ago, I was afraid of wanting anything. I figured wanting would lead to trying, and trying would lead to failure. But now I find I can't stop wanting. I want to fly somewhere in first class. I want to travel to Europe on a business trip. I want to get invited to the White House. I want to learn about the world. I want to surprise myself. I want to be important. I want to be the best person I can be. I want to define myself instead of having others define me. I want to win, and have people be happy for me. I want to lose and get over it. I want to not be afraid of the unknown. I want to grow up to be generous and bighearted, the way that people have been with me. I want an interesting and surprising life. It's not that I think I'm going to get all these things. I just want the possibility of getting them. College represents possibility. The possibility that things are going to change. I can't wait.[117]

For anyone fighting against all odds for a better life, what a moving scene this is!

When people enter our churches, do they pick up—from the pastor's tone of voice, from the congregants' postures, from the path laid out before them—that the church is the "possibility place"? If they are willing to journey forward, who knows the amazing, incredible doors that God will open? The church—no other place offers as much! It wouldn't be such a bad slogan: _____ Church: The Possibilities Place!

---

117. *Friday Night Lights*, "Underdogs," NBC, January 7, 2009, written by Peter Berg and Buzz Bissinger, directed by Jeffrey Reiner, http://www.imdb.com/title/tt1216621/.

Of course, it really helps if you believe in the potential of the people you are trying to reach, *tipping the tower* in a major horizontal, outward projection. Is this your message: "We believe in you, and therefore, we are going to invest in and develop you for God's great purposes"? The *poema* principle: You are his poem, his piece of art to perform works *"which God prepared in advance for us to do"* (Ephesians 2:10). What a promise: God has gone before them for what they will fulfill! This truth you must pursue tangibly by pointing them toward your path.

One day, I busted up at the sight of a scrawny, nerdy-looking twelve-year-old sporting a T-shirt printed with the words "Babe Magnet." T-shirted or not, pastors and other visible church leaders are magnets for the Christian life. No offense intended, but I came up with this crass-sounding adage: "Pastors are hookers." Not in the usual sense of the word "hookers," of course. But the presenter's role is to hook people to come back and then guide them onto a path. *Back and then forward.* This is reason enough to polish up those messages. Your church is paving the way for God's supernatural possibilities.

In a larger sense, the most significant thing that your message can do is to prepare hearts to step onto your path. (If they settle for a sermon, they might miss it!) Hearing Jesus' call through your words, they begin a journey of transformation in the context of community, practices, group life, engagement experiences, and mission-skill development. If you don't believe in what God can do with this form of discipleship, yours will not be a great church. Believe in it! Make sure your team shows up ready to take people on an exciting adventure where God will do unimaginable things.

## BEYOND "FIRST IMPRESSIONS"

From a design view, think more deeply about your greeting ministry. Every church wants to reach new people. Consider the four levels that you will have to target if you are to claim that they are actually being reached.

Level 1 - Contacts: Warm welcomers

Level 2 - Connectors: Following-up relationship-builders

Level 3 - Connections: Ongoing relationship in groups/ministries

Level 4 - Calling: Inspiring people to a new vision

The first three levels are necessary, and they typically require a lot of work. But that fourth level, in my view, is when the person is truly reached by the church. It relates to personal dreams and aspirations. What is going to solidly close the back door to your church? It's when people become part of something great, something visionary for their lives! This is why your path is so important. It's the way to zero in on Christ's calling for each person.

———

Let's not get ahead of ourselves, though. Reaching wider circles creates new waves of responsibility. The "step IN" stage leads and grounds people in the true faith. Then, after laying solid their foundation, you must be ready for their next link in the journey—the vital spiritual practices that will launch them forward in the mission call of Christ. Just like God, we must love them too much to leave them where they are.

We now move from IN to ON. Hook them back and then send them on the journey of their lives!

## REFLECTIONS

1. Take time to evaluate what you are doing to reach each of the three sectors identified: (1) the hurting, (2) the searching, and (3) the dreaming. Don't be discouraged if you're not doing much. Begin where you are!

2. Who within your picture can be catalyzers to developing your "step IN" stage? List specific names, and pray for those individuals. Then devise a specific strategy for how you are going to mobilize them.

3. What could you see your church offering, specifically, that you are not now offering to reach farther into your community?

## REMISSION TAKEAWAYS

1. The church has an enormous responsibility to welcome the limitless number of those within reach of the cross of Christ.

2. Creating the space for individuals to land, connect, and process will broaden the effectual range of your church.

3. Divinely placed experiences enable Christians to have inroads and insights for mission.

# —11—

## STEP ON

It's a dangerous business…going out your door.
You step onto the road, and if you don't keep your feet,
there's no knowing where you might be swept off to.
—Bilbo Baggins, in J. R. R. Tolkien's
*The Lord of the Rings: The Fellowship of the Ring*

Growing up in the 1980s, I became an avid fan of the San Francisco 49ers' football dynasty. Following my team year-round, I devoured any and all information available and even subscribed to a special news release called the *49er Report*. Everything seemed right and good, until the tipping point. I reckoned my fanaticism had crossed a line when after the 49ers lost the NFC Championship to those hated Dallas Cowboys, and I actually cried. Idolatry has many victims.

Despite the strange soul wreckage I suffered, I found that something redeeming did come from my love affair with this football team: I had the opportunity to witness one of the true paradigm shifts in sports history. The revolutionizing change came from the brain trust of Bill Walsh, who created a strategy so unique that it acquired its own name: the "West Coast offense." Within Walsh's offensive system, a relatively new statistical category popped up: RAC, or "run after catch." This stat skyrocketed in prominence during the Montana-Rice years, when Walsh instructed his quarterbacks to hit receivers "in stride, on the break, at the numbers." He deemed anything outside this tight quadrant a bad throw.

Why so specific? Walsh aimed to turn receivers into runners. By having the quarterback throw unpredictably on first downs instead of thirds, and by designing plays to get the ball into a receiver's hands at a place where he could then run, he changed the game. With undeniable scoreboard success, every other NFL team began to emulate aspects of the 49ers' thinking. Today, RAC (sometimes referred to as YAC, with Y signifying "yards") is an integral part of football terminology.

———

As to potential, we have come to the life stage of parallel magnitude. In the church, it is so critical and mismanaged that I have made two hard assessments, not just one.

IN – **ON** – UP – OUT

In the purest sense, the "ON stage" addresses initial discipleship. Every church should pay close attention to what is occurring with those who are newer to the faith if it is serious about making disciples. My first-year doctoral research examined twenty churches, ten of the megachurch variety, on this very subject. I compared what I saw being either enacted or neglected to what the Bible portrayed. For the purposes of *ReMission*, the following are two major critiques.

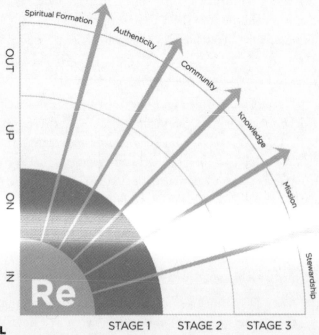

**RE-MISSION MODEL**

# #1 HARD ASSESSMENT: DECISIONS OVER DISCIPLESHIP

Why would someone of David Platt's stature take aim at, of all things, the traditional prayer of salvation?[118] If you were to corner the pastor, author, and president of the influential Southern Baptist Convention's International Mission Board, do you think he would be up in arms about churches creating a moment of decision? Certainly, a decision point of belief and repentance is valid based on Scripture; as it says in Romans 10:9, *"If you declare with your mouth, 'Jesus is Lord,' and believe in your heart that God raised him from the dead, you will be saved."* What he sees, and what he is riled up about and railing against, is the disconnection between salvation decisions (the uttering of the prayer) and the making of real disciples. His response to the controversy: "My comments about the 'sinner's prayer' have been deeply motivated by a concern for authentic conversion"; and then: "What kind of faith are we calling people to?"[119] He is pointing out a huge issue in the church, one we must always work at rectifying.

A better way beckons, but it will take your leadership moxie to pull it off. Here is the principle: You must *link salvation decisions to discipleship.* The Scriptures contain many stories to support this connection. It should not be lost on us that when the bleeding woman touched Jesus' garment, sensing the suctioning of his power, he stopped in the middle of a crowd in order to discover who had touched him. (See Mark 5:24–29.) His disciples were miffed at him for jamming the traffic flow and throwing a monkey wrench into the day's agenda, saying, "You see the people crowding against you, and yet you ask, 'Who touched me?'" In short, they were saying, "Lord, why do you bother with such a small thing as someone bumping you?"

What Jesus did here should raise major questions for all churches, especially larger ones, where size increases anonymity and depersonalization. Like the disciples, we must ask: Why was it so important for Jesus to know who had touched him? Why couldn't he have just made a mental tally that another human had been helped, and let it go? We could expand

---

118. "David Platt, "Why 'Accepting Jesus in Your Heart' Is Superstitious & Unbiblical," YouTube Video, 2:56, conference message, posted by VergeNetwork, April 11, 2012, September 6, 2014, https://www.youtube.com/watch?v=JPhEEzjU8xQ.

119. Lillian Kwon, "David Platt Still Addressing Controversy Over 'Sinner's Prayer' Remarks," *Christian Post Reporter* (June 29, 2012). Available at: http://www.christianpost.com/news/david-platt-still-addressing-controversy-over-sinners-prayer-remarks-77462/.

the question more broadly and ask: Why, in the enormous scale of his ministry, did Jesus not just address the masses, and let the chips fall where they may regarding specific individuals? Why did he have to get so personal?

The answer is profound. Jesus knew this principle: *Follow-up creates followers.* Making followers is what he came to earth to do! It's why he often stuck around after his healings in order to locate the recipients for a second, more intimate, encounter, where spiritual formation could begin. (See, for example, John 5:14; 9:35.) He didn't come to merely save or heal people. Nor did he come just to gather crowds in order to gain attention or feel important. When you study Jesus, make special note of the potency of his second, after-the-event encounters.

> JESUS KNEW THIS PRINCIPLE: FOLLOW-UP
> CREATES FOLLOWERS. MAKING FOLLOWERS
> IS WHAT HE CAME TO EARTH TO DO!

By singling out the bleeding woman—the one who thought of herself as so insignificant that she would sneak up secretly from behind Jesus, touch his dangling garment, and then slip away unnoticed—he communicated to her just how valued she was! Called out from her obscurity, she came forth, falling to her knees before the throng of onlookers, and publicly admitted to having been the one who had touched him. Jesus then esteemed her as his "Daughter" and commended her faith, assuring the relationship not thinly by a stealthy healing, but publicly and personally by the promise of his word![120] As to her future ministry, she was now fully in his court to be his conduit of hope to others. Every ounce of her body and soul was healed in that moment. She became whole.

Contrast Jesus' way with the strategy of most churches. We offer reports on how many were saved during our services, whether 5 or 12 or 109. Do we ask who was touched? Do we inquire after their names, their stories? Do we really know? Are they now solid in their standing and

---

120. Green, *Evangelism in the Early Church*, 65.

spiritual projection? Or was their declaration of faith just a fleeting moment in time? Did they come and go as the nameless and the faceless? The words of Jesus should haunt us. The woman with the issue of blood was no mere bump or notched number to be tallied by God, but rather a precious daughter to be welcomed and celebrated. She had experienced something of meaning beyond her comprehension. By virtue of her faith, she deserved to be affirmed, established, protected, and empowered. This is true for every person coming to Christ under your stewarding. Like Jesus did, do we feel their decisional gravitas? By circling back like he did, we can solidify their faith and secure their followership, which will involve their influence, as well. (I call this "The plus-1 skill: Circling back." It's what must always happen after the impact of the 10 base skills.)

> THE CALL TO FOLLOW CHRIST IS A CALL TO BECOME HIS DISCIPLE. WE'RE NOT TALKING EASY BELIEVISM BUT A COMMITMENT THAT INVOLVES LEARNING AND GROWING, BEING IN CLOSE RELATIONSHIP WITH OTHER LIKE-MINDED PEOPLE, AND BEING IN A COMMUNITY TRAINING ENVIRONMENT.

Granted, it's not always easy to make the discipling connection happen. When I studied what churches were doing in terms of follow-up, Laurie Beshore of Mariners Church in Newport Beach admitted, "Results of people moving from a Sunday-service decision into the new believers' class were abysmal." There are two factors that can help. The first is in the big picture. Whenever you see a gap between decisions and discipleship, it usually indicates a lack of relationship. So, when the church becomes more missionally engaged with members who have been well equipped to come alongside their not-yet-believing friends, we see greater fruits of discipleship. The relational closeness with an established believer supports the transformation of a new Christian. Ideally, we want our missional Christians to disciple new Christians forward (either one-on-one or in a group/class setting). You must be intentional with vision and materials if you desire to see your disciples making disciples.

The second way to address the gap has to do with how you dial in your communication. "Decisions less disciples" is a problem. We can turn that sucker around. Instead of the pastor merely making a salvation call, make the call about discipleship. The call to follow Christ is a call to become his disciple. We're not talking easy believism but a commitment that involves learning and growing, being in close relationship with other like-minded people, and being in a community training environment. Your path should be similar to Acts 11: Antioch. With full expectation of their taking the next step, link them directly and immediately to your discipling vehicle.

On big gospel-call days at Sandals, Matt Brown would direct dozens, sometimes hundreds, to walk into an overflow location to talk for a few moments about their discipleship, and to explore the journey class beginning at the church. This smart strategy created a hand-off to another leader. It also created the space for our team to minister one-on-one, which began the discipling process right there. You can't make them get on board, but you can make it very clear what the call of Christ entails.

I know it's much easier to bypass this step. You can wash your hands of it, saying: "The Holy Spirit will handle it." You can rationalize, "As long as there are decisions made, we are a great church." But that isn't so! You might be failing to make disciples. If someone truly had been unsaved and came to Christ (many who respond are not getting saved for the first time but were simply never discipled; they keep coming forward to claim salvation, wondering when the decision will finally "take"), don't we have a responsibility to help him or her into a strong spiritual understanding and entry into a fruitful life as a Christ-follower?

If there is any doubt lingering in your mind, let me add this thought: The first steps of a new believer are more important than you may think. There's a truism that says, "You never outgrow the basics." That which new Christians learn in this early stage will set the course for their entire Christian lives. Grace formation, and other foundational practices, are gifts that keep giving; they remain essential for growth. If new believers do not develop in these ways, they will be stunted, spiritually. New believers are also a thrilling group to work with. Why? Because it's among new believers that awesome stories abound of the influence of the gospel at work through you!

Having worked with and authored materials on the discipling process, I'd like to share with you a concept that will elevate your disciplemaking dynamics.

*Establish Faith by Instilling Practices*

From a study of twenty churches, one of my critiques was that they taught but did not instill practices. Consider the difference. Instead of telling people to read their Bibles, we introduced a devotional pattern to empower them to get the most from the Bible. Who is responsible for their spiritual growth? They are! They will need to be "self-feeders" of the Word of God in order to be effective in their mission field. As Beth Moore writes, "We all need to study the Scriptures for ourselves."[121]

When I developed a devotional pattern, I wanted to achieve more than just having others observe the Scriptures. The popular acronym S.O.A.P. (Scripture, Observation, Application, Prayer) is not sufficient, in my view, because we can observe the Bible and yet not deduce what God intended for us to see. Mere observation often misses God's thought. When people observe and then say, "It means _____ to me," we must stop them and say, "Who cares what you think? Are you omniscient and all-wise? It matters not what you or I may think; we must find what God thinks and intends for us to retrieve and receive. We want God's ideas for our lives." After hearing how to dig out the main idea from a passage of Scripture, one person said to me, "I will never look at the Bible the same way again." A more mature Christian admitted, "I was struggling to get anything from my Bible reading. This pattern has entirely changed that." Another wrote on our class review, "The devotional pattern F.I.R.S.T. [is] so powerful!"

The acronym FIRST provides a means for spiritual nurture. It is both a pattern for putting God first in one's day and a contextual method for hearing God's voice. The letters signify the following:

F: First in the day

---

121. Beth Moore, *To Live Is Christ: Joining Paul's Journey of Faith* (Nashville, TN: B&H Publishing, 2001), 122.

I: Idea of the passage

R: Relate it to life

S: Seek God in prayer

T: Take it with you[122]

*First in the day*: The Bible sets forth what is to be our top priority—putting God first in our lives. Matthew 6:33 says, *"Seek first [God's] kingdom and his righteousness."* Without being legalistic, let's not be afraid to give people some structure to their schedule by having them begin each morning by reading God's Word and praying.

*Idea of the passage*: Each Scripture passage contains a "big idea." Understanding Scripture properly requires digging out the intended theme of the author. We give people four digging tools to discern the main theme in group discussions: (1) big-picture context, (2) patterns of words and phrases, (3) emphasis, and (4) key verse. Once they think they've got it, we have them boil it down to a single-sentence principle. (Note: Everyone finds this task difficult at first. It's a skill to be honed. Role-playing/demonstration and practice will help people to "get it.").

*Relate it to life*: Having discovered the principle, we let it speak. How does this "idea" inform, help, direct, correct, or challenge us? We learn to study the Bible, and allow it to study us.

*Seek God in prayer*: Freshly informed as to the relevance and challenge of the idea, individuals are to seek its fulfillment in prayer: "God, help me have the courage to apply your truth in my situation." Or, "Give me your power to live out this truth from your Word."

*Take it with you*: Having spent time in the Word and prayer, the people head into their day being mindful to live out the Word.

Initially, I care far less about their scriptural breadth as I do about their learning how to be infected by the big, transformational ideas of God's Word! For those who fill pulpits, do you know what marks the most powerful preaching? In an article on what TED (Technology, Entertainment and Design) Conference speakers know, guess what was number one on

122. Gary Comer, *First Steps Discipleship Training: Turning Newer Believers into Missional Disciples* (Eugene, OR: Wipf & Stock, 2014), 30–33.

their list: Teach one idea.[123] The best preachers get this. Sure, you will develop points, but each subordinate insight must flow from the same singular idea in order to give your message a focal punch. It is my earnest opinion that most "list preaching" (and there's a whole lot of it happening) guts the Bible of its power. Masterful preachers extract the principle and have the discipline to cut away all the clatter and dissonance in order to let God's Word speak!

My acrostic is adaptable. Sandals worked it into their "R.E.A.L." value, with the E standing for "extract the main idea." We want to hear the authentic voice of God, don't we? If you teach people how to dig out the author's idea, they will find God speaking into their lives every day. Again, this skill requires a trained eye. Over the ten weeks of my First Steps Discipleship Training, the participants practice this skill in groups for eight consecutive weeks.

Here are some "big ideas" pulled from our group breakout sessions. As you read them and their correlating interactions, envision the amazing conversations that could happen among your own people.

Luke 5:1–11 (Jesus calls his disciples to "fish" for men instead of for fish)

Idea: "To follow Christ in his mission, you will have to leave lesser dreams behind."

Group: What specifically do we need to leave behind in order to follow in Jesus' steps?

Mark 1:1–8 (John the Baptist's forerunning ministry)

Idea: "God uses humble messengers to prepare responsive hearts."

Group: How can we clothe ourselves in humility with those outside our faith?

Mark 9:2–13 (Jesus' transfiguration)

Idea: "At times, we will not understand the glorious things that God is doing."

---

123. Jessica Stillman, "5 Secrets of Public Speaking from the Best Ted Presenters" (November 8, 2013). Available at: http://www.inc.com/jessica-stillman/ted-speakers-on-presenting-public-speaking.html (accessed March 22, 2015).

Group: Can we discern any of the wondrous things that God is working in our lives right now?

Mark 15:16–20 (The soldiers mock Jesus on his way to Calvary)

Idea: "How you are treated does not change who you are."

Group: Where do we need to stand strong in our identity as Christians?

John 15:1–8 (Jesus' parable of the vine and the branches)

Idea: "The only fruitful life Source is Jesus and our connection with him."

Group: What is it that we must do to maintain our walk with Christ?

The prayer part of the pattern may be a sensitive area for new believers and must be developed in the right way. In the devotional pattern, we prepare them prior to asking them to put prayer into practice. Consider the testimony of a man who found himself in a church service standing by a crying woman and was asked to pray over her. Though he had attended church for years, he had never prayed out loud for anyone. Fortunately, God didn't bail him out; with quavering voice, this man eked out a string of words on the woman's behalf. How could this have happened? How did this guy belong to the church without ever learning to pray? Sermons are not well suited for imparting skills; and for many, prayer is a learned skill. Though every church has its prayer warriors, if you are making new believers, you will have to help them break through with prayer. Just like that guy who found himself put on the spot with knees shaking, believe me when I say that anyone praying aloud in public for the first time will be frightened.

THOUGH EVERY CHURCH HAS ITS PRAYER WARRIORS, IF YOU ARE MAKING NEW BELIEVERS, YOU WILL HAVE TO HELP THEM BREAK THROUGH WITH PRAYER.

We have taught thousands to break through with prayer. Many have thanked my teaching teams for not just talking about prayer but actually having them practice it. And here's how we do it. Teaching people to pray out loud in community with others is best done using simple "help me" prayers. The first time around, in a group setting, they will say one or two sentences. That's it. "Help me, God, to learn how to pray." "Help me, God, to relate to you as my loving heavenly Father." "Help me, God, to seek your will, not mine, in this situation." The whole occasion takes less than a minute. The next time the group meets, they will do it again, having a bit more latitude on what to pray for. And the same will be true of the next session. Like riding a bike, once they get it, they will have gotten it for life!

There are other vital practices to be taught, such as confession, abiding, community fellowship, and service. What we are doing is not merely offering instruction but rather teaching and leading people into the formational development of skills and experiences that will enhance their transformation dramatically. Many of their spiritual journeys will exceed the walks and impact of longer-term Christians simply because they were well trained.

## #2 HARD ASSESSMENT: MISSED MOMENTUM

If we think in terms of *ReMission*, where influence already exists, momentum matters. Unlike your prototypical long-term Christians, newer believers have something absolutely vital to your movement: unsaved friends. When I asked the participants in one of our First Steps classes how many of their friends were outside the church, one person replied, "All of them." If you can't see the potential in that, you need to get your eyes checked and put on some new gospel glasses!

Bradley, a young man with a giant hoop in each of his earlobes, told me, "I've never read anything in the Bible before." His friends hounded him over what he was doing, going to church. "I want to be able to explain what I believe, but I don't have the understanding to do that," he told me. We bear a responsibility to ground and prepare such people as Bradley.

This is precisely what Jesus did in his pivotal post-resurrection ministry, which Luke, in his gospel, quantifies as a 40-day period. What was Jesus doing? It might initially sound funny to us, but he was following up with new believers. Think about it: The Twelve spent three years walking with him, and yet they did not put all the pieces together. Peter denied

Jesus. Thomas doubted him. They were all disillusioned. Peter, the leader, even tried to stop Jesus from going to the cross. The disciples may have been followers of Christ, but they were not believers in the full sense. Their human fragility was on public display.

So, Jesus stuck around, coming to them again and again with nine resurrection appearances, including an extended stay in Galilee, where it all started. He "opened their minds" to the Scriptures, revealing the prophetic plan of God, both already fulfilled and to be fulfilled, and his vision for this message to reach the whole world through his disciples. (See Acts 1:1–3; Luke 24:45–49.) In essence, he was grounding and equipping them to become his missionary movement. In the post-resurrection age of the gospel, this is our vision for new believers.

The church must adopt the same IAS (influence after salvation) thinking. For this to occur, two catalytic things must happen. First, you need to be reaching nonbelievers. Without people coming to salvation, the movement will go dry, like a sluice gate blocking the flow of water. This is why churches that cater only to transfers get stuck. Second—yes, I'm saying it again: The church needs to come alongside those who are new to the faith, to equip them with mission skills.

*Empower Mission by Instilling Skills*

I wrote *First Steps Discipleship Training* with Christ's pattern in mind. Based on what he modeled in the post-resurrection period, the 10-week program intends to turn newer believers into missional disciples. Of course, by providing them with tools, we are putting the gospel "in stride, on the break, at the numbers." With *First Steps*, we are building a strong foundation of discipleship, and teaching them how to engage evangelistically from the get-go. When you do this, you will see results.

In your sessions, helping to ground new believers in the gospel is a double-edged sword that will accomplish two vital things: (1) assurance of salvation and (2) equipping. They need a full understanding of the gospel for themselves, as well as the ability to present it reasonably to others. We sit in the salvation subject for a while, drenching them in God's bottomless grace, and then we build the kind of reasoning for their faith that works in our culture. We rid ourselves of such tired lines as "I believe the Bible because it says it's God's Word" (circular reasoning). I believe the Bible because there is no other explanation for its unity and prophecies unless it's inspired by an outside-of-time Source, God. From the get-go, trainees learn how to talk intelligently about their faith. In the first course, we give them specific faith-sharing skills.

Neophyte Laurie writes down six names of nonbelievers to be praying for regularly. When you ask your new believers to make a missional prayer list, they don't draw big blanks like many long-term Christians do. After receiving training on how to go about sharing her faith, Laurie reported that on one day, God opened up conversations with four of the six people whose names she'd written down. Brimming with excitement, she said, "I did what you taught us to do. Every conversation was amazing!" One of those people came to faith during the time Laurie was taking the class.

Mary Jane embraced the Christian faith in our exploration class and then connected her friend Wayne to the next session. Now, having been trained, Mary Jane continues to influence others, while Wayne has come to faith and is now trained to reach his friends. A participant told me, "I have three of my family with me today at church. Months ago, I never would have imagined that I would be doing this!" Is this how you view new believers? Are you thinking "influence after salvation"? Let's dump the wimpy follow-up term, and start using the far more visionary, and more biblical, term "follow forward," instead. "Following forward" on people's salvation so that they influence others in the same way often requires having eyes on the ground. One day, I received this message via e-mail:

> Hello again Gary, I would love to go to the *Steps to Faith* course, but I've been having difficulty attending because of my Starbucks schedule. I feel like I am so close to getting to know God, but not quite there yet, and I really feel your course would help me. Do you teach any other similar classes for beginners/new believers?[124]

Did you notice where this young woman said she is employed? I am thinking we'll start a discovery group to help her and also to reach out to her many friends at work! Can you see how to work it?

---

124. Kara Mitchell, e-mail to author (October 12, 2010).

Merle arrives at class with a major attitude. As the class interacts, he interjects with some of the typical hard-edged questions. Never surprised by this, we welcome his honesty (yet we don't allow a bad spirit or belligerence to disrupt the whole class). Remembering our desire to attract those at the outer edges of Christianity, we do our best to provide answers while maintaining the dignity of the questioner. After this exchange, I knew more was required, and so I made a personal call to Merle. When he realized my interest in him, the walls dropped, and we had a good heart-level talk.

At the end of the course, I collected the class members' evaluations, which had been printed with this closing remark: "Keep journeying with us. You are loved here." On Merle's evaluation, he wrote just beneath that remark, "I am beginning to feel that." When I bumped into him a month later, he apologized for being "such a jerk." Christ's love had broken through! The guy was suddenly transformed. He had begun reaching out to his unsaved friends. One of them, a casual atheist, challenged him, "Show me one miracle, and I'll come to your church." Merle's response? "You're looking at it." His friend said, "You're right. You have changed." The guy started coming to our church and is now in the faith!

## GOOD DESIGN IN THE CHURCH SERVES ITS PEOPLE AND MAINTAINS THE GOSPEL'S FORWARD MOMENTUM.

Good design in the church serves its people and maintains the gospel's forward momentum. It means newer believers get connected with the body, become established in their faith, and then start moving forward in the exciting mission of Christ. It takes perceived-to-be-second-stringers and raises them as stars!

My catchphrase "The movement starts with us" is remarkably true. What do the following Bible characters have in common: the Samaritan Woman, Ananias, Philip, Lydia, the Roman jailer, the demoniac, Crispus, and Saul of Tarsus? Answer: They were all new believers who had enormous impact! They demonstrate a prolific gospel reach, the expansionary dynamic of our message.

Get on the mission side, and you'll discover that God's vision is always bigger than you thought. Why was it important for Ananias to go to Saul? Look at God's declaration in Acts 9:15: *"This man is my chosen instrument to proclaim my name to the Gentiles and their kings and to the people of Israel."* The persecuting outsider Saul (aka Paul) became God's lead to the Gentile world. The sequence went as follows:

Ananias → Saul → Gentile world → Gentile churches

In our sessions, we open the trainees' eyes to how significant their engagement can be. Consider these other sample impact sequences:

Philip → The eunuch → The court of Africa → Broader Africa

Jesus → The Samaritan woman → The nearby town → The entire region of Samaria

Jesus → The demoniac → The Decapolis → The Decapolis region

Paul → Lydia → Lydia's household → The city of Corinth

When believers make their lives strictly about their own spiritual consumption, about their own faith story, the movement stops. It's true. The entire movement doesn't stop, of course; but the movement through them halts in at least three places: (1) their direct sphere of influence, which includes all the not-yet-believing-people they know personally; (2) their friends' spheres of influence; and (3) the broader circle of "friends of their friends."

It's why mission-less Christianity is a death knell for the faith. When you focus exclusively on your own faith—when your personal spiritual growth is the primary objective—you get stagnation. We must go out to be healthy and grow. Some think that the systemic answer is found in merely getting beside people who are distanced from any church or Christian influence. Here is why I believe that is not our sole issue. Many of our church's members do not know how to reach the unbelievers who are right within their own circles, within their existing reach: family members, neighbors, friends, colleagues, playmates, or members of their close community or another group to which they belong. Since they are ineffective with the people they know, the movement does not proceed to the wider circles of people they do not know (the networks of their friends). In other words, we don't have just an isolation problem solvable by saturation; we have an efficacy problem that must be solved by skill development and greater relational investment in the lost all around us. If we raise the ability of Christians to influence others for the gospel, the movement will take off beyond our bearings.

As a final word of faith for our study, I ask you not to underestimate what God wills do through *you*. If you are willing to get *out of yourself* and *into reaching someone else*, he will multiply his movement well beyond your capacity to fathom. Reaching one reaches many. It's the way of God. It's the way of his kingdom.

———

As your new believers grow, they will begin to hunger for greater food. The spiritual leader must be ready to satisfy that developing appetite. Many of your people have been in the faith for some time. God always has bigger things in store for his children. The next chapter will help you enter that stage. It's time to help them to step UP!

## REFLECTIONS

1. Why are leaders reticent to ask unsaved people to commit to discipleship (in lieu of merely acknowledging a decision)? Make a mental list of reasons, or write them down.

2. Do you think Jesus' question *"Who touched me?"* (Mark 5:31; Luke 8:45) is challenging today? How so? How can you and

the people you lead be more sensitive to the needs of the people around you and them?

3.   Discuss what is happening with your new believers. How well are you doing in grounding/discipling them? How many people are being saved through their influence? What needs to be started or shored up?

## REMISSION TAKEAWAYS

1.   The call to follow Christ is a call to discipleship.

2.   New believers are already positioned as the frontline of the movement.

3.   We have a biblical responsibility to ground and equip all new believers to be missional disciples.

# —12—

# STEP UP

Give me a lever long enough…, and I shall move the world.
—Archimedes

Every human being possesses the yearning to rise. Something inside us knows we were meant for more. Inside every church are people who wish that their spirituality could find another gear. They may be faithful attendees. They may have listened to Bible messages for years on end, and yet, with all their accumulated knowledge, they feel that their Christian life is stuck in first or, perhaps with a grinding of gears, second. As much as they want to, they are not sure how to shift in order to attain a higher speed and a greater sense of fulfillment.

The "step UP" stage is specially designed to take Christians to higher echelons of empowerment and satisfaction. It embodies the spirit of the words of the apostle Paul in Philippians 3:13 (NKJV): *"I press toward the goal for the prize of the upward call of God in Christ Jesus."* In this stage, you will be seeking the spiritual equivalent of a physical PR ("personal record," a cross-training term). Since Christian growth is progressive, the idea of each of us improving is in alignment with God's perfect will. He, being love, always desires that our lives count in better and bigger ways.

To realize your personal best, you have to ask climber-type questions. Here, you are openly searching for what is missing or needed in order to attain the next tier. Whatever that is, in the lives of your people, you seek its discovery. This means there will be occasions to stop and assess a hindering block or a critical area. What will get them up and over? Is it surrender?

Healing? Sharper skills? Certain knowledge? Support? Engagement? Focused placement? More practice? What is it? Each of their roles is important to Jesus and his church. If it's possible to identify what is missing, you will. Where you can celebrate and capture God's developing story, you will do that, as well.

———

Regarding your mission discipleship, the "step UP" stage creates linkage to your larger vision. If, as a body, your people move together, synergy will help everyone move toward the collective calling. Broken down, it will entail their growing further in your specified core values (such as spiritual formation, authenticity, community, knowledge, mission, and stewardship).

Participation in the "step IN" and "step ON" stages gets people in the faith and starts them moving forward. Next, you want to get them moving UP! Though you will be reinforcing the foundational practices (from the "step ON" stage), from time to time, if you don't build upon that foundation with higher intensity, you'll find that the bigger goals of the path will be harder to reach. All that is to say, this stage is vital.

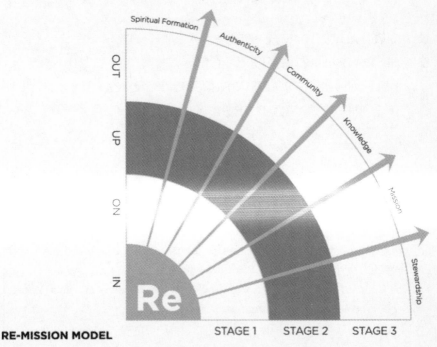

**RE-MISSION MODEL**

### IN – ON – **UP** – OUT

Moving people into mission for the long haul is a qualitative challenge. The beauty of the Path design is how the sequential stages allow for reinforcement and refinement. Intensive, highly practical, and engagement oriented, the "step UP" stage integrates training with life experiences. Your planning team must come together to flesh out their engagement in precise, doable terms, and to assume oversight of the activities.

As you lead the "step UP" phase, be honest about expectations. "Progress, not perfection" should be your motto. Admittedly, moments will surface when your people feel as if they are stepping down, not up. It's how the spiritual life sometimes works. When we seek growth, we discover that getting more truthful with ourselves feels harder, not easier. We know that the upward path will take us first through the valley. But once the course is set or the breakthrough occurs, the hills are never far away. The greater climb commences. The "step UP" stage also does something that is absolutely vital for growing churches. See if you can relate to the following scenario.

> IF YOU DON'T OFFER PEOPLE A PATH INTO
> THEIR NEXT BIG STEPS OF GROWTH,
> YOU SHOULDN'T BE SURPRISED WHEN YOU SEE
> THEM HEADING OUT THE BACK DOOR.

At first visit, the new couple said that your church was "so wonderful." They could not sing enough praises about you! A mere six months later, you get the heart-dropping text letting you know that they have left for another ministry. What happened? How did these fan favorites, once some of your biggest fans, turn to play the Judas card so quickly? Let's break it down. Your one-dimensional wonder lost its warm fuzziness. As soon as they moved beyond the initial growth stage, to their spiritual credit, they began to desire something more. When the opportunity for that step presented itself from another church or para-ministry, they jumped to a faster-moving train—to grow deeper, to get equipped, and to move into mission. If you don't offer a path into their next big steps of growth, you shouldn't be surprised when you see them heading out the back door.

You close that sucker by creating a vehicle of significant growth—one that serves as a kind of tracking app on people's development. Get them moving in a big way into community connection and Christ's cause, and you can preempt their exit strategy. Of course, your vision is not to keep them in the pen but to disciple them in the missional sense.

## COMPLEMENTARY DESIGN

A keen design observation that we have made is how the key values work complementarily. Look at the list below and the corresponding graphic. Each value plays a vital part in shaping a missionally effective Christian.

"Up" Values:

Relational skills – Key to mission

Knowledge – Key to mission

Authenticity – Key to mission

Spiritual formation – Key to mission

Stewardship – Key to mission

Each value is critical. Consider, for a moment, just how linked up people are to the unbelieving world around them. If your people lack basic relationship-building skills, you can kiss their evangelistic influence good-bye! The ability to relate well with others, to form ongoing relationships built on trust, is crucial not only to their quality of life but also for their ability to further Christ's cause. For this reason, the holistic approach of a sequential path makes a lot of sense. It gives you time to evaluate people and zero in on growth areas, so that they can reach their full gospel potential.

When it comes to relational skills, we chose to start at the most basic level. You might think that it would be wise to jump to advance concepts; but in our dysfunctional world, we cannot assume that people have gotten good relationship training in their families. On the topic of being a better conversationalist, Michael Hyatt has shared five secrets. Notice how each one deals with some aspect of being self-aware and also sensitive to others. These secrets are very basic, but many people miss them:

#1: Listen with your heart.

#2: Be aware of how much you're talking.

#3: Hit the ball back over the net.

#4: Ask follow-up questions.

#5: Provide positive feedback.[125]

If we are honest, some of your people (and even you and me, from time to time) are flubbing all five! We don't listen empathetically. We talk too much. We don't respond in a thoughtful manner to what others have said. We don't ask the critical follow-up questions to discern what's really going on with someone or how to help him or her. And we say little that is positive and uplifting. Then, we complain that we don't have better relationships or any notable influence for Christ.

If you are to make effective, missional disciples, your people must grow in multiple areas. By design, the "step UP" stage addresses this challenge. Now, think with me of how the value of knowledge serves the sphere of mission.

## UP: KNOWLEDGE

From a distant spectator's seat, it's not hard to surmise some things about James Cameron, the screenwriter, movie director/producer, and industry mogul. Having produced and directed two "little" box-office blockbusters, *Titanic* and *Avatar*, he is obviously well off and possesses considerable clout in Hollywood. Yet when his follow-up documentary, *Titanic: The Final Word with James Cameron*, aired, I saw something far more estimable. After completing the production of *Titanic*, Cameron was still seeking answers to what really happened on the fateful night of April 14, 1912. For this, I give him credit—he's a truth seeker! To assist him in his quest for an accurate analysis, he assembled a dozen or so qualified Titanic-obsessed friends. Let's just call them "the fellowship of the ship."

125. Michael Hyatt, "5 Strategies for Becoming a Better Conversationalist: What Leaders Can Learn from a Good Game of Ping Pong." Available at: https://michaelhyatt.com/5-strategies-for-becoming-a-better-conversationalist.html (accessed May, 18, 2014).

The documentary revealed that Cameron was not satisfied with all the assumptions that had guided the writing of the ship's sinking as depicted in the original movie. He knew that although they'd gotten much of it right, some key mysteries remained unsolved. I am sure you would love to know all the places where the speculation behind the original script went adrift. To me, there was one part that stuck out and stirred passion for my faith.

A primary feature of the film story was how the great ship split apart. From the public hearings following the tragedy, we know that this detail, in the retelling, was not accepted. Titanic Historical Society "experts" did not believe such a thing could occur. Even when one of the survivors, Ruth Blanchard—twelve years old at the time of the sinking—described how she had watched the vessel rip in two, and how everyone in her lifeboat was talking about the phenomenon, conference officials grabbed her microphone and qualified her remarks, saying, "This was just her perception because the funnel had fallen." On the grounds of civil engineering, the original reports were deemed unreasonable and were consequently dismissed.

The belief that the ship went down intact remained the most popular position until 1985, when Bob Ballard used marine robotics to explore the wreck, proving once and for all that the eyewitnesses were right! The *Titanic* had indeed torn in two when the front compartments of the ship had filled with water, lifting the back, which created stress beyond the ship's ability to bear. Unlike in the film, which shows the back end of the ocean liner going vertical, the stern lifted only 23 degrees.

This is where their dialogue got interesting. The "fellowship of the ship" spoke vehemently against the censorship of Ms. Blanchard and the reinterpretation of history. With righteous indignation, one researcher said, "I wish she [Blanchard] would have taken the microphone back and said, 'Were you there?'" With fiery zeal, the group zeroed in on the preeminence of eyewitness testimony, questioning the dismissal of the corroborating voices by saying, "They can't all be having hallucinations!"

On another detail, the witnesses had described colored flares being shot into the night sky. Although the movie producers speculated that this detail might, in fact, have been accurate, they didn't believe their viewers would accept it, and so they used only white flares in the film. Yet again, the wreckage vindicated the testimony when underwater cameras bumped into an unused flare bundle with colored canister tips. In the end, as to accuracy, no one got it right—no one but the eyewitnesses.[126]

As modern-day Christians, we find that whole cultures, philosophies, religions, and so-called "experts" marginalize eyewitness testimony of history's most significant person every single day. Islam, the second-largest religion (at the time of publication), denies it outright. The magnitude of Jesus' life, death, and rising relegate the *Titanic* telling to something meaningless and immaterial. Yet so little credence is given to four detailed Gospel accounts that come to us from multiple intimately involved, corroborating eyewitnesses. This is tragic. It does show us, though, how the church must sharpen itself.

CHURCH PLANTERS TODAY MUST BE ABLE TO ADDRESS THE PREVAILING THOUGHTS AND DEMONICALLY ERECTED "PRETENSIONS" WITHIN THE CULTURE. THE CHURCH MUST RAISE UP WRITERS, BLOGGERS, RADIO HOSTS, MEDIA CONDUITS, FILM PRODUCERS, APOLOGISTS, AND EVANGELISTS.

As leaders, we must raise up our people to enter into the all-important conversation. Church members must learn how to have respectful, loving, constructive dialogues with unbelievers in the marketplace, the neighborhood, and elsewhere. Church planters today must be able to address the prevailing thoughts and demonically erected "pretensions" within the culture. The church must raise up writers, bloggers, radio hosts, media conduits, film producers, apologists, and evangelists. Will the future church be ready to face the next ideological landslide that is coming if we are not producing critical thinkers willing to meet people right where they are?

126. *Titanic: The Final Word with James Cameron*, BluRay, directed by Tony Gerber (USA: National Geographic Channel, 2012).

Up 239

This explains why, in this stage, we make it a requirement for participants to read one or two top-level education books (from a compilation of recommended titles and corresponding summaries) and then write their thoughts on the content. We are losing the literacy battle, and we need to shore up our position on the frontlines by opening the mind conceptually, broadening vocabulary, and building the confidence of people to engage with a culture in a thoughtful way. Reading is still one of the most potent means of getting it done. We also ask select members to read oppositional books, for how can we raise our people if they haven't sat in and sized up the culture's thinking?

Reza Aslan's book *Zealot*, a scholarly deconstruction of the biblical Jesus, is a *New York Times* bestseller. I talked with a literary agent who had bought the author's fallacies hook, line and sinker. Can your people counter the widely circulating notion that the biblical Jesus is the fabrication of Gospel inventors? Would they be able to pinpoint the errant thought, and enter into constructive conversations? If not, don't expect them to be able to justify their faith. The great majority within Christendom today cannot defend their convictions—a sad commentary on our churches. Vincent Bugliosi's agnostic critique of religion and atheism, *The Divinity of Doubt*, is another of the kinds of books that reveal what people out there are thinking.[127] Don't be afraid to let your people hear the other side and wrestle with it. That's what education is all about. If you equip them with knowledge, their ability to interact meaningfully will rise exponentially. They will be sharp and ready!

For your up-and-coming missional leaders, let them enter the HD living-color story of the early church in Michael Green's magisterial work, *Evangelism in the Early Church*, with its 55-page bibliography of original sources. Though the academic reading will be tough trudging at times, the payoff in depth is worth it! Also, your people can journey into the guiding parameters of how to examine the veracity of one's faith in Mark Mittelberg's *Confident Faith*.[128]

---

127. Vincent Bugliosi, *Divinity of Doubt: The God Question* (New York, NY: Vanguard Press, 2011).
128. Mark Mittelberg, *Confident Faith: Building a Firm Foundation for Your Beliefs* (Carol Streams: IL: Tyndale, 2013).

There was a final twist to Cameron's inquiry. It comes from another documentary that he co-produced for The Discovery Channel called *The Lost Tomb of Jesus*. In this piece, Cameron and his colleagues make the claim that they discovered the actual tomb where Jesus and his family were laid to rest—the rather ominous implication being that the resurrection never occurred, at least in the physical sense. The basis for this assertion derived from ossuaries (containers or burial chambers for human bones) with etched-in-stone inscriptions that apparently included the names of Jesus' kin.[129]

As soon as this "new finding" went public, archaeologists quickly chimed in to set the record straight. First, this tomb was not a new discovery, and no one had ever drawn such a conclusion. Second, the names that were etched were common in their day; the equivalent would be finding such surnames as Smith and Jones in the Yellow Pages. Third, this grave was not even located in the hometown of Jesus' clan—a contradiction of the burial practices of poor Judean families. Topping it off, the biggest irony of all was how easy it was for Cameron and his colleagues to disregard the historic record.[130]

If only Cameron had the foresight and integrity to apply the same rationale for the resurrection that he would later use for the *Titanic*. Cameron would have been one of Christianity's greatest advocates! Who, may I ask, is going to win this guy to our side? I'll put on a black tie. I'll hold a wine glass and hobnob at those celebrity parties. Maybe we could produce some world-class Christian movies. If I were moving in his circles, I'd be pursuing deeper dialogues with him, for sure. I'd appeal: "After venerating the voices of the great ship's survivors, how can you now be so cavalier as to disregard the first-century biblical accounts? Could all those eyewitnesses have been hallucinating? You are being hypocritical, my friend. Why believe a romanticized version of history instead of the one that really occurred? Like the Titanic Historical Society experts, have you written off the eyewitnesses because what they described was just too unbelievable? Come on, searcher for truth—your life and eternal destiny are at stake!"

129. *The Lost Tomb of Jesus*, Streaming/DVD, directed by Simcha Jacobovici (USA: James Cameron & The Discovery Channel, 2007). Available at: https://www.amazon.com/James-Cameron-Presents-Lost-Jesus/dp/B000RE6RYW.
130. John Ortberg, *Faith and Doubt* (Grand Rapids, MI: Zondervan, 2008), 94.

My true point, though, comes down to this question: Are we raising up sharp, independent thinkers who can meaningfully engage with the secular thoughts of our day? As one of my colleagues noted, "The lack of intellectualism is no virtue in the church." In Matthew 22, consistent with his pattern of reading positional starting points, Jesus provided the Pharisees and Sadducees a series of intellectually compelling stumpers, proving that the Spirit and the intellect work in concert! Maybe I'm asking for a lot here from your Path, but let's acknowledge that "knowledge" is an important piece to raising culturally savvy Christians. Ideas infuse the mission equation in every sphere: neighborhoods, the marketplace, academia, and the media.

## UP: AUTHENTICITY

The "step UP" stage will also raise the bar of spiritual formation. The truth is, all Christians have their hang-ups. Sometimes, those issues are enough to sideline believers from serving in the church. At the very least, they can create an enormous distraction that may immobilize a potentially fruitful Christ follower. No doubt, a spiritual battle rages.

At a Catalyst Conference, Pastor Louie Giglio used the design of an elevator to illustrate the intent of the gospel. As Giglio noted, "The elevator's function derives from the counterweight." The concept is simple: *If you are going to go up, something heavier must come down.* His big, singular idea: When Christ came down, he became the ultimate counterweight.[131] This was a home-run message!

In the spiritual realm, Jesus' descending to earth in the incarnation not only has the power to lift us up to heaven; it is also meant to pull us upward in every earthly challenge we face. His promises are plain, such as the one we find in John 10:10: *"The thief comes only to steal and kill and destroy; I have come that they may have life, and have it to the full."* Although there may be times when the Lord allows us to endure hardships for the purpose of refining our character, it is incredible to consider that he has all the capacity to do just what he promised. Jesus routinely lifts people from the muck and mire

---

131. Louie Giglio, "Catalyst West Session 6" (presentation at the Catalyst Conference at Newport Beach, California, April 18, 2013). Partial transcript available at: https://dustn.tv/catalyst-west-2013-louie-giglio/.

of sin, from doubt and despair, from apathy or complacency, from waste and obscurity, and from the powerless limitations of their circumstances.

To help our missionaries-in-training reach higher ground, we require them to do two very personal things: (1) identify their partner and (2) identify their triggers. *Identifying a partner* involves establishing a relationship of candor and confidence with a fellow path-mate. The aim is to move from isolation and secrecy into community connection and support. (2) *Identifying triggers* means asking oneself: "What behavioral tendencies leave me vulnerable to, or set up for, personal or spiritual attack?" A fantastic conversation! In some cases, you may want to invite the entire group to pray for spiritual deliverance over someone. Keep in mind your team will need to be guided, and they may need wisdom and structure for recovery in order to sustain long-term victory.

As Jesus hyperbolized with his lines about "pulling out one's eyeball" and "cutting off one's hand" (see Matthew 5:29), radical measures must be taken to overcome sin. Do you need to crucify something? As C. S. Lewis wrote, the only way to deal with the lizard of lust whispering on your shoulder is to kill it![132] In the language of recovery, "Half measures availed us nothing."[133] J. Oswald Sanders wrote, "A leader is a person who has learned to obey a discipline imposed from without, but who then imposed on himself a much more rigorous discipline from within."[134] Each member must assess his or her personal patterns in order to rise higher for Jesus. Where your people start out in the class should not be the same place as where they finish. Many will look back at this stage as the moment they began to break the stronghold. Set a strong projection. Establish needed connections. Let's move together into Christ's upward call!

## ENGAGEMENT LINES

When it comes to mission engagement, this stage focuses on the gaining of experience. In addition to ministering at the neighborhood level,

132. C. S. Lewis, *The Great Divorce* (New York, NY: HarperCollins, 1945, 2001), 106–112.
133. *Alcoholics Anonymous: The Story of How Many Thousands of Men and Women Have Recovered from Alcoholism*, Fourth Edition (New York, NY: Alcoholic Anonymous World Services, 2001), 59.
134. J. Oswald Sanders, *Spiritual Leadership: Principles of Excellence for Every Believer* (Chicago, IL: Moody Publishers, 1967, 1980, 1994), 67.

look to raise your people along many fronts: community compassion, mission projects, and planting efforts.

In a conversation with Sandals' staff, the late renowned author/speaker Dallas Willard mentioned how the church must reach the "up-and-in" as well as the "down-and-out." It's a helpful distinction. Naturally, compassion ministries target the disenfranchised. Yet we must also target the "up-and-in" power players of the city if we are going to maximize our cultural impact. Every city has its key decision-makers who are positioned to create change. Their advocacy for resources and church partnerships opens big doors.

> NATURALLY, COMPASSION MINISTRIES TARGET THE DISENFRANCHISED. YET WE MUST ALSO TARGET THE "UP-AND-IN" POWER PLAYERS OF THE CITY IF WE ARE GOING TO MAXIMIZE OUR CULTURAL IMPACT. EVERY CITY HAS ITS KEY DECISION MAKERS WHO ARE POSITIONED TO CREATE CHANGE.

I will always remember the day that Teresa, the head of Child Protective Services in our city, came to our Steps to Faith class. Anna, one of our leaders, flagged me down and asked, "Is she coming to your class?" Another gal working in foster care pulled me aside to express how excited she was. Teresa ended up coming to Christ, and then she was discipled in our First Steps training program. A top player in the city got aligned with Jesus and his mission!

Focusing efforts to the "up-and-in" usually requires a different skill set. You are looking for people who are comfortable attending meetings and mixing at cocktail parties, walking with the higher-ups of society. Not everyone can do that. So, it usually begins with a vision, then identifying the right types of leaders in your church body.

Then we have the "down-and-outers"—precious people on the margin of society. Sandals Church is famous in some circles, and infamous in others, for the mission known as JC's Girls. Launched by the church in 2003, it started when a young woman named Heather, newly removed from the strip club scene, felt led by God to begin a ministry to women in the "industry." But she didn't want to do it by herself. Our women's ministry leader, Lori Albee, had the courage to take the first partnering steps of bringing Jesus to local women in this environment.

When the idea was initially presented, Lori said, "When was the last time I allowed myself to be remotely uncomfortable for God?" In her first trip to a club with Heather, the two women purchased lap dances to get some alone time with some of the girls who were working. Lori later described how she had expected some "skanky" gal to come walking out; instead, it was a beautiful young girl who could have been her own daughter. It cut her to the core. She told me, "God knew what I needed to see that first time." She and Heather proceeded to share with this young woman how much Jesus loved her and how he was reaching toward her, and would be waiting for her. The young girl broke down and cried. She couldn't believe what was happening, that they had come to her that night. One of their stated goals was for the women to know that there were Christians who were not "haters."

Lori told me about one young woman who said she'd often thought of showing up at church but feared she would turn into a pillar of fire. Intuiting the next steps, Lori and Heather decided to offer a place for these women to go. Thus began the gatherings of "JC's Girls." Organized as a mission, they initiated various outreaches and also set up a table at Adult Industry Conventions to reach out and communicate what they were about. Because of their ministry, many women came to Christ and walked out of the sex industry.

As you might imagine, these efforts stirred up great controversy within the church and were met with tremendous opposition. Nasty articles were written. Local pastors expressed their concerns to Matt Brown. Yet even after JC's Girls was discontinued in 2008, the movement swept into other cities and still exists today.[135] One of my friends, Marisol, is deeply vested in this outreach right now, bringing gifts and notecards with words

135. Lori Albee (women's ministry director), interview with the author, August 3, 2012.

of affirmation at establishments near Rockaway, New Jersey. Marisol says, "We go because, if we don't, who will?"

Let's be clear: Starting and developing a ministry like this takes leadership guts and a willingness to courageously follow God's Spirit. Along with key member Heather, the catalyzer was Lori Albee. She had the leadership stature, along with the sincerity and sweetness, to make it a viable reality. These are the gutsy leaders we must tap or raise to reach our cities.

## CHURCH PLANTING

Every church should multiply through new plants. According to Dave Ferguson of Exponential, only 4 percent of churches in America are reproducing.[136] To till the soil, host churches must become incubators for kingdom-expansion births. Your path allows you to identify and train the next line of church planters. You must take on Jesus' eyes for seeing their potential, and then groom them to be skilled, godly leaders of the gospel movement. Since not everyone is cut from the planter's cloth, it is wise to use assessment services to give aspirants affirmation and guidance. I have performed many assessments with Southwest Church Planting Network. Because the self-awareness learning curve is high, a probing examination is very valuable in the screening process.

> MORE AND MORE CHURCH PLANTERS ARE BI-VOCATIONAL, WHICH MEANS THERE ARE MANY LEADERS IN MISSION-FERTILE WORK ENVIRONMENTS.

Finally, being open to new forms and new wineskins will keep us dialed in to a shifting culture. More and more church planters are bi-vocational, which means there are many leaders in mission-fertile work environments. The simplicity and adaptability of the house church and various micro-church/marketplace expressions also makes the planting process more doable, organic, and impactful without a large outlay of financial support from a mother church. We need waves of simple multiplying structures to

136. Dave Ferguson, "Dream Big" (presentation at Exponential West, October 4, 2017).

penetrate the new, emerging world. Agencies such as Fresh Expressions, which originated in the UK, provide a template for how churches can start mission-focused, ecclesial gatherings (targeting outside groups and niches such as: bikers, artisans, bowlers, locals, addicts, athletes, etc.) to reach the estimated 40 percent of North Americans who will not attend the weekend services of the institutionalized church.[137] In our post-Christianizing world, the "Come to us" mantra should not define or limit us anymore. We also need more racially diversified, multiethnic church plants. Pastor Jonathan Bilima of Relevant Church, a growing church plant in our city, has championed this vision, saying, "We have a cross-cultural perspective. The cross brings us all together."

## HARD ASSESSMENT: REUNION WORTHY?

With all the preceding chapters, I placed the hard assessment up front. In this chapter, however, I feel it fits best here, near the conclusion. I trust you will see why as you read on.

The television show *Lost* quickly became a cultural phenomenon with a gigantic following. When, after six seasons, the producers finally chose to call it a wrap, the closing episode stirred up much anticipation (and sparked the planning of more than a few viewing parties). Everyone (13.5 million in America, plus viewers in nine other countries) sat on the edge of their seats, wondering how they would end it.

Fittingly, the finale's script focused on viewers re-experiencing the deep connections that had occurred between the cast members. In a series of projections of scenes from their future lives, the characters bump into significant others from their past, whereupon the physical touch unleashes a flashback to the island and a simultaneous realization of who this person was and how much he or she used to mean. Each revelation became a rite of passage to the final reunion.

Left unresolved amid the tension was Jack's story. With all the main cast members gathered, Kate, in her sweet yet direct way, was the one interceding to get Jack to join up with the group. The writers aptly named

---

137. Chris Backert, "Fresh Expressions: How the Church is Changing to Meet the Needs of a New Generation," (presentation at the Great Commission Research Network conference, October 20, 2017).

him Jack Shephard, emphasizing his role as the primary leader, or "shepherd." Not that the others weren't leaders, but he was important. For the reunion to be complete and right, it could not occur without his presence. He had to be there! For the viewing audience, the build-up conjured what *community* is all about. Jack's dad synthesized the sentiment: "The most important part of your life was the time that you spent with these people.... You needed all of them, and they needed you."[138]

Pondering the conclusion of this epic TV series, I found myself thinking in terms of our relationships as Christians. It stirred within me a disturbing question, one that needs to be asked in your own life, church, and/or organization: How many community experiences have you shared in, large or small, such that, if they were to organize a reunion, it would be incomplete without *you*? Some of us are shrinking down sheepishly, saying, "I don't think they'd even notice my absence. Would anyone really care if I wasn't there? I don't think so!"

Such contemplation makes us feel exposed. But the point goes beyond the pain. Again, how many journeys have you shared with others that required your being there? Think for a moment about your current circles—the people you are journeying with right now. How *reunion-worthy* are your connections? It's a great question. And it's the one I have asked again and again when designing a path. You might think it's simply solved by your attending church or coming to your group meetings, but you'd be wrong. I've had many people come through our church, hear our class teachings, and join various groups, without "it" ever happening. Many come and go without experiencing any sense of this transcendence. Across the land, countless numbers of people participate in endless Bible studies, without any "reunion-worthy" results.

It begs the question, What is it that takes community to these memory-making places? Don't you, as I do, want your life to have that depth of resonance with other people? I've noticed, getting older, that long-term friendships matter. Ministry partners who've battled side by side for Jesus matter in the memory column. Why is that? Isn't it because you participated in something profound? Whether or not you recognized it at the time, if the season was guided around God's purposes, chances are, it represented your life at its very best.

---

138. *Lost*, "The End," ABC, May 23, 2010, written by Damon Lindelof and Carlton Cuse.

My church college group held a thirty-year reunion. It was weird! Time-morphed, grey-haired, no-haired, grown-up twenty-somethings showed up. I found myself saying, "Oh my gosh, is that you?!" As we all reminisced together, we basked in the blessing of an amazing chapter. It may have been cloudy then, but in hindsight, it could not have been clearer that we shared something "reunion-worthy." People had grown spiritually. Some, myself included, had been literally transformed. We had stretched and served "on mission" alongside one another. Because of the battle waged and the toil shared, it had come to mean something more. In answer to our question, most likely, you will have to get more involved, more invested, and more intentional. You will need to go deeper together, be stretched, and get out there on some limb for God! Can you see how you must widen the target beyond a series of teachings? It was from this prophetic assessment that we knew classes alone would not do it. People needed communal experiences. The class extensions became the design feature that took it into the experiential, transforming it into something richer and more memorable. What you must aim for will take people into the missional heart of Christ.

Perhaps your current course is just now beginning to evoke something "reunion-worthy." Or maybe you haven't even begun to enter those places, relationally or missionally. Don't settle for less than creating environments and experiences that leave people wanting more and keep people coming back.

———

The next chapter addresses the ultimate stage, "step OUT." You can't miss this one!

## REFLECTIONS

1. Can you perceive this stage in your church body: the Christ-loving person who is not rising into mission prominence like he or she could be? Share your immediate thoughts on the value of this type of second-level training.

2. What ideas came to mind as you read the PR (personal record) intention of the "step UP" stage?

3. Can you see how this next stage will enable you to develop and identify leaders for your engagement structures: community, compassion mobilization, church planting, etc.?

## REMISSION TAKEAWAYS

1. Zeroing in on higher levels of mission training will make a definitive difference in your church or agency.

2. Church leaders and members alike need specific assignments to undergird their growth potential.

3. Christian community and mission engagement combine to make church experience exceptional.

# —13—

# STEP OUT

Ultimately, a church's health is measured by its sending capacity,
not its seating capacity.
—Rick Warren, foreword to Craig Ott and Gene Wilson,
*Global Church Planting: Biblical Principles and Best Practices
for Multiplication*

Congratulations on reaching the highest step of the discipleship path! That shows something. They say that the cream rises to the top, right? This is, of course, what a sequential path does—raises your people to a new level. Of the four steps, you will find the final stage to be the most visionary. The class and materials will invite your people to dream. Not pie-in-the-sky dreaming, but the kind of training that equips them to pursue the realization of kingdom goals. In this stage, you will inspire them, and they, in turn, will inspire you!

Whether you lead a church, a mission organization, or another type of group, your specified vision should seep into the interactions you have with those you lead. Not only will this enable you to drive key values further, but this quadrant eyes the associated values through an idyllic lens. You will adopt the highest standards, not expecting perfection but rather chasing hard after Christ in formation, transparency, sacrifice, service, courage, and fruitfulness. This is only fitting for people of faith, who, despite their limitations and flaws, are connected with a miraculous God who chooses to use ordinary people to accomplish extraordinary feats. Your church or group will be sowing potent seeds. Though you may not reap immediate fruit in every area, how thrilling will it be to see the harvest in the months and years ahead? It's exciting to create anticipation for what God can and will do!

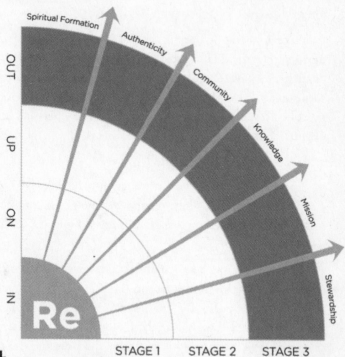

**RE-MISSION MODEL**

To show how this stage works, let's highlight the value of stewardship. In lieu of teaching basic stewardship principles and practices of the earlier stages, here, you will be asking members to ask themselves the big stewardship question: "What does God want to do with the totality of my life, including my gifts and resources?" That inquiry will take your people into another stratosphere of thought, and some may contemplate giving significant portions of their time, talent, and treasure. It will stir their minds and hearts to go big and to be all in!

Likewise, in setting the mission value, you are not merely focusing on building mission skills and experiences; you are asking: "Where is God leading you to invest for the long haul?" In this stage, you will task each person with drafting a personal mission statement. Not that anyone has to have it all figured out, but you want your people to begin thinking in tangible and strategic ways about the unique part they will play in advancing

God's kingdom. Thus, you will be asking, "What greater things does God want to do through you? And what will your particular story be for his kingdom work?"

Like an artist before his canvas, you frame the picture. But it will be up to each individual to color it in. At this point in the progression, the participants have already taken out their paintbrushes; you may have even seen some strokes of brilliance. Yet we also know that God has much more in store. That is what is so exciting about the Christian life: We go further up and farther in!

IN – ON – UP – **OUT**

Here, we see how the path is composed of four "I's": Invite, Involve, Improve, and Inspire. Each person stepping into your church is included in the faith, involved on a path, improved by levels, and then inspired to dream.

This final stage, appropriately, assesses personal gifting (a survey/interactive process given as either an extension of the second stage or a means of stoking their passion in the third!). Their *gift-shape* is a directional key to be discovered. Our infinitely personal God has ordained his people's strengths. We must help his people to discover and use their natural and spiritual gifts without their losing sight of the prime mission directive. As vital players in God's harvest fields, they have been assigned an awesome plan. Let's make sure they don't miss it!

> WE MUST HELP HIS PEOPLE TO DISCOVER AND USE THEIR NATURAL AND SPIRITUAL GIFTS WITHOUT THEIR LOSING SIGHT OF THE PRIME MISSION DIRECTIVE. AS VITAL PLAYERS IN GOD'S HARVEST FIELDS, THEY HAVE BEEN ASSIGNED AN AWESOME PLAN.

For many, it will be in this stage that greater mission dreams take root. One day, I noticed that the initials of the path are: I.O.U., followed by Out.

How cool! It made me think of Paul's stated obligation to the gospel (see Romans 1:14). Moderns may want to avoid such language, yet Paul understood that his salvation could not be merely internalized. Paul's statement "I am obligated," as well as Isaiah's "Send me" upon his being cleansed (see Isaiah 6:8), have something powerful in common. These men were not merely reached; they were *re-missioned*. They had powerful experiences that undeniably resulted in the bestowing of God's mantle upon them. Later in his life, Paul voiced, "I was not disobedient to the heavenly vision." (See Acts 26:19.) Hopefully, in this phase, your people have an epiphany, or an encounter with God, that will result in their coming to a similar, pivotal place. Though some will be called to affect their own culture, community, or city, others will hear the call to global missions.

Having addressed local mission threads along the way, in this chapter, I give special treatment to the international picture. Like the 59-mile aqueduct of the Romans, Jesus calls us to go to the ends of the earth.[139]

## HARD ASSESSMENT: AMATEURIZATION

It is sobering to admit how unprepared for the mission fields we can be. All you have to do is take a wide-angle-lens view of global religions to get an overwhelming sense of this. Consider the major categories using the acrostic "THUMB":

Tribal: Animistic—the spirit world.

Hindu: Pantheistic—God is the cosmos.

Un-religious: Secular—the lost world.

Muslim: submitted ones to Allah's law from his greatest final prophet.

Buddhist: the middle way's noble path of escape.[140]

In the spirit of the visionary, teachers must grab their Indiana Jones hat, whip, and pistol—the adventure is out there! Modern mission's founder William Carey was accustomed to saying, "To know the will of God, we need an open Bible with an open map." Education is fertilizer for mission. Learning about the world and its diverse peoples and cultures is one

---

139. "Watering Ancient Rome," *PBS NOVA* (February 22, 2000). Available at: http://www. pbs.org/wgbh/nova/ancient/roman-aqueducts.html (accessed October 14, 2014).
140. https://joshuaproject.net/resources/prayer_videos.

challenge; learning how to reach others and facilitate mission within those cultures is another matter altogether. It invokes the proverbial critique: "If you can't reach someone here (in your own culture), what makes you think you can reach someone there?" To illustrate just how wide the preparation gap is, let me share an observation from one of our murkiest mission fronts.

EDUCATION IS FERTILIZER FOR MISSION. LEARNING ABOUT THE WORLD AND ITS DIVERSE PEOPLES AND CULTURES IS ONE CHALLENGE; LEARNING HOW TO REACH OTHERS AND FACILITATE MISSION WITHIN THOSE CULTURES IS ANOTHER MATTER ALTOGETHER.

―

As I munched naan and sipped coffee with a seasoned missionary in West Bengal, India, my brain brought forth a scene from the movie *The Matrix*. It was not a direct parallel but rather a tributary idea that began to shed light on a concept that is difficult to wrap one's head around. I had come to the other side of the world seeking this insight. Hang with me, here. By the way, you may not have observed it lately, but Hindus live all around us. We do business at a Postal Annex with our Hindu friends. India, at a 97 percent non-Christian census ratio for its billion-plus populace (the U.S. is only 330 million), holds the largest unreached people group on the globe.[141]

According to the film script of *The Matrix*, a particularly perceptive man named Neo (played by actor Keanu Reeves) is drawn to a place entertaining the idea that something about the world is amiss. Through his digital wanderings, a door has cracked open, and it appears as if someone is there. In fact, if you have seen this pop-culture flick, you know that the

―――――――――――――――――――

141. Joanna Sugden and Shandoor Seervai, "Where are India's 2011 Census Figures on Religion?" *The Wall Street Journal* (January, 9, 2015). Available at: http://blogs.wsj.com/indiarealtime/2015/01/09/where-are-indias-census-figures-on-religion/.

movie portrays the real world as something different from the visual world we are living in. What is visible to the eye is merely a computerized façade termed "the Matrix."

Searching for and believing in Neo's possible messianic-like role to save Zion and the human race, Morpheus and his crew intervene, entering the Matrix to extract this seemly average young man. Incrementally, at first, so as not to overwhelm Neo, Morpheus provides glimpses of the alternative reality. But this is not enough. The only way for Neo to come to grips with the shocking truth is to see it for himself. Thus, Morpheus offers the choice of the red pill or the blue pill—and down the rabbit hole Neo goes! Losing his lunch—welcome to Wonderland—and being coaxed out of utter shock, he begins to piece together the stark, stripped-back version of true, earthly reality.

Now, we're the ones who are going to do something that feels weird. We, too, must go down the rabbit hole! Think of *The Matrix* storyline, and then invert it. Let me explain why we must do this. What I am suggesting is that Hindus, from their cultural viewpoint as passed down by their ancestors, accept an otherworldly reality already. Unlike materialistic Westerners, they look at the invisible, cosmic world as the real one. This is what the Vedas, Upanishads, and their Sanskrit scriptures have pointed them toward. Other than their love for the game of cricket and their hatred of neighboring Pakistan, Indians can agree on this. And an understanding of this inverted mind-set cannot be overstated, and should not be underestimated, if you are seeking to reach these people.

It's here that the illustration of *The Matrix* helps. It explains why our appeals for what has occurred in the physical, historical world (such as Jesus' life, death, and resurrection), and its verifiable proofs, are a moot point to Hindus. Did you get that? Moot. All our attempts at convincing dissipate without anything sticking. According to their worldview and their wiring, the finite world can never adequately explain the infinite. So, our telling of Jesus' life and divine intervention simply gets absorbed into the myriad of gods they believe in, all of whom are believed to represent one cosmic, all-encompassing reality.

As a result, trying to persuade Hindus with a rational line of argument doesn't work. It would be like trying to convince Morpheus to change his whole view of reality based upon the falsified Matrix. That could never happen. In classic Western thinking, which includes the theistic cousins Judaism and Islam, evidentiary proof is everything. However, to the Hindu's mental and philosophic orientation, it means little or nothing. Hindus do not reason classically, as did the Greeks of old, or today's Westerners. Rather, a bigger concept of reality, outside the present world, drives their thought processes.

The missional implication, of course, is huge! The starting point in reaching Hindus is elsewhere, along an inverted axis. The biblical worldview that you and I hold dearly has not changed. Nor have the absolute truths about God, human beings, and Christ's intervention. What we are learning about Hindus' *starting point* is crucial. If we stand a chance to reach Hindus, the path to truth must begin from an unconventional angle.

Being clueless of this dynamic in my years of college ministry, I see now what occurred with my international student friend Raj, from India. After building a friendship over several months, we began having deeper conversations about religions—Christianity and Hinduism, in particular. Pursuing my Western, rationalistic line of thinking, I pointed to Christ's divinity in classic terminology. Yet I learned the hard way that all my honed, apologetic training, frustratingly, went nowhere. I had no comprehension of how Raj was wired. The result? We spun wheels in our dialogues. There was no place to gain traction or to get any aspect of the gospel to stick.

Though the path to reach Jewish people or Muslims, with their theistic tethers, has rational hooks, the quest to reach a Hindu cannot begin with the same presuppositions. As soon as we are able to drop the classical thinking, then we can get onto what speaks and appeals to these minds conditioned by pantheistic brushstrokes.

Metaphorically, we are like Team Morpheus entering another world, interceding to bring Neo into reality. We must dive in, personally and commutatively, to bring Hindus into the full experiential and eventual reprogrammed awareness of Christ. Can you picture their mental screen flickering and then glitzing as the truth bumps up against the false grid?

HINDUS ORIENT THEMSELVES GODWARD MUCH
MORE THAN WESTERNERS. IN THIS, THEY ARE
FARTHER ALONG THAN EUROPEANS AND THOSE IN
THE SECULAR PARTS OF NORTH AMERICA IN TERMS
OF THEIR FORM OF "SPIRITUALITY."

As for conversational openings, one has to understand Hindus' orientation. Interestingly, Hindus orient themselves Godward much more than Westerners. In this, they are farther along than Europeans and those in the secular parts of North America in terms of their form of "spirituality." They are immersed in religious thinking and have millions of gods with temple worship practices providing a baseline as they seek to rise in spiritual standing. Their religion sits within a "caste" system, which prescribes where people are located in the ascension, from the upper-echeloned, priestly Brahman class all the way down to the lowly, despised Dalits. (This system of human valuation has propagated great injustices, by the way, but we won't get into that here.)

Avoiding what is counterproductive, we do not "fight" them on the rational front. Instead, we invite them to hear about, and to see for themselves, the experience that we have with our God, the One who is "fully integrated" to meet their every need; the only One who can guide them into all truth and bring tremendous blessings. This discovery process of learning, seeking, and experiencing becomes the bridge to the realization that Christ is the transcendent One!

Heading northward from Kolkata to Siliguri on a trip in India, I interacted with my cabbie about his three human-looking gods on his dashboard. "That's Calle," he said. Later, I had the opportunity to converse intimately with Mari, a Hindu mom, with her two daughters nearby. As she explained, "Brahma, the Creator Supreme God, has no form." Can you see the eventual angle on that one regarding Jesus? (See John 1:14.) Thus, the gods serve to help human beings (who live outside the infinite) to understand and relate to him.

From this woman's perspective, religious devotion involved all of life. It wasn't just about keeping religious rituals but rather something she embraced as a way of living. Doesn't that sound Christian, my friends? Ultimately, within pantheistic thinking, they hope to eventually work out their karma, to get off the incarnational wheel and enter the "One." This all makes reasonable, good sense to a Hindu. When we ended the conversation, she was thrilled to receive a Bible from me, assuring me that she would read it. I prayed for God to bring a friend or a group alongside her to secure her comprehension of Christ.

## MISSIONS TRAINING 101

You can see how Christ's paradigm of influence is going to be dynamic in each mission context when you: (1) start where they are, (2) read what they need, and then (3) know where to take them.

If we are to have influence, we have homework to do. Reaching people from other mind-sets, even ones hostile to Christianity, can seem overwhelming. There is only one way forward, and that's preparation. It is the church's responsibility to raise its members to be effective missionary influencers. We start with educating our people about our world. Peer-group learning with those on mission to reach their city or nation can be a means of informing and also providing needed wisdom. We may not be able to learn about and interact with people of every different faith, but we can gain general principles about being wise and sensitive as we use our own faith to build bridges to the unsaved, and apply them with people we associate with in our day-to-day circles preparatorily.

The pattern set by Christ, *Start where they are*, is enormously helpful in every mission context. As trainers, we can help our members be less overwhelmed by giving them a breakdown of the beginning step. Again, in the field, the effective missionary does not have to know everything. This point takes some of the intimidation out of it, thank God. But our people do need to know two things: (1) What the person or people group believes, and (2) The level of conviction held by the person or people group.

Let's start with question 1: What does the person or people group believe?

The conversation always starts with them. Probe with questions. Draw out their point of view. Your members do not need to master the innumerable variations of Hinduism, nor must they know everything about the two main branches of Islam (Sunni and Shia) and their offshoots, like the ultra-conservative forms of Salafism ("salaf" means past or preceding, denoting a call to recover the primitive Islam, which idolizes its earliest followers),[142] nor are they to become experts in every aspect of Buddhism; but they will need to comprehend the beliefs held by any particular person they are trying to reach. As an Indian missionary friend of mine revealed, "Most Hindus are not pure pantheists." What is taught in the classroom is not always adhered to on the street. Drawing out what they believe simplifies and personalizes the engagement. Let the person or group fill in your understanding. Realize that you are building a relationship with the person, not having a onetime interaction. Be patient, be kind, be understanding. Listen. Know that if you are respectful, you will have a chance to continue to talk with those you desire to reach, and will eventually have an opportunity to share your faith in a natural way.

## SOME PEOPLE ARE RELIGIOUS ONLY BY ASSOCIATION, AS A MEANS OF IDENTIFYING WITH THEIR PARTICULAR CULTURE, AND NOT IN TRUE CONVICTION.

The second question is: What conviction level does the person or people group hold?

This is another vital distinction. Are his or her beliefs nominal (in name only)? Or is the person devout? Some people are religious only by association, as a means of identifying with their particular culture, and not in true conviction. There is a huge difference between someone who is nominal versus someone who is devoted, no matter his or her belief system.

142. Stephen Prothero, *God Is Not One: The Eight Rival Religions That Run the World* (New York, NY: Harper Collins, 2010), 51–53.

The answers to these two questions will provide critical information on how to proceed, shedding light on what it will take to reach them for Christ. Teach your people to apply these questions faithfully.

After the December 2015 terrorist attack in San Bernardino, California, some members of my missional group and I had a splendid dinner with a local imam named Imaad and his wife, Jabira. Sitting down together, we enjoyed the delights of a Hindi-Pakistani restaurant and friendly conversation getting to know one another. Throughout the evening, I asked a variety of questions, some personal and some religious. I wanted to learn about the imam's path into his lead role. Imaad shared that he had begun his schooling in the Qur'an when he was very young. During those early, formative years, he actually memorized the holy book of Islam.

Later that evening, one of our members, Pam, shared her testimony. As the conversation broadened, Imaad praised the sacrificial love displayed by Christians who were helping the Syrian refugees, and stated that Muslims admired us for our charitable works of self-sacrifice. He even went so far as to say that Muslims have a lot to learn from Christians. Pam looked Imaad in the eye and told him that she would die for him. Though her statement may seem a bit extreme, it was well-received in the moment, as an expression of deep friendship. Though we all were looking for ways to frame the ongoing relationship (my first step was playing basketball with Imaad and his flock at the mosque!), I knew from the conversation that reaching someone like him would be a monumental task.

What do we know about the imam Imaad? He is a devout minister of Islam and has even memorized their scriptures. I left that initial meeting still sizing up the challenge of sharing Jesus with him and explaining various aspects of Christianity. I knew he would not be reached by loving Christians but rather by a loving Christian with the apologetic skill to eventually back him into a corner. This guy needed to be won to the truth.

Consider the following testimony of Nabeel Qureshi, from his book *Seeking Allah, Finding Jesus*:

> I needed a friend, an intelligent, uncompromising, non-Muslim friend who would be willing to challenge me. Of course, not only would he have to be bold and stubborn enough to deal with the

likes of me, but I would have to like and trust him enough to dialogue with him about the things that mattered to me most.

Little did I know, God had already introduced us, and I was already on a path that would change my life forever.[143]

Here is the generalized path I developed to reach the religious person. Notice the sequence.

Openness ▶ Truth ▶ Courage ▶ Faith ▶ Influence

When our missional group attended an event at RZIM (Ravi Zacharias International Ministries) on Islam, the seminar title was carefully crafted: "Understanding and Answering Islam." Why not just "Understanding Islam"? Don't we just need to love Muslims to Christ? Like Nabeel, the people at RZIM realize that it is impossible to reach Muslims outside of answering Islam. We must sharpen ourselves (and others) to bring God's truth into a false system.

In contrast, consider the starting point of Nasra, who had never read anything in the Qur'an. Such is common among Muslims. Many of them receive their Qur'anic instruction from their local imam. Nasra was a Muslim of low conviction. When she opened the Qur'an and began comparing it to readings in the Bible, she was shocked at what she found. Kris and Jamie, members of our church, drove into Los Angeles, where they dropped off Kris so that Jamie could pick up Nasra (for Muslims, male-female protocol states that men do not even shake hands with Muslim women). They followed this routine for many weeks on end. Nasra finally came to faith and is now a Christian apologist!

Of all the categories of unsaved people, the religious person of a different culture is particularly difficult to reach because his or her beliefs are not merely tethered to the rational faculties but are also bound by sociological loyalties. This is why I call these types of converts to Christianity the "heroes of faith." It takes an incredible amount of courage to turn from the long-held beliefs of one's family and culture in order to embrace faith

---

143. Nabeel A. Qureshi, *Seeking Allah, Finding Jesus: A Devout Muslim Encounters Christianity* (Grand Rapids, MI: Zondervan, 2014), 117.

in Christ. They are the ones who fulfill the words of Jesus in Luke 14:26: *"If anyone comes to me and does not hate father and mother, wife and children, brothers and sisters—yes, even their own life—such a person cannot be my disciple."* The extent of one's difficulty with culture change will vary, depending upon his or her starting point.

> THE RELIGIOUS PERSON OF A DIFFERENT CULTURE IS PARTICULARLY DIFFICULT TO REACH BECAUSE HIS OR HER BELIEFS ARE NOT MERELY TETHERED TO THE RATIONAL FACULTIES BUT ARE ALSO BOUND BY SOCIOLOGICAL LOYALTIES.

In my travels abroad, it has struck me as a major barrier, an obstacle that's almost impossible to overcome—how the sense of belonging, in a religious sense, is reinforced through family rituals, cultural connections, names, dress, media, laws, customs, calendar events, and ideological concepts. Observe a Muslim, Buddhist, or Sikh in full garb, and you'll get what I mean. How daunting it is to break through real and perceived barriers alike, when so many religious strands are interwoven around one's identity.

This explains in part why, in missions today, there is so much focus on creating movements. How much better to baptize Muslims in groups than as isolated individuals? This was the insight and strategy expressed by Greg Livingstone in his book *Planting Churches in Muslim Cities*.[144] He saw the advantage of the urban context, where the anonymity of the city afforded individuals a chance to do their spiritual searching under the radar.[145] Over twenty years ago, Livingstone understood how paramount was "gospel key" communication. He writes, "Muslims are led to that experience by being helped to envision how their deepest needs can be satisfied by a

---

144. Greg Livingstone, *Planting Churches in Muslim Cities: A Team Approach* (Grand Rapids, MI: Baker Books, 1993), 38.
145. Ibid., 163–172.

living, caring, powerful Messiah who, if called upon, is personally available as mediator between God and people."[146] (See Qur'an 3:45.)

Creating communities of belief and mutual support is smart in that it recognizes the cultural barriers that exist. Movement ideology is strategic for other reasons. We want to reach whole groups and tribes, not just rogue outliers, to get sociological forces swinging in the direction of Christianity. Books such as *Miraculous Movements* and *A Wind in the House of Islam* highlight this importance, and how the dynamic can occur. Communities of support also put the onus for God's movement where it should be: among the indigenous peoples. It is good for Westerners to admit that the potential impact of the gospel lies not with us but with them. In truth, coming from the outside, we cannot touch the passionate love that they have for their own people.

Everyone must learn Christ's pattern and principles for gospel influence, but creating the places and pockets for new followers to land and learn makes following feasible. More will be reached and discipled when real community undergirds their courage. As you are coming alongside others and sharing your faith, projecting a picture of their future helps (Skill #8: Projecting). They may have never even contemplated what their life would mean, or how it might look, if they were Christians. We must help them consider what that real possibility could be, and then create anticipation for making that step.

Developing strategies apart from understanding a person's starting point—his or her worldview and any major cultural barriers to Christian belief—will lead only to spinning wheels. Dialing in our efforts to the right faith-formation process will garner results. Believe me, there are many missionaries, both abroad and at home, who have not been effective, not because God wasn't powerful enough, or the gospel wasn't personally relevant, but because they were not well tuned to the requirements of faith formation. As to preparation, you always work from the outside in—from their worldview to the barriers to embracing faith—to get the picture of what your faith-formational activity will need to look like.

---

146. Ibid., 140.

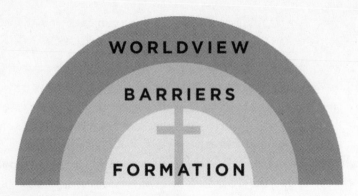

## TRENDING THE GLOBAL CHALLENGE

Do you recall the opening words of Galadriel in *The Lord of the Rings?* "The world is changed. I feel it in the water. I feel it in the earth. I smell it in the air. Much that once was is lost...." Her soliloquy could not be more resounding for modern missions. The global panorama is a moving landscape, and *whatever lies ahead will not be what it has been.* Just as every snowflake is unique, God does not copy. Frontier leaders do well to stay on their toes, observing, adapting, and shifting strategies as they go.

How fascinating that France, a country with only 8 percent evangelical Christians,[147] has produced the TV series *Les Revenants,* translated "The Returned." The show depicts the nation's pervading skepticism as teenager Camille reacts to Christian dogma, "I don't believe that bullsh-t." The 2012 program (MA rating) was awarded an international Emmy for best dramatic series. Indeed, it was artfully crafted and carried a spiritual dialogue. Confounded by reported sightings of deceased persons reappearing (not as zombies), the Police Captain (C) and the local Priest (P) have the following exchange:

P: Don't worry about Simon. He's dead. He's nothing but a ghost that she'll soon forget about.

C: Was Jesus considered a ghost when he came back?

P: Why bring that up?

C: He was here. Physically speaking in flesh and blood?

---

147 "Are Revival Fires Burning in France," *Christian Newswire* (February 1, 2016). Available at: http://www.christiannewswire.com /news/438705507.html.

P: You can't take things so literally.

C: I'm a cop, not an intellectual. I need to understand. Chloe learned Jesus was resurrected. Is it for good or not?

P: The question is irrelevant.

C: What do you mean? Do you believe it?

P: Of course.

C: So if you were told...that people returned...were resurrected... you'd believe it?

P: Faith is what's important. Believing is more important than seeing. The rest is a mystery.

C: My job is revealing mysteries! Do you believe it or not?

P: You don't ask the right questions.

C: You don't give the right answers.[148]

That discourse just blipped on the French radar! The potential for movement is everywhere, even in the hardest of soils. We need many more missionaries who are trained and mobilized to penetrate these regions. The primary responsibility lies with the leaders of local churches.

Over a decade ago, when I first taught pastors in Kenya, I mentioned the term "atheism" in one of my talks. After the lesson, Kenyan leader John Njoroge, now with Ravi Zacharias's team, stated, "Gary mentioned atheism. That is coming here." I was taken aback to realize that it wasn't there already, but his prediction came true in 2015, when atheism grew markedly in his nation. Based on various reports, shifts are also taking place in regards to evangelism, in that long-used crusade methods are proving less effective. Will Kenya move from its modern-minded mainstay to embracing postmodern forms of authenticity? We'll just have to see, won't we? What ground currents are afoot with the youth that the old guard hasn't yet seen? Such missiological measures are vital to gauge.

---

148. *Les Revenants*, "Victor," French TV, December 3, 2012, written by Fabrice Gobert and Emmanuel Carrère, directed by Fabrice Gordert, https://www.netflix.com/watch/70295932?trackId=200257859.

Allow me to frame a few factors that currently exist as we go forward into the newly emerging global community. Here are some takes on trends in missions. May they inspire your vision and stimulate your dreams.

## TEAMS AND TERMS

Shrinking are the days of solo savior-missionaries sent as the lone gospel representatives to unreached people groups across the globe. Leading churches now send teams of people who provide one another with intrinsic support and who are better able to spearhead indigenous church-planting efforts.

Working as a team makes good sense—and it will likely seem much more attractive and safe to your people, as they see mission couched within community. In other words, they think it's exciting to go on a long-term, thrilling adventure with friends! Approaching the mission challenge this way has benefits for the participants and also for the sending church. When your team lands, there is a higher level of home-church involvement and awareness, which is exciting for the church—for those who remain behind.

Coupled with the team emphasis are elongated terms of service (i.e., long-term mission efforts), where relationships and language mastery can ferment into real influence. One of Sandals' mission teams in Turkey had set the bar high, with a ten-year minimum commitment for those doing an in-country stay.

## REGIONS AND RISK

With the cat out of the bag regarding our proselytizing intentions, the gospel message, with its beloved Bible, is now outlawed in dozens of countries. News flash: Add Russia to the list.[149] Missionary "anonymity" is a new watchword. In some contexts, aggressive telling can create backlash to our kingdom aims, and may end up causing trouble for those coming behind. Again, we must be as shrewd as serpents and as innocent as doves. (See Matthew 10:16.) This wisdom is a growing reality to manage missions endeavors both locally and globally.

---

149. Mark Woods, "Outrage at Russia's 'Unconstitutional' Crackdown on Religion, Evangelism," *Christianity Today* (July 13, 2016). Available at: http://www.christiantoday.com/article/outrage.at.russias.unconstitutional.crackdown.on.religion.evangelism/90527.htm.

With rising awareness, we know that a major section of the globe is primarily unreached. The 10/40 Window fits the apostle Paul's vision to go to where no one else has gone before, or where few Christian missionaries live, relatively speaking. That sector includes Europe, the Middle East, India, and Asia. In our current scenario, dangers and persecutions are real possibilities. Talking to my two boys before heading to the Middle East, I referenced J. K. Rowling's classic tale in which Sirius Black says to Harry, "What's life without a little risk?" It's a timely point, and one that must find Christian hearts. What's life when it's played too safe, when our ship remains anchored to the shore? And what are ships for? We need courage if we are to reach the greater world. The church has always grown by the blood of its martyrs.

> ## WE NEED COURAGE IF WE ARE TO REACH THE GREATER WORLD. THE CHURCH HAS ALWAYS GROWN BY THE BLOOD OF ITS MARTYRS.

Pushing the church forward is a sovereign God who has overseen and orchestrated the paths of men since time began. From his inexorable hand over Abraham and the line of faith, to the protective diversions of a young pregnant Palestinian couple on pilgrimage to and from Bethlehem, to the expansion of a new faith in the hostile climate of the Roman Empire, God has always achieved his aims in the context of risk.

Teaching evangelism in Middle Eastern environments presented me with a new learning curve. Imagine living in a culture where it's hazardous to talk about your faith. Sudanese Pastor James Aldama belongs to a contingent of people who immigrated to Egypt during the civil war. He told me, "In Sudan, you could talk to anyone, but here, trying to convert a Muslim is illegal." We knew that when we had entered the country in order to train church leaders, our activity was considered unlawful, as well, and could result in deportation—or worse! Stepping onto the soil of the 10/40 Window caused me to meditate deeply on Jesus' "man of peace" motif.

Reaching people in unfriendly environs requires making a read on the person you are sharing with, one who has the character not to harm, and one whose character can be a conduit to others. However, let me add, being with them (the Sudanese), I was impressed by their boldness in stewarding the gospel. They knew what was at stake!

## MULTIPLICATION AND EMPOWERMENT

Far more than the North American church, foreign mission leaders today think in terms of multiplication. There is good reason for this. The bulk of my time in India was spent shadowing a man working with Disciple Making Movements (DMM), where multiplication through discovery Bible study is everything.

Now, the context of post-Christian North America and the religious climate of India are light-years apart. To demonstrate just how far removed they are from each other, I observed how group expansion was fueled by the sheer volume of closely related family members coming to Christ, which often included the leader's own spouse, kids, and closest of kin. Can you imagine a North American pastor founding a church by reaching his own spouse? This is what it's like to do mission where 97 percent of the people identify with Hinduism or with another faith that isn't Christianity.

Gathering regionally, leaders came forward to chart their efforts, showing the network of groups they had launched. Beginning with evangelistic focus, searching for the catalyzing *man of peace*, they launched a group where people were reached and baptized, and then key members broke off to work the same progression. Multiplication ideology is critical in these regions because creating a movement is the only way to make a dent for the kingdom of God. The web of relational networks acted as kindling to the fire.

We concentrated our time with pastors/leaders in two cities in two of the twenty-nine confederation states that comprise India where diversity seemed to mark the territory the most. The individuals best able to read the regional distinctions were the indigenous leaders. The Bible Discovery method worked well because it avoided trying to win converts through the convincing game. This method simply lets the Word speak and bear practical fruit, trusting that influence will come over time. The order isn't "believe, belong, behave" but rather "behave, belong, believe."

Finding what works for a culture—the contextualization of the gospel—is a practice that's biblically founded. Paul was especially savvy when it came to this method, saying, *"To the Jews I became like a Jew, to win the Jews....I have become all things to all people so that by all possible means I might save some"* (1 Corinthians 9:20, 22).

The relationship between cultural identification and Christian distinction for Muslims is hotly debated. A man using the pseudonym John Travis created a template to rate the extent of cultural association on a scale of C1 to C6. Take a moment to read a selection of his delineations:

C3 believers have Muslim backgrounds and call themselves Christians.

C4 believers identify themselves as "followers of Isa the Messiah."

C5 believers are viewed as Muslims by the Muslim community and refer to themselves as Muslims who follow Isa the Messiah.

C6 believers are perceived as Muslims by the Muslim community and identify themselves as Muslims.[150]

The above spectrum prompted the saying, "C4 and no more" (which is my position), but not everyone agrees on this point. Assimilation of culture facilitates the reaching of people, but there are limits. Within each culture, what must we rejoice about, reject, or redeem?[151] Many aspects of culture can be celebrated—those that are morally neutral. Yet some cultural mores may be inherently evil and thus require dissociation (such as the practice of hunting for someone's head). Other facets may be honorable but require Christ's redemption. For example, the word Muslim (meaning "submitted one") is not wrong in concept; the tension is that it stems from a false religious system.

---

150. John Travis, "The C1 to C6 Spectrum: A Practical Tool for Defining Six Types of 'Christ-centered Communities' Found in the Muslim Context," *Evangelical Missions Quarterly* (October 1998), 407–08.

151. "Christ and Culture–Part 1: Rejoice, Reject, Redeem," YouTube Video, 45:04, conference presentation on July 20, 2015, posted by Illuminate, September 12, 2015, https://www.youtube.com/watch?v=-IaJixvbL_I.

As we work through these evaluations, we must be quick to listen and slow to judge. Missionary Ronna said this of her methods of processing: "He who thinks he knows something knows not. I had to release the need to be right, to come to an answer inside the context of love and relationship."

> IN NO WAY ARE WE TRYING TO PROMOTE WESTERN CHURCH VALUES. THE FUTURE CHURCH NEEDS TO BE FULLY TIPPED FOR EVERY PEOPLE GROUP. IT MUST CUT THE REINS OF CONTROL, POURING INTO NEW FORMS THAT FIT EACH CONTEXTUAL SITUATION.

In no way are we trying to promote Western church values. The future church needs to be fully tipped for every people group. It must cut the reins of control, pouring into new forms that fit each contextual situation. Who is positioned to make that call? Often, indigenous Christians see the lines better than we do. Let's trust them to run with it! Under the missions agency Serve U, my role is training leaders to synergize Christian movements. One of the liaisons we support is an African pastor who oversees an interdenominational network that we formed in extension to our conferences. We do the same thing in Egypt, training and networking with pastors and leaders. If you are a pastor-equipper and haven't yet gone out into the frontier to train, may I encourage you—please go! Translators will take your words and make them even better. It will bless your soul to see your name and notes scribed in Swahili, Arabic, Mandarin, or Hindi. When you return home, you will find that God has broadened your mind as to what he wants to do through you and your people.

## SUPERNATURAL FAITH AND POWER ENCOUNTERS

One of the thrilling things about missions is how it engages our supernatural God. Partnering with Ethnos Asia, some close friends have journeyed into closed countries where the government opposes Christian gatherings and gospel proliferation.

On one trip to communist Vietnam, smuggling in hundreds of Bibles, anxiety mounted as my friends anticipated passing customs with their spiritual contraband in hand. Upon entering the checkpoint, suddenly, they heard a loud snap. A commotion followed, with PA announcements rerouting all the baggage checkers to deal with the crisis—the conveyor belt had ripped apart. With this distraction, the team walked their bags of Bibles through security unchecked and unmolested. Marveling, they exclaimed, "Only God!" These types of rich faith-building experiences await your people as they step out and participate in his movement.

Satan adjusts his strategy regionally, keeping his minions underground in rationalistic cultures, and overtly engaged in places of religious perversions. In the lives of religious people holding superstitious leanings, the gospel often advances through power and dominion. Confrontations with the demonic realm—through prayer and intercession, and sometimes through signs and wonders—are more commonplace in those cultural contexts, and become ways for lost religious people to see the superior power of Christ's name. Though this is unfamiliar turf to most Westerners, it parallels the overt demonic activity we read about in the New Testament. From Zion to Zeus, as the gospel extended outward, God revealed himself miraculously. (See, for example, Acts 14.) I see this as a positive thing overall. Being exposed to the spiritual battle does wonders to ignite people's faith and passion.

## TENTMAKING AND PARTNERING

From Paul's mission-supporting livelihood, tentmaking puts Christians in countries to contribute tangibly to their new homeland and legitimize their presence, while creating a platform for sharing the gospel.

As to partnering, besides denominational agencies, many solid organizations exist to support missionaries and teams: Frontiers, New Tribes Mission, Pioneers, and Ethnos Asia, to name just a few. It is comforting to know that others have gone before you—others who have insight on how to spearhead God's mission thrust.

Allow me to conclude this chapter with a story of a recent encounter.

## SWEET CHARIOT

Embarking from LAX, I selected a seat on the Emirates Airbus, only to find myself sandwiched between two rather intriguing international gentlemen. One, a big-shouldered man from Nigeria in the aisle seat, had me scrunched in the middle. During the sixteen-hour flight, he passed on all meals, preferring shots of liquor instead. Not surprisingly, he slept most of the journey. The other on my left, by the window, was a Middle-Eastern man. Later, in conversation, I learned his name was Mahir, and he was a Muslim from Lebanon on his way back home after visiting friends in the U.S. He came across as sensitive, educated, and unassuming.

As the flight began, and before I had engaged in any conversation with these men, I could not anticipate where things might go, discussion-wise, with either seatmate. Honestly, I was in no rush to find out. Having made this trek many times, I knew that this aerial leap was brutally long. So, observing the proper pace and checking-out period for any new relationship, I remained passive, unengaged. I intuited that my laid-back posture would facilitate eventual conversation; had I been overly assertive, I might have thwarted any chance of talking. From the nonverbal cues, my sober-minded friend had already picked up something about me: I am an easygoing guy who prefers a less aggressive posture. I was "safe," at least impressionistically. We didn't say a word to each other for nine hours.

Finally, a natural moment occurred where we exchanged introductory pleasantries. Actually, by that time, both of us welcomed a chance to talk. When I learned that he was from Lebanon, my mind's newsreel began racing, and I said to myself, *Wow, isn't that one of the more volatile places on our planet?* He spoke generally about his home country, and I proceeded to inquire more specifically, trying to understand his culture and the religious climate, as well as to gain insights on my new friend. I learned that Lebanon divides almost evenly between Muslims and Christians (Maronite Catholics, Orthodox, and other groups—the largest Christian presence of all Arab nations).[152] I also learned that there is a significant French influence from the early colonial days, with noticeable vestiges remaining in

---

152. Oinkysmith2, "A Forgotten Population: Christianity in Lebanon," *Digital Journal* (March 3, 2007). Available at: http://www.digitaljournal.com/article/131869.

the language and culture alike. Eventually, in the exchange, I probed him directly about his faith.

It came as no surprise to me when Mahir identified himself as a Muslim. He wasn't shocked when I shared my Christian identity. We talked about his family, and Ramadan, as the holiday was nearing its end. I worked the conversation toward our commonality, just as the apostle Paul identified himself with the Athenians by saying, "I see you are very religious…." (See Acts 17:22.) I observed that we believed some of the same things, especially in that we both held to theistic worldviews. Thus, I made a resonating connection, emphasizing unity rather than division. After touching on our common beliefs in God as the Creator, we discussed how all three theistic faiths—Judaism, Christianity, and Islam—agreed with the big-picture stamp of our world. How different we were from those of pantheistic origins, who believe that God and the universe are one—like the Hindus sitting directly across from us. The content of our conversation, at this juncture, had not been all that significant, but setting the right tone sure was.

Then I added that, as he already knew, there were also major differences, especially when it came to Jesus. However, it was too early to go there. We kept to a more agreeable line of conversation, sharing thoughts on Middle Eastern versus American culture, for a while.

Eventually, I began to feel my way into a deeper dialogue. I inquired about his family's faith connection, knowing how strong that mooring is for a Muslim. Seeking to draw out his thoughts, I acknowledged that someone coming from a devout family has ties that are difficult to break. Even if someone wanted to believe something different, or came to the place of believing another faith was true, it would take a lot of courage to do so. I put this out there early on, knowing that it is often the crux of the issue.

Framing forward, I made the point that something as important as the tenets of our faith should be something we can discuss openly with others. He absolutely agreed with me. He had had some rich conversations with people of other faiths, and he shared that he had observed how some were not able to have an open discussion. He even mentioned that they needed to "think for themselves." Yes! I seized upon it. That was just what he need-ed to do!

Making sure to honor his personal devotion where I could, layer by lay-er, I moved our conversation from broad agreement into a more specified discussion on why he should reconsider Jesus (Isa). Here is how this hap-pened: When I brought up the basic Christian beliefs about Jesus, at one point, he offered the Muslim viewpoint on how Jesus did not really die on the cross. Of course, if Jesus was just one in a succession of scores of human prophets, then what would have been the big deal or difference? Relegating Jesus' life and death to that of a mere mortal guts the entire meaning of Christianity. Already obvious to him, I acknowledged that this would be one area where we would disagree; but then, I asked if it would be okay for me to share my rationale for my belief. He said, "Sure."

There are reasons to believe Jesus did die on the cross. The first I men-tioned was that the crucifixion event was predicted. I could tell this fact grabbed his interest. I embellished further, saying that in Psalm 22 (the Psalm of the Cross), the psalmist refers to crucifixion 400 years before it was ever employed as a means of carrying out capital punishment. Also, the prophet Isaiah gives a vivid, living-color account of Christ's suffering on the cross 700 prior to Jesus' birth. (See Isaiah 53.)

Another reason is history. Picking up that he was educated and ex-posed to the global climate, I asked if he had seen the movie *Schindler's List*. He shook his head no, so I shared with him the inspiration behind it. The producers, including director Steven Spielberg, sought to counter the notion that the Holocaust was a myth.[153] As shocking as it sounds to us, there were some at the time who were actually saying this well-attested tragedy never occurred. This is why the movie concluded with the living descendants of Schindler's Jews placing flowers at his grave. The film was made for historical record.

---

153. In his Academy Award-winning acceptance speech for *Schindler's List*, Spielberg made a verbal appeal on the importance of history, calling out teachers and saying: "There are 350,000 survivors of the Holocaust alive today. I implore all the educators watching. Please teach this in your schools!" Available at: https://www.youtube.com/watch?v=1HKTYYX50hQ.

I then said, "How would you feel if people started saying that Mohammed was not a real person? That all the big events in his story never happened?" I sensitively appealed, "You would be offended, wouldn't you?" He nodded affirmatively, saying, "It would be an injustice." Then I drew in closer, looked him in the eye, and said pointedly, "We can't just go around dismissing history." In the New Testament, we have four detailed accounts of Christ's life. In each, there is a detailed, realistic description of Jesus' public death on a cross.

I continued, "The accounts are amazingly accurate depictions of death through asphyxiation, where a person can no longer breathe. Modern medicine informs us that when the heart fails under this kind of duress, the lungs fill with a water-like periodic fluid. John's account notes that when the Roman soldier speared Christ *to ensure he was dead*, water and blood poured out. This detail preceded the medical knowledge to explain it."[154] He sat there, listening intently. Nonbiblical historians of the period also affirm that Christ was crucified and buried, as well.[155] Softly now, I said, "The Muslim position takes all this documented history, and essentially tosses it in the trash."

I leaned even closer, wanting to get to a more personal place. "If Jesus is God, then his death was for *you*. He died for *your sins*. We all have sins, don't you agree?" He said, "Yes." I went on, "It is through the cross that he atones for sin and can secure for *you* eternal life." I then asked if had he ever looked at the accounts of Christ's death for himself. "No," he replied. (Note how he had blindly believed what others had told him.) I encouraged him to do what he had advocated for others—to think for himself. At that point, rather off-the-cuff, I insinuated that perhaps I should give him my Bible. I noticed how he perked up at this hinting. I paused to ponder who I was sitting next to, and where he was heading. He wasn't going to be able to mosey down to the Bible bookstore, was he?

That was when I started contemplating actually giving him my cherished teaching Bible, its pages filled with my many meaningful notes. I had

154. See Lee Strobel, *The Case for Christ: A Journalist's Personal Investigation of the Evidence for Jesus* (Grand Rapids, MI: Zondervan, 1998), 198–200.
155. *Josephus Complete Works; The Antiquities of the Jews*, trans. William Whiston (Grand Rapids, MI: Kregel Publications, 1960), XVIII.3.3.

to weigh the decision. Following up with him later, I asked if he could get a Bible. Again, I saw the obstacle and the taboo nature of such a quest. It became a no-brainer. Here was the chance for him to read the Bible for himself. I gave mine to him.

Before doing so, I did show him some of the prophecies, and explained the rationale behind the devotional notes. Muslims don't understand why we write in our Bibles. We see Jesus as the gift of God; they see the Qur'an as God's gift. They practically worship the text, as if it were divine art. You wouldn't scribble on a masterpiece, would you?

> MUSLIMS DON'T UNDERSTAND WHY WE
> WRITE IN OUR BIBLES. WE SEE JESUS AS THE
> GIFT OF GOD; THEY SEE THE QUR'AN AS GOD'S GIFT.
> THEY PRACTICALLY WORSHIP THE TEXT,
> AS IF IT WERE DIVINE ART.

Though it made me feel vulnerable, I left him my name, address, and phone number, in the chance he would decide to call. It was an amazing conversation, and I didn't want to fall short in extending him the opportunity to talk more, especially since I sensed the Spirit moving. A connection had occurred. His heart opened. He truly listened. I prayed for God to do his miraculous work in this man's mind and heart, and for God to take it forward and do what was needed to reach him. Sitting there, I wondered if I would see him one day in heaven.

Later, I ruminated on how awesome it was for God to show up so swiftly. Stepping up to serve internationally, only hours off the tarmac, I had a conversation that felt every bit the equivalent of what took place between Philip and the Ethiopian eunuch in Acts 8. There was a man traveling back to his home country, and God had positioned me in an airborne chariot to talk about Jesus in the truest of ways. Like Philip, I had succeeded to connect some dots. This man needed to see who Jesus really was, and God had sovereignly positioned me for such a moment. As the airplane lights were lowered, some travelers slept, while others chose a movie to watch. I rejoiced in this man's openness to my words, to think for himself, and to read the New Testament accounts.

———

The end is near. The end of this book, I mean. The closing chapter is next.

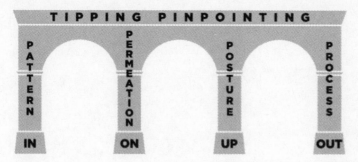

## REFLECTIONS

1. Discuss the six values—spiritual formation, authenticity, community, knowledge, mission, and stewardship—and how you could see a high-level focus helping your people. What would you need to tackle first?

2. Do you believe this stage can help your people to be captured by the call of Christ? What are some tangible ways you can help them catch the vision and passion?

3. Evaluate what have you done with missions thus far and then how can you raise the bar with your path.

4. What obstacles do you foresee that you will need to overcome in order to implement this visionary training? List them in detail.

## REMISSION TAKEAWAYS

1. The third stage creates a contagious vision for people to dream big for God.

2. Mission statement and clarity of gifting are critical undergirding directors.

3. We need more preparation to face the global challenge.

4. Education is mission fertilizer.

5. Developing and sending teams is something all churches can do, especially with great partnering organizations available to help.

# —14—

# LEADING LEGACIES

I am sorry if I'm the one to break this news to you: you were born
into a world at war, and you will live all your days in the midst
of a great battle, involving all the forces of heaven and hell and
played out here on earth.
—John Eldredge, *Waking the Dead*

Watching the smoke from his cigar waft upward, I contemplated
the contours of his bronze, sea-weathered face. These were not
the features of a common tourist. Looking more like a prizefighter still
standing at the final bell, this steely character emanated a gaze you see only
in someone who has paid an inestimable price. He had sailed solo all the
way from South America to Catalina Island. Once he arrived, not being
the type to take selfies (if you know what I mean), he casually asked me to
take his picture with his small craft in the background.

As he sucked on the stogie, I could not help but absorb his accomplishment. Unaware of the details surrounding this stranger's voyage, I
felt strangely honored to be taking his photograph. Peering into his eyes,
I could tell that it meant something to him. A connection occurred, momentarily. I, too, know what it's like to sacrifice for a dream. I am mindful
of leaders like you who have made a journey. Although I will not have the
privilege of knowing all of you or getting a chance to hear the particulars
of your leadership progression, with all its joys and perils, I do know this:
Many of you have sacrificed, perhaps even suffered, for your church and for
the Lord. (If perchance my sentiment is not yet registering, your crucible
is odds-on coming.) As with the man I encountered that day, I sense your

passage hasn't been easy. God has imparted to you a vision, and you have been willing to fight it out for his cause. You would not have read this far if this were not true of you. So, I'm confident this describes you; and, my brothers and sisters, please know I will pause anytime to take your pic!

Since we have come to the end of our time together, I have chosen to close the book on an intimate level. I will share with you some of my personal battles, between myself and God, as they have played out in the mission arena. I trust you will see yourself in them somewhere. My hope is that my transparency will nudge you forward to the place of having your dreams, your resolve, and your hope rekindled or rerouted like mine.

———

I have never gone on a mission trip that was not fraught with fear. But one excursion to Africa, Egypt, and India surpassed them all. Departing to Egypt in the wake of the military coup of President Morsi and his Muslim Brotherhood party, I felt as if we were heading into a hornet's nest. Like déjà-vu, it evoked the memory of my 1986 trip to the Philippines, which nearly got scuttled due to the coup d'état deposing Ferdinand Marcos. In Cairo, the U.S. embassy had shut down. I had not appreciated the value of embassies until that moment. Visions from the film *Argo* ransacked my mind. I couldn't shake it. An aura of anxiety hung heavily over that leg of the trip.

Landing first in Nairobi, we learned that within an hour of our grabbing our luggage, the Departures section of the airport had burned down. Bizarre! We watched the news reports, nervously wondering whether we would be stuck. Various comments we overheard about our host town also unnerved me. The burgeoning truck stop was now headlining papers as "The Wicked City" because of its high rates of murder and prostitution. High walls with steel gates were necessary at the orphanage where we were staying. Security personnel actually had bows and arrows ready to fend off attacks. What era are we in? I secured my door with a padlock but still found it hard to sleep with the strange sounds echoing through the ventilation holes, as well as voices and dogs barking in the streets outside. Waking abruptly to the Muslim call to prayer alarmed my soul to the spiritual battle at hand. Then again, there was the uncertainty of Egypt, and my perpetual consciousness of my loving, anxious wife back home. "I need you to come back," she said as I was leaving. The combination of it all felt oppressive.

Before departing the States, I had succeeded in pushing it all back, deflecting the concerns of friends, just as we'd done before our missions trip to Tijuana, when I knew we would not be in the crosshairs of the drug-dealing cartels, contrary to what the media would have you believe. I told others we'd be fine. But now, with the unrest in Africa as the kettle began to boil over in Cairo, a sense of fear—or, I daresay, dread—began taking root. Perhaps the fatigue from a lack of sleep and the process of reorienting my body clock played a part in my feeling a bit overwhelmed. Lying on my makeshift bed inside the mosquito netting (yeah, malaria prevention), I realized something was off. However, that something wasn't related to the circumstances of the trip; it related to myself. Something was off with me. Why was I so fearful?

Seeing the situation with unusual clarity, I called foul on myself. I was not right, spiritually. I had never identified this type of heart-sin so minutely. I knew I needed to figure this out immediately, or else the vertical misalignment of my relationship to God would render me paralyzed. I couldn't afford to have that happen. So, in a moment of insight, I repented.

This fear has only one antidote: God Almighty! Crying out to the God of heaven, I claimed the name of Jesus and declared aloud, "I will not have the spirit of fear over me for the rest of this trip." I began perusing the Scriptures, claiming their truth and promise. *"The LORD is my shepherd… though I walk through the valley of the shadow of death, I will fear no evil, for you are with me; your rod and your staff, they comfort me"* (Psalm 23:1, 4). I found myself drawn into a time of reflection on great people of faith who lived amid constant fear. We take our security for granted, but they didn't have that choice. David, in the Psalms, writes rather obsessively about God's protection. For a decade, he was on the run with a mile-wide target on his back. Jesus himself navigated his way through malicious, murderous murmurs from scheming zealots; demons; and plotting Pharisees. The realization of this gave me hope. Living abundantly in a fearful climate is possible.

I knew full well that the problem was no one's but my own. Skimming through Exodus, I imagined the Lord reassuring me, saying, "Gary, my son. Think of who I am. I know Egypt. I've been there from the beginning. Don't you remember Abraham, Joseph, and Moses? Have you forgotten my vulnerable parents fleeing from Herod's deathly swipe? Do you think I can't handle your journey into Egypt? I know 'unstable.' I do 'unstable' all the time."

I recalled God's words to Joshua: *"Be strong and courageous."* (See, for example, Joshua 1:9.) Later that night, my phone beeped to indicate a Facebook post. It popped up out of the blue from an old friend, asking whether I had watched the movie *Courageous*. Marveling, I thought, *I just got texted by God!*

Almost immediately, my heart began to change. The next morning, I awoke as a totally different person. Out for a predawn run, I discovered that the high-gusting winds had swept clear the African sky. When I looked skyward, I saw the constellation Orion gleaming boldly and brilliantly, declaring to me, and to the whole universe, "Your God is a warrior!" Spiritual acuity had descended. The circumstances remained the same, but I had rediscovered my center. I would trust in the Lord—the Maker of heaven and earth; the One who walks before me, hems my days, and directs my every step. I stood with vertical strength. God was with me! I never came out of it. Even in Egypt, when my young Muslim seatmate warned me, "You are coming at the wrong time," or when the reports of deaths and attacks against the Coptic Church filtered into the conference, or when we drove through a stirred-up, "tire-burning" Cairo, fear had no grip on me.

Friends, I don't know if you have ever faced the paralyzing properties of fear or dread as I have. Perhaps I have bigger timidity issues than most. I know that many people have faced circumstances that were exceedingly more harrowing. But fear, by its very essence, does not even have to be in the present. So, I can guess that you, too, know the experience. My question is, Has God backed you deeply enough into his corner that you've found your small self before the enormity of his greatness?

Along the line of missions, do you ever find your heart faltering when you hear God's call to reach this world? Do you feel a hindering hitch when you consider what it will take to make your church missionally lethal? We all know it's easier to default into planning impactful church services. However, to teach influence skills to your people—to take on big challenges in your neighborhood and city; to risk launching a new church; to get serious about penetrating the dark places of the city or the hostile sectors of the globe—is different.

How does it feel to draw up plans to penetrate the 10/40 Window? Does the illegality of our gospel business conjure any scary images? How does the word *Jihad* strike you? Stepping out or contemplating the idea of following Jesus into a region of inherent risk, would you ever wonder if you would be okay? Ever hear that pestering, sinister voice say, "Don't do it, because something might happen"? Friends, let's talk some sense into ourselves. Our God is mighty big! Don't refrain because of unbelief. Don't succumb to the safety-first, security-driven voices from those around us who *don't know God* or don't have a grid for risk. Mothers and spouses, because of their concern for your well-being, can also unwittingly hold you back.

> OUR GOD IS MIGHTY BIG! DON'T REFRAIN BECAUSE OF UNBELIEF. DON'T SUCCUMB TO THE SAFETY-FIRST, SECURITY-DRIVEN VOICES FROM THOSE AROUND US WHO DON'T KNOW GOD OR DON'T HAVE A GRID FOR RISK.

I am not saying we should be reckless; and, let me be clear: We weren't being heroes on this journey. If they had told us it wasn't safe, we wouldn't have gone. As to training others to reach Muslims, when we talked of *obeying God rather than men*, we did so with a stature unbeholden to anything that we said. The pastors knew we had come in spite of the conditions. In the lead group, one voiced, "You knew it was unstable, yet you still came. We are strengthened by that." Those words blessed me! I'll go to my grave wearing that metaphorical necklace of honor. God had many purposes for sending us. One was to bolster the courage of these leaders. Another was to bolster my own courage. I was so glad to be on the right side of faith and not the wrong side of fear.

The sooner we get it, the better. Like David learned, being backed into God's corner again and again is not such a bad thing. Remember when he hid in a cave? (See 1 Samuel 24.) God was on his side. The Lord was present with him. Looking upward, David knew that when we entrust our lives to God and hide beneath the wings of the Almighty, his covering is sufficient. Is it time to get truly vertical? I will call it out declaratively: May fear never hold *you* back from doing all that God wills for you to do. May your church or mission become a major force in the spiritual war of the coming decades!

## THE OTHER WING

While consulting with pastors, I have identified a need for supplemental vision. I'll admit that this insight came to me from a place of personal pain. I recall volunteering at Sandals Church for about a year. (A side note: Volunteering somewhere can be epic from an educational standpoint. If you ever decide to volunteer somewhere, make sure you pick either a top-level church, a Fortune 500 company, a cutting-edge mission agency, a local safehouse, or a rehabilitation center. Or, put on a disguise and see what it's like to just sit at your church for a couple months.) Though I love the church, ironically, it was when my involvement was at the lowest ebb of my life, with the least personal visibility, that God taught me some of the biggest lessons I've ever learned.

Working up from the literal bottom in a large church, my new stint at Sandals was a very difficult thing to do. As a leader who was accustomed to calling the shots, I was suddenly outside the decision-making sphere. It was as if God was saying to me: "Shut up and submit!" There were times when I came perilously close to dropping out. Fortunately, I had something ancillary going for me, which I eventually termed the "other wing of the plane." This concept, which I stumbled upon, may help you, too. Let me explain.

As I uncannily began to rebuild a local ministry and found myself grasping for straws, there was another beckoning dream connected to what God was doing in me, and the vision for writing. When I came dangerously close to a ministry crash, this "other wing" provided the necessary lift to keep me in the air. I wouldn't have made it otherwise. Over time, I recognized that God had bestowed a gift upon me. In the moments of diving emotions, I focused on the other wing and thereby found stability amid feelings of displacement and uncertainty. I was able to keep course, somehow. In the bigger picture, God used that other wing to keep me right where he wanted me—volunteering at Sandals. Eventually, I joined the church's ministry staff. While the leadership initially struggled to figure out what to do with me, God knew what to do, pouring out his Spirit for influence—indiscriminate of my past, position, or paycheck.

I often broach the idea of the "other wing" with pastors. Sure, you have your all-important church ministry, but what is the other dream that God is birthing in you? I am not trying to pull you away from a singular aim. I know we must keep ourselves tethered to the grindstone. Church-planters must think of nothing else. You know, that "take a deep breath, and hope to see you on the other side" type of thing.

> YOU NEED TO REALIZE THAT GOD INTENDS
> TO DO SOMETHING THROUGH YOU IN THE LARGER
> REALM THAT WILL BLOW YOUR MIND.
> HIS PLANS FOR YOU ARE GREATER THAN WHATEVER
> YOU ARE ENVISIONING RIGHT NOW.

Get this: Your church or mission is not the only measure of your life. Nor is it the exclusive focus of God. Sometimes, church can be a big-time bummer. People are sinners. Just because they're Christians doesn't mean they can't be giant jerks at times! Statistics tell us that one third of pastors will be fired sometime in their career. Many will be greatly disappointed. Most of us will be hurt. I am not trying to depress you, but a little realism goes a long way in ministry.

What has God divinely determined that *you* would contribute—perhaps to the greater church, or to your denomination, or beyond your local ministry? What is your "other wing"? You need to realize that God intends to do something through you in the larger realm that will blow your mind. His plans for you are greater than whatever you are envisioning right now. You need to be open and sensitive to the Lord's leading. Will Mancini describes the power of it: "A defining moment occurs; a particular call from God collides with a concrete need," resulting in "an atomic energy release, filling the leader's heart."[156] The church has many problems and is in desperate need of *your innovating touch*! What will it be? A book? A video series? A needed ministry? A collaborative partnership? A new mission arm this world is crying out for?

Know this: Before your great revisionist work is done, you will have had to face opposition from within and without—foes you cannot underestimate. In *The War of Art*, author Steven Pressfield captures the battle well:

> *Genius* is a Latin word; the Romans used it to denote an inner spirit, holy and inviolable, which watches over us, guiding us to our calling. A writer writes with his *genius*; an artist paints with hers; everyone who creates operates from this sacramental center. It is our soul's seat, the vessel that holds our being-in-potential, our star's beacon and Polaris.

> Every sun casts a shadow, and genius's shadow is Resistance. As powerful as is our soul's call to realization, so potent are the forces of Resistance arrayed against it. Resistance is faster than a speeding bullet, more powerful than a locomotive, harder to kick than crack cocaine. We're not alone if we've been mowed down by Resistance; millions of good men and women have bitten the dust before us.[157]

I don't know what God wills to go after within you to prepare you for what's ahead. But I do know that he loves clean, humble, imperfect vessels. You serve a God who bleeds over injustice and his kingdom cause. He's

---

156. Will Mancini, *Church Unique: How Missional Leaders Cast Vision, Capture Culture, and Create Movement* (San Francisco, CA: Jossey-Bass, 2008), 73.
157. Steven Pressfield, *The War of Art: Break Through the Blocks and Win Your Inner Creative Battles* (New York, NY: Black Irish Entertainment LLC, 2002), 8.

looking down for someone to pick up his righteous mantle. If you are to sustain such an undertaking, then you will need to make a serious attempt at applying the process of Nehemiah 1. Have you ever noticed his threefold progression? Here it is: (1) See it, (2) weep it, and (3) pray it.

First, see the deficiency. As Nehemiah described in detail the dire condition of God's beloved city, you must see the situation with striking clarity. When God gave me the assignment of penning *Soul Whisperer*, I did not see Jerusalem's walls breached, but rather the frontline message of utmost significance being lost. Something divinely precious lies in danger. Is it time to walk the rubble and kick some stones? Look carefully. Assess the situation. Take off the rose-colored glasses. Don't underestimate the power of this birthing piece. You have to *see it*. What is wrong? What must be dealt with and changed? What are the real consequences to lives, the gospel, and God's glorious kingdom?

Then, to summon the emotional courage for the fight, you must *weep it*. This gets personal as you sit in it. Make sure you allow yourself the space to feel the hurt of life, the void of need, the loss of hope, the lack of purpose. When Paul entered Athens and saw that the city was full of idols, he was *"greatly distressed"* (Acts 17:16). Don't fear this visceral experience. In it lies the power behind your pulse. Do your homework. Listen to interviews. Hear actual voices. Experience it. Find some fire and passion for that which breaks God's heart. What is it like to be in those shoes?

FINDING THAT BIGGER VISION PIECE FOR YOUR LIFE WILL BROADEN YOUR VIEW, CREATE NEW INSPIRATION, AND SUPPLEMENT YOUR SPIRITUAL HEALTH.

Lastly, we get to desperation. Here, you *pray it*. "Oh, God, I am here to do your work of rectifying this evil, this thing that I just cannot leave be." "Lord, I know that I cannot do it without you. I do not have, in and of myself, what it will take: partnerships, inspiration, strength, resources, team. I plead with you now, Lord of the universe, mover of hearts of kings, come down for your cause!" Then, and (in most cases) only then, will you be commissioned for God's work.

Finding that bigger vision piece for your life will broaden your view, create new inspiration, and supplement your spiritual health. So many pastors are beaten down within their own picture, feeling stuck in the stagnant ponds of their own making and needing fresh outlets of cool water running over their parched souls. Often, like I did, you just need something else to create lift and keep you afloat. These types of stirrings, shared with trusted colleagues, will renew your spirit. They will open hopeful conversations laced with opportunistic thinking. Of course, the leadings that materialize have to come from the Lord. We all know that unless the Lord builds it, we'd better forget it! (See Psalm 127:1.) Ask him for his divinely ordained design to unfold. You'll know his answer if it's big. In faith, be willing to have him shape and forge you for the assignment.

## HARD ASSESSMENT: *REMISSION*

What I had seen prior to undertaking this project was the need to *ReMission* leaders to become truer, closer, and better at empowering God's people. It was crystal-teary-eyed-clear to me that pew-sitting and soaking up information passively will never produce the vitalizing character and mission muscles that are needed for our time. No matter your position within God's kingdom, as a Christian, you have the calling and capacity to make a life-changing difference, wherever you are planted or are seeking to go. I set out to implant the following ideological hooks:

1.  You are the primary shaper of mission, carrying the mission mantle to others.

2.  You have the power and responsibility to shape a mission culture. Erecting the four pillars can get you there, but you will need to drive those foundations deep.

3.  You increase your people's influence projection directly in two ways: by *tipping* and by *pinpointing*. Horizontal dynamics unleash an ever-expanding, penetrative, empowered church body. Let it pour!

4. You must give your people a clear path into mission. Meet them where they are at every stage, and then lead them forward into Christ's full vision.

Because execution is so crucial, please don't miss the intimate implementation steps I have outlined for you in the Afterword.

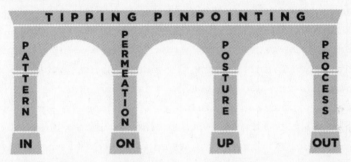

Regarding this great challenge, Jesus has his own words to you, my friend. I will now share a childhood memory that illustrates the manner in which his words came to me.

## FACING UP TO JESUS

The cold feel of barbed wire topping perimeter fences seemed more fitting for a prison than for a junior high school. Oddly, the feature matched the reputation of the inner-city institution Lincoln Junior High. A logistical oversight resulted in our eighth-grade basketball team's being dropped off during recess without even one adult chaperone present. A gang of students, upon seeing us in our uniforms, made a beeline over to us, ready to defend their turf. We felt like meat tossed into shark-infested waters.

With a demeanor that was less than cordial, one of their ninth-grade football players engaged our team leader, an African-American student named Lucius Green, in a bit of street-level trash-talk. After a few back-and-forth barbs, this guy grasped his own shirt, ripped a piece from it, and threw the scrap of fabric in Lucius's face. I had to admit, his way of picking a fight was dramatic. What a warm welcome we were getting! A coach arrived in the nick of time, but the tough guy stuck around for the fight after the game. (By the way, we were the best basketball team in all of San Diego County, and we destroyed Lincoln's team on the court.) Though

Lucius was ready to rumble afterward, a parent intervened to cut off the impending action, and nothing ensued.

There is a lot that I cannot recall from my growing-up years. Vague memories from myriad events hover in my mind. However, I will never forget the moment when that young thug tore a piece from his own shirt and threw it in LG's face. The gesture had such flair! Being gentle, loving, kind, and gracious, our Lord is nothing like him; yet it was a manly Jesus who brandished a whip to drive peddlers from the temple. Still, as a Christian, I never pondered that there might be a time when Jesus would pick a fight with me. It has happened only once, on a day when I was angry, crying out in frustration, and throwing punches with God in prayer over my obscurity. The usual silence stopped. Heaven opened. God came down. The spiritual showdown was as intense as if Jesus had ripped off a piece of his tunic, thrown it my way, and said, "Why, Gary, do you care so much for your concerns?" My feeble voice broke as I attempted to justify myself before him: "But I am leading your church, Lord. I am your servant." Undeterred, Jesus stared me down, as if to say, "Should I really care about your standing or status? What is truly driving you? Is it your dream or mine? Be honest, now."

Gulp!

Though his words were not audible, the cornering was as real as the moisture of another's heated breath. After he called me out, I fell to my knees, confronted. His dream or mine—which was it? Forced to see my self-ambition, I came kicking and screaming to the place of surrender. Like the young rich ruler (see, for example, Matthew 19:16–30), I underwent soul surgery. I had to give up my dream for his. As you can imagine, that moment altered the trajectory of my life. It was the hinge that swung open a new door. Everything changed.

I began to find a new courage. Shedding a part of myself like a snake sheds its skin, I found myself being more like the biblical Timothy—speaking more boldly than ever for the Lord's cause, even if it meant saying something that would not make me popular; challenging the system; disclosing my own darkness, in spite of any risk to my reputation; standing for innovations that bucked the status quo. I detached from self-preoccupation, reckoning that it didn't matter so much what others thought of me, only what they thought of God and the efficacy of his church. It was liberating. *ReMission* had come to me.

I trust you've had your morphing moments, as well—times when God has spoken to *who you need to become*. His love will not allow you to squander your calling, but it may look different from what you'd expect. Just as he questioned Peter three times, "Do you love me?" (see John 21:15–17) and answered negatively Paul's thrice-made thorn-removal request (see 2 Corinthians 2:7–9), the divine voice comes to each one of us. Surely, it will be custom-fitted to your situation. If the heavenly encounter is not already blinking for you, perhaps it's forthcoming. I've prayed for the readers of this book to have that kind of necessary encounter anew. As deep calls to deep, God redresses us for his mission call. In this co-crucifixion, all glory returns to him, does it not?

EVERYONE HAS A SPHERE IN WHICH TO REACH OTHERS. WE MUST LEAVE OUR LAME EXCUSES BEHIND AND THEN MOVE OURSELVES AND OUR PEOPLE INTO PROPER POSITIONING, EQUIPPED WITH SUFFICIENT ENGAGEMENT SKILLS FOR THE GREAT STORY TO UNFOLD.

It is in this spirit that I am asking you, Whose dream are you chasing? The question might seem like a simple query for church leaders, but I submit that it is nothing of the sort. Is it your dream, your vision for the church, a passed-down cultural replication? Or is it God's dream? What lies at the end of your labor? Are you making standard churchgoers who hang on your every word, or kingdom Christians who are pounding on the gates of hell? The underdrawing of the Master cries out! Friends, I am not speaking down to you. On the contrary, I know how important you are to this whole *ReMission* equation. It's because of who I am addressing as you stand at your significant kingdom post that I bring this encouragement and challenge. I trust I am not the only one who needs the laser of *ReMission*. I am praying for you to have a holy moment. Are you on your knees? Allow his searching spotlight to invade your soul, as the psalmist did in Psalm 139:23–24. With his confrontation, God swings the channel of influence wide-open. Everything pivots here. It marks a leader after God's own heart. Are you ready for a divine tattoo?

As we lead the children God has entrusted to our stewardship, every believer must look at Jesus and his mission in the mirror. I don't care who they are: how educated, how accomplished, how heralded, how wealthy, or how lowly. God is not handing out "Get Out of Mission Free" cards. How are they doing in reaching people outside the faith? No doubt, Jesus will have pointed words for them, too. Everyone has a sphere in which to reach others. We must leave our lame excuses behind and then move ourselves and our people into proper positioning, equipped with sufficient engagement skills for the great story to unfold. For this work of God to be fulfilled, it may start with one person, or with just a few of us. But to truly change the world with the life-changing message of our Savior, we need congregations of all sizes to run to the battle with a new mission projection.

## FIGHTING WORDS

This book has championed the need for a new kind of catalytic leader. I have simply offered what comes from the Lord's handiwork of my life and experiences. Allow the storytelling prowess of renowned fantasy writer Christopher Paolini to reveal this truth and its significance.

> "I have done the impossible," she said, the words hoarse and broken. "I made a sword when I swore I would not. What is more, I made it in less than a day and with hands that were not my own. Yet the sword is not crude or shoddy. No! It is the finest sword I have ever forged. I would have preferred to use less magic during the process, but that is my only qualm, and it is a small one compared with the perfection of the results. Behold!"
>
> Gasping the corner of the cloth, Rhunön pulled it aside, revealing the sword....

Overcome by a sense of reverence, Eragon reached out toward the sword, then paused and glanced at Rhunön. "May I?" he asked.

She inclined her head. "You may. I give it to thee, Shadeslayer."

Eragon lifted the sword from the bench. The scabbard and the wood of the hilt were cool to the touch. For several minutes, he marveled at the details on the scabbard and the guard and the pommel. Then he tightened his grip around the hilt and unsheathed the blade....

"Are you well pleased, Dragon Rider?" Rhunön asked.

"More than pleased, Rhunön-elda," said Eragon, and bowed to her. "I do not know how I can thank you for such a gift."

"You may thank me by killing Galbatorix. If there is any sword destined to slay that mad king, it is this one."[158]

What God forged through the cross is life-giving, eternity-altering truth to every person and tribe. It is why Paul urges every believer to fit his feet with *"the gospel of peace"* (Ephesians 6:15) as part of the Ephesians 6 armor of God, and rightly so. It is the gospel that brings peace between a holy God and sinful man, thereby leveling all barriers to eternal and earthly reconciliation.

Yet, in the wider context of "powers and principalities" that rage (see Ephesians 6:12 NKJV), it is not only the gospel of peace, but also the gospel of war! Nothing does more damage to the kingdom of darkness than the message of light. Nothing strikes at the stronghold of our enemy with more consequence than when the gospel is received by captive souls. This means God's people are privileged carriers of a great weapon. Still, most Christians know little about how to pick it up, much less how to wield the divine gift of power. This, in my view, is our premier discipleship void, and it's one of the gaps I set out to close when God first stirred within me the vision of *ReMission*.

Paolini's Inheritance Cycle, of which *Brisingr* is the third novel, conjures the discipling theme in the title of its 52nd chapter: "A Rider in Full." This chapter tells of the master-artisan elf Rhunön, who forges and then

---

158. Christopher Paolini, *Brisingr* (New York, NY: Random House, 2002), 679–80.

bestows upon Eragon the Excalibur-like sword, the ultimate weapon. Now, Eragon's fully armed with what he needs to do the great deed—the deed that he alone can fulfill; the deed that will turn the tide for the whole world. With Brisingr, his personalized sword, he will land the death blow against the evil king.

> TELLING YOUR PEOPLE TO TELL OTHERS ABOUT JESUS IS NOT ENOUGH. THEY NEED YOUR GUIDANCE ON HOW TO RELATE AND COMMUNICATE THEIR FAITH IN NATURAL AND EFFECTIVE WAYS.

Church leaders, I appeal to you—play the role of Rhunön to your people. Honor the gift that belongs to them: the gospel. Then, give them what they need to fight and win—the necessary skills and knowledge to wield its power. Telling your people to tell others about Jesus is not enough. They need your guidance on how to relate and communicate their faith in natural and effective ways. In the Addendum, I have included detailed descriptions of the 10 influence skills for your trainers. Work these skills into the practices of your people to reach many more lives. Godspeed!

Developing your people's mission skills is partly what this book is about. I have shaped you to sharpen them. For their growth, and for the sake of the movement, let's make disciples in full. Let's empower them to enter the enemy's keep, sever his clenching claws of death, and return hearts to the true King.

> The Lord will punish with his sword—
> his fierce, great and powerful sword—
> Leviathan the gliding serpent,
> Leviathan the coiling serpent;
> he will slay the monster of the sea.
> —Isaiah 27:1

My final thought: During this year of writing, I watched the film *The Walk*, which relates the story of the French high-wire artist Philippe Petit who came to New York City to tightrope between the newly constructed Twin Towers. He and his team showed up to do something so outrageous that no one imagined it possible. In 1981, having thoroughly planned the covert and illegal operation, they succeeded in securing a cable between the towers for Petit's high-wire act. When he finished traipsing back and forth, he was arrested, only to be released soon thereafter and celebrated by people throughout the city and then all over the globe.

Petit became such a city favorite, he decided to stay in New York. In order for him to return to the very spot, to remember and relive the triumph, he needed a tourist's ticket; yet, in his case, because of who he was and what he had done, officials at the Twin Towers scratched out the expiration date and scribed instead the word "forever." It fit. Walking that line mattered for the whole line of Petit's life.

WHEN YOU TEACH AND APPLY MISSION KNOWLEDGE, PRINCIPLES, AND SKILLS OF ENGAGEMENT, YOU ARE CATAPULTING PEOPLE OUT OF THE MUNDANE AND TEMPORARY, AND INTO THE ETERNAL REALM OF WHAT TRULY MATTERS BECAUSE IT LASTS FOREVER.

Down at the deepest motivational pools of the spiritual life is the question of why we are here. Of all the words in the dictionary, of all the terms spoken in the world's vernaculars, nothing quite rivals "forever" in gravitas. C. S. Lewis titled one of his provocative essays *The Weight of Glory* to depict how it is Christians who carry the glory of others. What you and your team do in the mission realm matters—not just for the line of your lives, but for the larger line. When you teach and apply mission knowledge, principles, and skills of engagement, you are catapulting people out of the mundane and temporary, and into the eternal realm of what truly matters because it lasts forever. How wonderful that God privileges us with the opportunity to accomplish such a feat. It is in that horizon that your reward awaits.

Mission matters to precious lost souls. It matters for members' discipleship. It matters for the church's vitality. It matters for heaven's joy. It matters for God's expanding glory. It matters for your crown. In all these ways, it matters…forever.

———

The Afterword, which I have included next, is a special section focusing entirely on the implementation of *ReMission* within your ministry picture. Join me!

# —Afterword—

## IN THE TRENCHES OF REMISSIONING

> There are only two options regarding commitment. You're either
> in or out. There's no such thing as a life in between.
> —Pat Riley, renowned NBA coach

One day, I thought to myself, *What if we'd had a different Jesus?*
What if the Son of God incarnated in the same exact moment of
time, with the same name, with all the same scenes and settings to work
with, and yet was missing one simple ingredient: a sense of urgency for the
Father's mission—what would that have looked like?

His accumulated time in his Father's house would not have been limited to a disappearing act by a twelve-year-old (see Luke 2:41–52) and a few
other sit-ins staged at the temple halls during his thirty-three years. Had
he been missing an urgency for mission, crowds would have frequented
the temple to hear him expound upon the Word of God, and also would
have seen his playbill for the surrounding synagogues. He would have been
a man well-known in the religious community, and not so known in other circles. In fact, the "friend of sinners" slur that marred his career and
reputation could have been avoided altogether. He would have been less
resolute and more accommodating to the powers that be. There would have
been no reason to rock the boat so much with the religious establishment.
Satan's early offer of the world's kingdoms (see, for example, Luke 4:5–7),
though voiced by an uncomely source, would have made pragmatic sense to
this Jesus. Consider all the good he could have done! His life would have
been spent doing great charitable works for people all over the planet.

With a lessened urgency for mission, Christ would have lived a safe,
comfortable life, for the most part. Jesus would not have been a threat to

the dominions of darkness. As to priorities, his time running around with those riffraff fishermen would have needed to be curbed back. His conversations with marginalized and immoral people would not have made his agenda, either. With the slight alteration of his character, he would have lived much longer than thirty-three years, too. Freed from the tyranny of mission, his life could have been full and prosperous. The world would have been blessed by his righteous presence, and his teachings would have produced exceedingly larger volumes of content. He would have been balanced, well-rounded, and stable in temperament. Fewer tears. More politeness. Less passion. When he saw the fig tree barren of fruit in the city of Jerusalem (see Mark 11:12–25), instead of reacting violently, he would have acted more like a tree hugger. Yes, one could make the case that a kinder, gentler Jesus would have been a better one, and greener, too.

Why does this little segue of thought seem so surreal? Or even heretical? Of course, we cannot conceive of Jesus' being anything other than who he was and is. He is no gutted, half-baked poser, but the real deal in every way. He is *"the way and the truth and the life"* (John 14:6). We follow him today because the Father's love and mission made him something other, something powerfully transcendent and dangerous, something that was beyond the established order, something not of this world! Vulnerable and accessible, merciful and zealous. My leader friends: Walk in his footsteps. Be the kind of leader that your church needs! Break from the establishment. Please.

Just as Jesus passed his movement baton to his disciples, so must you do with your followers. Your church, group, or agency must bear the distinct marks of the Father's mission if you are to fulfill his mandate. This means you must break the mold and be more than the attractional model, which is limited in its scope of reach (increasingly so every single day); you must also do more than renewal thinking, which is ineffectual in its equipping goal. You must get *ReMission* happening through the bulk of the body. You have a new metric. Don't let it slip through your fingers. Let's seize your moment by discussing some critical links of execution.

How do you get this moving with your people? How do you get *ReMission* in motion and working for you? Those questions are the reason I've included this extra chapter on implementation. I know we're covered a lot of ground. It might feel overwhelming to you. So, I want to cut to the chase and give you some clear steps on how to go forward with *ReMission*—steps that will flesh out the concept a bit. I wrote this section as if I were doing a sit-down consultation with you. If I were seated across the table from you, I would begin by affirming your stature and successes. Many churches and groups are seeing missional fruit. To their leaders, I say, "Good job!" I also know that some of you are legacy leaders/members already, and quite astute in the mission arena. I hope this book has sharpened your mind and honed your abilities for completing God's noble task.

Even though we see some fruit, we are far from realizing our full potential. Even in strong churches or groups, we might be achieving only the standard 20 percent—or even less, from the leader testimonies I have heard—of what God wants to do and build, missionally. The body of Christ is not what he intended it to be. Not yet! So, I'd like to offer you a few hooks and levers that will help launch the content forward into your church body, group, or agency in a practical way. Throughout this book, I have leaned into a metaphor to backdrop our grand theme. I will lean into it one more time and leave you with two ideas I hope will stay with you and guide your structure-building. Let's *ReMission*!

———

The innovations of the Romans had fascinating backstories. Ironically, the architectural movement was set in motion by an accidental discovery that the volcanic earth embedded in thick strata at Pozzuoli, a seaport near Naples, had super-structural powers. It produced something new as limitless as the imagination: the fabricated stone we now call "concrete."[159] The second innovation tapped that expanded their capability was the arch. Again, it was simple and rudimentary. The arch was a gift of civil-engineering geometry. The capstoned, weight-bearing design allowed engineers to erect tall, tiered arcades at the necessary heights.[160] The discovery of concrete and arches paved the way for creating structures that could serve the needs of large population centers with fantastic results! The ancient system

159. Daniel Boorstin, *The Creators: A History of Heroes of the Imagination* (New York, NY: Random House, 1992), 108–10.
160. Evan Andrews, "10 Innovations That Built Ancient Rome," *The History Channel* (November 20, 2012). Available at: http://www.history.com/news/history-lists/10-innovations-that-built-ancient-rome.

channeled substantially more water to the city of Rome in the first century than was supplied to New York City in 1985.[161]

Two equivalent catalyzers undergirding your gospel expansion are (1) mission mind-set and (2) leadership placement. One is the concrete, the other is the arch. These architectural features have great potential to release the gospel in expansive ways.

## #1 MISSION MIND-SET: CREATE BUY-IN FOR NEW ARCHITECTURE

As a leader of a movement, you need to create a massive level of *buy-in*. The *Oxford American Dictionary* defines *philosophy* as "a theory or attitude held by a person or organization that acts as a guiding principle for behavior." If *ReMission* has now entered your ideological framework, you now have the challenge of cementing the same principle within the minds of many others. Wherever you may be in that construction process, I boldly predict that convincing your followers will not be easy. To illustrate, consider this e-mail I received from a pastor who had been under pressure to return to a singular service:

> After the event when we were all together there is increased talk about why we don't permanently go to one service. I've tried to help the staff realize that even though one packed audience is very motivating and exciting for everyone, this is not an easy or simple decision to make. Your experience with multiple churches is so extensive that your thoughts would be invaluable.[162]

Though he sought my input on a specific issue, he had a more generalized problem, in my view. There were several valid reasons for his church to consolidate its worship services, and I put some of those before him; but the justification his staff had been giving him—that one service would allow everyone to be together at the same time—was not one of them. Lacking focus and a guiding compass, his membership was not thinking missionally, and it was undermining this pastor's church in multiple ways. Arguably the best book on breaking the barrier to church growth and bursting through the proverbial ceiling is *The Myth of the 200 Barrier*, in which Kevin Martin claims that the answer lies in reshaping congregational

---

161. Hodge, *Roman Aqueducts & Water Supply*, 191–207.
162. Anonymous, personal e-mail to author, May 17, 2014.

mind-set.[163] According to Martin, if you transform the mentality of your congregants into a mission mind-set, you can be on your way to the next level. Creating mission mind-set is like applying cement or mortar to your structure. It always begins with the pastor and top team leaders, elders, and staff members, but it must work its way down into the body. Your people must see the church, and their very lives, through mission-minded eyes.

For anyone who would tackle this challenge with a preaching series, let me reiterate—it will not happen that way. The average churchgoer is already so inoculated to that kind of charge that you will not puncture his or her veneer. To the contrary, mission mentality must build from a multilayered infusion strategy. I love the Heath brothers' Velcro illustration in *Made to Stick*: "If you look at the two sides of Velcro material, you'll see that one is covered with thousands of tiny hooks and the other is covered with thousands of tiny loops. When you press the two sides together, a huge number of hooks get snagged inside the loops, and that's what causes Velcro to seal."[164] Their point: "Great teachers have a knack for multiplying the hooks in a particular idea [to make it stick]."[165] Let me add that great leaders find multiple ways to get key values rooting deep in those they lead.

"Multiplying the hooks" is all the more necessary for you, since you are trying to create substantial change in a church culture that is preconditioned against you. The three main areas—culture, channel, and charting—are all vital for your success. Let's now break down these areas into smaller steps. I realize it will develop differently depending on your context. For the sake of identification with your situation, and to make corresponding references ahead, I've listed six contextual types here, with a few notable distinctions (please note that this list is not exhaustive, by any means).

+ House church, missional group: Micro, organic network.

+ Church-planter: Start-up, core team.

+ Smaller church: One intimate family, associate pastor.

+ Midsize church: Staff management, multi-service, and cell infrastructure.

---

163. See Kevin E. Martin, *The Myth of the 200 Barrier: How to Lead Through Transitional Growth* (Nashville, TN: Abingdon Press, 2005), 37.
164. Heath and Heath, *Made to Stick*, 110–111.
165. Ibid., *Made to Stick*, 111.

+ Megachurch: Senior pastor figurehead, CEO of a major corporation. Chief of staff: Executive pastor over multiple staffed departments.

+ Regional heads: Bishops, directors, mission agency leaders, consultants.

Though the differences between heading a micro version, an intimate family, a larger multicell congregation, and a major corporation are vast in terms of scope and also required skills, what we all share is the great assignment. What will be true in every case is that in order for the Great Commission to expand and thrive in an outward manner, leaders must create buy-in with their key players. The pivotal first step is for you to decide to dump the tyranny of the urgent in order to pursue the priority of the call. Are you ready to clear your schedule a little? To make a value determination to stop doing certain things so that you can focus on the top priorities? Give yourself and your people time for this. Map it out on the calendar for multiple sessions. It is a challenge for church leaders to rise above the mundane demands of their job to redress what their calling is all about. If this significant new thrust is going to work, you must create the space for everyone to think together about building *ReMission* architecture.

Buy-in doesn't just happen. You have to build it, by educating, sharing, interacting, seeing, and doing. At the outset, there will be much to discuss. Let's just consider the culture-shaping aspects. Each structural theme has a vital question, as well as a proposed solution.

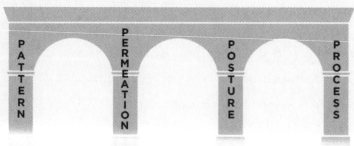

| **Q:** Do they know what they are trying to emulate? <br><br> **A:** Ten mission skills (of Christ). | **Q:** Does the mission training they need come in a form they can assimilate? <br><br> **A:** Engagement training model. | **Q:** How readily do they relate with others about their real sins, struggles and stories? <br><br> **A:** Pastoral modeling, Language: Sin Template. | **Q:** Have we identified the process steps for mission to unfold effectively? <br><br> **A:** Evaluation, Detailing, Collaboration. |

Of the three sections in this book, the one about shaping culture is the domain of top leaders. Unless something becomes a conviction of the pastor and his most intimate circle, it will never make it into the rest of the body. This kind of leadership begins with conviction, but it requires the skills of an artist. You are hewing and sculpting your culture to interface fruitfully with the world. The degree of your effectiveness is linked to the level that you see the four distinctions that will make a definitive difference for your people. I see it. Do you? You may have heard it said that "a mist in the pulpit is a fog in the pew." Here's my version of that maxim: "Cloudy eyes lead to unclear convictions and weak execution." Culture-shaping conversations must happen along each of the four vitalizing pillars. Ask the questions noted above of your team members, then seek ways to get the answer working in your unique scenario.

Eventually, given ample time with your team to process and deepen together, you will get into planning, which leads to setting—setting new objectives to pursue, new metrics to measure, and new benchmarks to surpass. In the book *Switch: How to Change Things When Change Is Hard*, the Heath brothers outline three ways to change the behavior of an organization. They use illustrative phrasing, so I will synthesize their key points simply: (1) earmarking for change (long-term planning), (2) emotional component of change (people's driving motivations), and (3) the environment for change (the training that undergirds it).[166] Interestingly, the authors' term for the third way is "Shape the Path." Sound familiar?

To achieve *ReMission* structure, you will have to think through how you are shaping your culture and how to implement a nonlinear, multistage path. In that training mechanism, you will create the environment needed to produce the change that will effect greater results for the gospel. The power of the path's hub design is that every step in your discipleship intersects with Christ's mandate. My word to you is to get started: IN and ON. That is, expand the range of your reach with non-believing types (IN), and create a discipling engine for newer believers (ON). Both actions will synergize conversion growth, discipleship, and mission. (If you have the leaders to hyper-jump to IN, ON, and UP, go for it!). Then, build the infrastructure by adding the other stages over time. If your training, activities,

---

166. Chip Heath and Dan Heath, *Switch: How to Change Things When Change Is Hard* (New York, NY: Broadway Books, 2010), 261.

and ministries are not missionally fruitful, then you must stop and ask yourself why. Be sure to ask routinely how you can create better alignment with mission. Every church ministry can find ways to reach more people. We honor those we lead when we challenge them to think strategically.

You are going to be enlisting key people and giving them new assignments. Remind them that change is good! This will necessitate carving out sufficient time to ensure a proper degree of vision permeation. The executive pastor must be on board and have tremendous clarity. The same will be true for the associate pastor of a smaller church. For the church-planter, your core team will have to be on board. So will your missional group or sub-ministry. In all cases, your staff and all designated trainers must get up to speed. Have you done the preparatory work to bring about alignment? What will it take? List the steps. Be patient, but also be determined. Consult with another staff member or an outside pastor to make sure you are covering all the bases. Time spent to raise their mission quotient (MQ) is one of the early steps. If they have not been reading this book along with you, select some chapters for them to read, then come together and discuss those chapters. Get the conversations stirring, and it will fertilize the growth you seek. By the way, let the reading stimulate your people's passions and ideas. Make sure to take notes, because some things that are shared in these discussion times will provide fruitful paths and partners for the future. Permeate. Collaborate. Go!

In these sessions, God will be faithful to give you the words for his cause, such as: "We are going to empower our people more." "We are going to see more fruit for the gospel and the kingdom." "We are not going to settle for allowing our people to remain as self-absorbed consumers of spiritual goods! We are going to get a path in place, so that our people become better trained. In that path, we will create structures and expect engagement for the gospel's sake. We are going to champion their stories inside and outside our church."

For *ReMission* to stick, as you work at it over many months, here are some tangible "hooks" to snag your people's "loops."

## HOOK #1: BLEED MISSION

Don't be afraid to open a vein. Other people will be more apt to catch your mission vision and passion if that mission and vision flows deep within you. A pastor friend commented about another leader, "I don't get much from him." When someone speaks about something that is a true passion, others usually can't help but listen. Comments emanating from studied, thoughtful conviction have power. Do your people hang around to be in the presence of you and your staff just to pick your brains or access the passion brewing in your hearts? What are you—decaf, blonde, bold, or espresso? Recall the scene in John 4 when the disciples see a hungry human being, and Jesus reveals his soul food—something they *"know nothing about"* (John 4:32). Does your missional drive run so deep within that others look at you and say, "Wow, I guess I need to grow much more"?

This spiritual dynamic is educationally fueled. Allow new insights to soak into your soul. Keep reading and learning. Reread important books and chapters. Over the months and years ahead, your people will pick up new levels of pathos as you talk, teach, and tout mission! And don't forget to get out there "in love" alongside lost souls who are precious to God, and share the rich stories of your engagements—the successes and the missteps alike. Model patience, perseverance, and humility before your people. Leading by example is never boring.

## HOOK #2: IDENTIFY MISSION TRAINERS/CATALYZERS

An avid NBA fan, I have my favorite nicknames: "Air Jordan"; "The Truth" (Paul Pierce); "The Splash Brothers" (Stephen Curry and Klay Thompson). However, my all-time favorite is the one given to two-time MVP Steve Nash: "The Nash Effect." What a term! Someone coined it to capture the impact of Steve Nash as the floor leader. Get him on your court, and all your other players rise. Everywhere he went, everyone else's stats improved. The Nash Effect.

As your church's "floor leader," do you have the "effect" going? Go ahead and write your last name in the blank (as long as you're not borrowing this book): The _____ Effect. The idea is simple: Everyone else becomes more fruitful for the gospel because of *you*! It's not about how great you are. The concept isn't vertical or pastor-centric. It's about horizontal empowerment—how great your people become because of *you*.

Again, depending on your context, what I am talking about will involve you directly, as well as select leaders. Hear me clearly: You and your key designees must become "experts" at mission training. This is critical. Even if you are working the mission training through your groups, someone needs to become the equipping catalyst of the movement. You can't do it yourself, with all that is on your plate as a leader. Prayerfully select someone trustworthy and tenacious to whom you will give the responsibility of working *ReMission* into your people (with your supervision, of course). This person will be charged with training the church body and any associated groups, and will be the "go-to" person for sharpening. It's absolutely paramount that this person teach the relational skills that all people can apply in their spheres of influence. Shun the telling paradigm, which is ineffective, and please forget the confrontational style—it's ineffective and, in most cases, not reproducible. In fact, you will likely drive your people away from practicing and living mission if you don't give them an approach that they will naturally embrace. Read for yourself, or have your key leaders study, my book *Soul Whisperer*, and work to become highly skilled at raising others to reach this world. Be sure to train others as equippers. Chapter 7 of *Soul Whisperer* focuses on effective compassion ministries in your city. Study it closely. The entire book will show you how to reach multiple types of individuals whom your people will be running into headlong.

Mike Breen's viral blog post, "Why the Missional Movement Will Fail," conveyed a sobering truth: "The reason the missional movement may fail is because most people/communities in the Western church are pretty bad at making disciples."[167] Spot-on! Here is where the ball can drop. Get your highlighter out right now. *If you don't teach the ten relational mission skills outlined in this book, you won't know how to measure your people's growth or their engagement, and all the investment you have made will go down the drain.* If we are truly serious about facing this glaring pitfall, we must help our people to learn specific skills within a model of relational engagement. Attempt to impart these skills through sermons or class instruction alone, and you will fail miserably. Trainers must walk alongside trainees for many months as they learn and practice how to relate to, connect with, deepen relationships with, and share with those outside the church. There is no quick fix. This process will take perseverance.

167. Mike Breen, "Why the Missional Movement Will Fail," *Verge*, http://www.vergenetwork.org/2011/09/14/mike-breen-why-the-missional-movement-will-fail/ (accessed January 6, 2016).

## HOOK #3: REROUTE DISCIPLESHIP STRUCTURES FOR MISSIONAL HEALTH

Christians who participate in Bible study after Bible study but make little effort to reach nonbelievers are not faithful disciples. We must adjust our thinking and our goals. We have to take remedial measures to rectify such ills as codependency, dysfunction, self-absorption, and structural disease. The great question beckons: What does it mean for each and every member to be a Christ-follower? I realize that this vision for the body's outer-influence potential goes against the grain of pastors I know who don't believe their people are capable of doing anything more than serving in an internal serving role. But the trainer sees so much more! Like the words in *Moneyball*: "Everyone else in baseball undervalues them….We'll find value in players that no one else can see….Like an island of misfit toys."[168] It was the belief in players nobody else believed in that challenged the highest payrolls of baseball. There it is—something that will set your group apart and ahead!

The *ReMission* leader redefines discipleship according to what Christ modeled during his life on this planet. A disciple, by definition, is to be like his teacher. (See Matthew 10:24–25.) Your "redesigned" definition must become pervasive. Hit on it, again and again, from multiple angles, training mechanisms, and structures. Ask, "How do our training and engagement apparatuses help our people to live it out?" No doubt, because Christ was all-in for the Father's mission, we have a high standard to emulate. Train your people to get alongside unsaved friends, and observe these fruits of their formation. They will grow in…

+ expressing healthy, active love.

+ sensitivity to nonbelievers' dispositions and the gospel's symphonic blessings.

+ compassion, as they fathom people's life condition and spiritual depravation without Christ.

+ service, by giving of themselves for Christ's cause.

+ authenticity and relationship-deepening patterns.

+ the skills of influence and missional leadership.

---

168. *Moneyball*. http://www.imdb.com/title/tt1210166/quotes.

- the knowledge necessary to reach distant minds and hearts.

- commitment to intercession.

- dependence upon the Holy Spirit's infilling and leading.

- the fruits of disciplemaking and eternal rewards.

- excitement about the part they play in God's greatest enterprise!

From studying the book of Acts, I came to qualify how the apostolic fellowship pattern was so different from what we see in our modern scene.

| The Apostolic Pattern<br>MISSION>HOME>MISSION |  | The Modern Pattern<br>CHURCH>SMALL GROUP>CHURCH |
|---|---|---|

Here's another way to phrase it: There's "fat" fellowship, and there's "fit" fellowship. Fit fellowship is the kind of community experienced by those who are exercising missionally. It's where "on-mission" activity sweetens the fellowship of the participants due to the sheer thrill of gospel-related engagement. When Paul and his band were going from town to town on a missionary task, stopping in various homes along the way (such as the houses of Lydia, Jason, Titus, Justus, and Mnason), their fellowship at those table stops was sweet and overflowing! Can you imagine the joy in the conversations that were had? There was so much excitement to share as the gospel penetrated and expanded to more and more people. God was using them! And that is how it can be for you when you develop mission rhythms for your people. But you have to create structures to get those rhythms in place.

An optimal starting point is to have your team study your community afresh. Look with new eyes, informed by a lens of mission, at the opportunities to serve, to get alongside others outside the church in the neighborhoods, community centers, and general places where non-Christian people congregate. Disciple your people to live the prime call of God. When it comes to mission engagement, the key word is *consistency*. What ongoing initiatives can you establish that will ensure opportunities to build relationships with new, unsaved friends? How can you get the broad core of your ministry to come alongside others in friendship for Jesus' sake? Get your people exercising.

## HOOK #4: ENSURE MISSION SUCCESSES

During a community group training, I asked those present at the house gathering to describe what they believed would increase their confidence to share their faith. Poignantly, Chris replied, "Actually reaching someone." He nailed it. Perhaps nothing will cement the mission mind-set more than success! And that truth puts an onus on leaders to walk with their people all the way into bona fide conversion/transformation results, celebrating every small victory along the way. If you train and teach a group, but, in the end, they didn't engage sufficiently, or persevere long enough to see a disciple or disciples produced, the members may lose heart. On the other hand, if you teach, organize, and work the process with them, God will show up miraculously, and they will be captured by joy! When this happens, you will be celebrating their wins along with them. That's why community baptisms and the public sharing of testimonies are crucial—they will encourage your members and also help others catch the vision for mission.

Let me add that you must *celebrate their engagement, not just their successes.* In fact, you will be amazed at how riveting it can be to interview members who are journeying alongside people who are still far from the faith. When you get the body engaged, the budding of stories begins. Imagine your people hearing a fellow member talk about an attempt to reach a God-accuser, an atheist, a Muslim, or a Buddhist. Ask informative questions: What has it been like to be with that person? What have you learned? How have you grown? Your people will be hanging on the speaker's every word, because, for the most part, they know little about mission, yet they long to become part of the great story.

# #2 REMISSION ARCH: LEVERAGE LEADERSHIP FOR EXPANSIONARY REACH

At the blueprint level, you must envision a style of leadership that the body can grow around and become mission viable. All church leaders, whether elders, staff members, or congregants, can serve as "structure" for mission flow. Remember, each stone in the arches of the Roman aqueducts was carefully placed, having its own weight-bearing capacity. Your team must be properly aligned with your mission and prepared to bear their leadership mantles.

## RAISE THE STRUCTURE

When I transitioned from my first church plant, one of the twenty big lessons I took away was that I hadn't been doing enough to raise up leaders. I kicked myself, because a pastor who mentored me, Matt Hannan, now in the Northwest, was particularly gifted at doing this. His disciples now cover the country and even the world. I had such a great example to follow, and yet I somehow failed to emulate his pattern—and Christ's pattern, for that matter. I did not make that mistake twice. Don't you make it even once! Invest in your up-and-coming leaders, and get them in place, so that mission can flow through your members.

The placement of gifting for the mission mandate is under your purview. We don't always get it right. There was a time when I thought I had my niche, but God's intervention spoke otherwise. Shot upward like a pinball, I found my path then ricocheting downward, bouncing and boxing me into the single slot of missional development. *God had returned me to my first love.* When I entered that sweet spot of strength, he released blessing! Whether a leader is novice or seasoned, everyone benefits from discovering and developing his first-love passion. God will not fulfill all that he has in store for your church outside "high definition." If your mission is LD (low-definition), God wants it to be HD. Take a splash of color and spread it wide enough, and it diffuses, losing punch. God says, "Be the dot! Be brilliant. Be powerful. Be noticeable. Be impactful!" When mission takes on an HD-brilliance, everybody benefits: you, your people, and the greater church, community, state, country, and globe.

The leader's role includes placement as well as development. You may have heard it said, "Leaders are born." Wrong! Dump that myth. Leaders are *made*. A leader must only be taught and given opportunities. John Maxwell's "Law of the Lid" applies here. Leaders' knowledge and abilities must rise in order for mission to reach higher levels. Let me encourage you not to wimp out on the hard parts. Have the courage to mirror back the corrective criticism they need! As to whom it is that you should hire, Seth Godin has sage words for the church:

> Great organizations are filled with people who are eagerly seeking to recruit people better than they are. Not just employees, but vendors,

coaches and even competitors. Most organizations seek to hire "people like us." The rationale is that someone too good might not take the job, might get frustrated, might be easily lured away. A few aim for, "so good she scares me." A few aim for, "it'll raise our game."[169]

Go after the best to get the best training dynamics possible. The problem with our hiring is not that we hire pastoral roles, but that we are not hiring nearly enough sodalically gifted mission leaders. We need more positions working the church's outer rim. Reshape your budget. Put your money where your mouth is! Please, when the *ReMission* Training Tour happens, send me your top men and women to invest in. Thank you.

## GUARD THE STRUCTURE

Unhealthy people can be like wrecking balls. At Southwest Church Planting, we urgently advise church planters to "watch and wait" before putting anyone into a position of leadership. While it's true that anyone can serve, not everyone should lead. Because planters feel pressed to make headway (with subtle and overt pressure from within and without), it's easy to make choices that end up backfiring. Church leaders should be humble, relationally healthy, and spiritually centered. Those descriptors can fit almost everyone—until you look deeper. Ask this key question of those you are considering for leadership: Do they have a history of leaving relational wreckage in their wake? Don't fall for the excuse that "It was the other person's fault," or you'll be next! The rule of thumb is to get people involved in serving and then observe them closely over an extended period of time before designating any as leaders.

When it comes to top leaders, such as elders and board members, the importance of the steps I just explained is magnified a hundredfold. At our church-planter forums, we've had veteran pastors disclose nightmarish stories of trusted people going AWOL. One told of an elder who suddenly turned on him, questioning the church's direction. When the pastor figured out what was going on and mentioned that it was rather obvious this elder should step down from his role, the man proceeded to dial up the entire church roster, raising doubts about the senior pastor's leadership

169. Seth Godin, "Raising the Average," (blog), June 13, 2016. Available at: http://sethgodin.typepad.com/seths_blog/2016/06/raising-the-average.html.

abilities. As a result, half his church members walked out! Later, the elder apologized to the pastor, saying he had been driven by pride. By then, the damage was already done. If you hire or mobilize in haste, you'll repent in leisure.

These types of leader issues create enormous distractions that will drain you of energy and detract from the time you should be spending doing what God wants you to do. When the time comes for laying hands on overseers, you don't need to assemble a big group. The point is not to make them feel included, to get them more involved, or to meet your need to placate their wishes. If you have even an iota of doubt about someone, do not put that person on your board. Wait, then proceed with caution! The Scriptures wisely warn, *"Do not be hasty in the laying on of hands"* (1 Timothy 5:22). Any doubts must be thoroughly resolved, and every choice of leader should be heartily affirmed by others you trust.

If you are a church-planter, you just received a warning shot across your bow.

## HELP THE STRUCTURE

Back in the day, we used to watch the political drama *The West Wing*. Leo McGarry, the president's chief of staff on the show, would occasionally bring in outside help. Sometimes, getting outside help is the best way to work through difficult decisions and make critical directional moves. Sadly, many churches never seek outside help. I am stunned by the number of churches with plateaued or declining membership that still think they have all the answers. They have settled and stepped off the learning curve, and it's killing them! Year after year, they stay within the confines of their status-quo thoughts, when the answer could be found quite easily, just outside their walls.

Coming into a church as a consultant, I notice certain things right away that others don't see, and I can say things that others won't—things that desperately need to be said and addressed. The potent combination opens the eyes of church leaders on how their church must change. Though change can be painful, the reward is always worth it. For the minor financial investment of bringing in a consultant, you can get the input and feedback necessary to make critical adjustments that can propel you to the next level of influence and growth, resulting in greater spiritual, emotional, and financial health. It's a worthwhile investment, considering all the time and money you will spend while spinning your wheels.

At a certain point in your preparatory work, you and the Spirit will be asking: "Are they ready to run?" You will know you've created sufficient buy-in when your people can run forward with it. How exciting to start taking new ground; to ignite a new learning curve; to offer new, better, revamped training; to raise the bar for the whole church. Let's run!

Let me encourage you forward with this thought: Great programs produce impact players. It's as true in the church as it is in sports. I daresay that if you go after this, you will not be the only one who wants it—your people will want it, too! Perhaps not all of them; but the core and the cream are looking for your leadership. Don't underestimate them. They want to go after the grand prize of the Christian life. They want to know where they are on the kingdom scoreboard. They are already asking those big questions: Who are we becoming? Are we making a dent? Are we fulfilling Christ's call? They want to win! And they desperately want to be part of something much bigger than a brand or a weekend service.

———

I am not into Bible numerology, nor do I generally attribute undue weight to happenstance; but it felt different on the day I passed through seven consecutive yellow lights. It happened right after I listened to a message on how to discern God's leading. The teacher had outlined three questions to ask oneself in order to identify the guidance of God: (1) Where has God dragged you kicking and screaming? (2) What is your desire? (3) Has God given you a revelation?[170] Driving away, I couldn't stop thinking about how I had experienced all three of those indications, and yet, at that present juncture, my life and my talents seemed rather wasted. I often murmured to myself that felt as if I had been put on the shelf.

When I began counting successive yellow lights, from three all the way up to seven, I became fixated on the number and its biblical significance. I

———

170. Guy Pfantz, "How to Discern Where God Is Leading You" (presentation at a Southwest Church Planting forum in Temecula, California, June 12, 2012).

started thinking, *How many years of feast and famine did Joseph predict for Pharaoh? How many days and trips around Jericho did it take for the walls to fall? How many seals, angels, trumpets, plagues, and bowls before the Lord returns?* In the Bible, seven is not only God's number for perfection; it denotes God's perfect rule. Seven lights? In the wake of the message I had just heard, it came at me like a heavenly dart: *I've got your future dialed in, Gary—don't you forget that, my beloved son!*

With laser-like precision, God has preordained your call. (See Ephesians 2:10.) As you elevate your dreams for your church, ministry, or mission agency, it will take time to build the kind of discipleship quality and "outfrastructure" that will ripple through your community. May honest, hard assessments continue to ignite your thinking and action! Keep his passion at your forefront. Persevere. Believe.

You probably aren't aware of the enormous doubts I faced while writing this book. One literary agent insinuated that I needed 300,000 to 500,000 recipients on my e-mail list (best-selling author Lysa TerKeurst has one million on hers) before a traditional publisher would take me seriously. Sizing up my menial figures, I gulped and choked on my foolishness. When I did sign with an agent, he shot me a line that sounded like it had leapt right out of *The Hunger Games*: "The odds are not in your favor." If this book could manage to find a publisher and then make its way into your hands, and then into your mind and heart, it testifies that God is greater than all the odds that were stacked against me. What I hope most for you, as you chase his dream, is that you'll find out even more how much greater God is than all that is stacked against you. Trust him as you lead your people forward. He is with you till the end of the age. He is, and will always be, the Great Steward of your life.

# PART IV
## —ADDENDA—

# —Addendum A—

## CONVERSATIONAL LINES TO REACH MUSLIMS

*It is He who has sent down the Book* [the Qur'an]
*to you* [Mohammed] *with truth,*
*confirming what came before it. And He sent down*
*the Taurat* [Torah] *and the Injeel* [Gospel].
—Surah 3:3, *The Qur'an*

**A**fter many years of involvement with our college ministry group, a Muslim student named Ashin came to Christ and was baptized. During my second church plant, when one young adult Muslim came to Christ over the course of a comparative book study on Jesus and Mohammed, two of his two close friends immediately followed him into the faith. Though they were ostracized initially, they hung in there and soon saw the fruits of conversion. Having said that, reaching Muslims presents an exceptionally high difficulty factor.

This reality is all the more sobering and heartbreaking when one considers that one in five people on the planet are now Muslim. With the higher fertility rates of Muslim families over most groups, Europe's Muslim population is expected to double by 2030.[171] And some American Muslim organizations have forecasted that by 2040, the U.S. Muslim population will jump from seven to 50 million.[172] Whoa. Can you see what is breaking upon us? Pause for a moment to take this in!

---

171. Ruth Dudley Edwards, "Will Britain One Day Be Muslim?" *Daily Mail* (May 5, 2007). Available at: http://www.dailymail.co.uk/news/article-452815/Will-Britain-day-Muslim.html.
172. Alan Shlemon, *The Ambassador's Guide to Islam* (Signal Hill, CA: Stand to Reason, 2012), 7.

In the chapter entitled "Step Out," I outlined a path sequence to reach people of other faiths. Given that Islam is all-encompassing for Muslims, affecting everything from their relationships to their cultural practices, every word in the sequence is critical: real openness, deciphering truth, courage to believe, and being God's instrument of influence to save others.

Openness ⟩ Truth ⟩ Courage ⟩ Faith ⟩ Influence

Even once a genuine openness has been established, winning Muslims to the truth is a formidable task. Given the gospel's call, how can Christians initiate meaningful, influential conversations with their Muslim friends? The first thing to see and accept is that influence will happen only inside a loving relationship. One-hit-wonder telling will achieve nothing. Steamrolling a Muslim with a canned evangelistic presentation won't work. Settle in for the long haul. You must journey with your Muslim friends long enough that they are able to actually hear and receive the gospel truth. Sahar, an international student from Saudi Arabia who converted to Christianity over a six-year process, explained to me the sequence that she has seen to be effective: "It's goodness, beauty, and then truth." Be holistic in your approach.

But, again, you won't see kingdom results if you do not challenge the belief system of Muslims. I want to share with you four conversational lines that have worked for me. After starting up a friendship, you must frame a safe conversation where both parties can express their views without the fear of altering or ending the friendship. Express this sentiment in your own words: "Obviously, we differ as to our beliefs, but I would love to get together and learn more about what you believe, and to share some of my beliefs, too. Please know our differences will not affect our friendship in any way." Now, your spirit and tone of communication should be safe, as well.

Once you get set to connect regularly with the person, possibly over coffee or tea, you can do two things: (1) Leverage his or her perceived authority with the Qur'an (I will explain this in further detail), and (2) Use philosophic arguments that have transcendent appeal. What I mean is, don't sit there and go tit-for-tat (he said, she said) between the Bible and Qur'an, or you'll only be spinning your wheels. A philosophic argument has the wings to rise above it all and hover over the person, causing him or her to think bigger and deeper. Yes, those are the kinds of discussions that can stir the mind and heart to search out truth.

Granted, this process will look different depending upon the person's degree of devotion and adherence to the Muslim faith, but we must begin where he or she is, and with his or her beliefs and their source.

## #1 THE QUR'AN'S VIEW OF BIBLE AUTHORITY

The Qur'an comprises 114 chapters, called "surahs." If you are reaching out to a Muslim friend, it would be good to get familiar with the book that is, for Muslims, the ultimate authority on divine truth. Though the Qur'an presents the prophet Jesus (Isa) as positive and even important, it also strips Christ of his divine nature. As long as Jesus remains just one of Allah's prophets, Muslims will miss Christ, salvation, truth, and an eternity with God.

Since the Qur'an holds such a high view of Isa, however, we can bridge a conversation about him that can stir the imagination. The statements made about Jesus in the Qur'an are fascinating for a Muslim to ponder. You may or may not know, but the Qur'an states that Jesus was born of a virgin, is the Messiah, lived a sinless life, performed miracles, raised the dead, was called the Word of God, and will return to usher in the end times. It also says that he did not die but instead was taken up to heaven by Allah. Interestingly, none of these things is said about Mohammed, even though Mohammed is far more revered than Jesus by Muslims.

In his booklet on Islam, Alan Shlemon models something that I teach in *Soul Whisperer*—the concept of "going to their side of the fence." That is when we begin the conversation from their religious source, not ours. This is new ground for most Christians. One husband, hearing that his wife had received the gift of a Qur'an from her Muslim friend, responded angrily, "Give it back!" Such an emotional reaction, though understandable because of its origins in the man's Christian loyalty, is shortsighted. It shows the lack of wisdom and mission understanding that exists among most Christians today. In North America, we presume to have a home-field advantage, seeing everything through our Christian lens and thinking everyone else must adjust accordingly. But when it comes to reaching people of other faiths, it is paramount that we see through their lens.

Shlemon outlines several reasons why it's a good idea to begin with the Qur'an, including that doing so (1) is minimalist (requiring a low degree of knowledge of the Christian), (2) provides source leverage, (3) establishes common ground, (4) is disarming, and (5) feels safer (for a Muslim!).[173] But the prime reason he advocates such an approach is this one troubling fact: *Muslims believe the Bible has been corrupted and is therefore an unreliable source.* This is what we are up against from the get-go. Authority is everything to Muslims. The corruption claim gets in the way of all the non-Qur'anic authoritative sources: the Taurat (Torah), given by Allah to Moses; the Psalms, given by Allah to David; and the Injil (Gospel), given by Allah to Jesus. Muslims are taught, and believe, that these other sources were altered and therefore corrupted; only the Qur'an has been preserved and protected.[174] So, beginning with their starting point, by using the very words of the Qur'an, we can reexamine this commonly held viewpoint and then build the needed bridge.

Here's the pivot point: The Qur'an does not actually say that these other, non-Qur'anic books of Allah are corrupted. In other words, there's a loophole to be explored. Key verses have been misapplied. Though this conversation gets a bit technical, it is a sound refutation that's well worth the effort. See if you can get your Muslim friend to rethink what he or she has routinely accepted, calling into question its trustworthiness. The most problematic verses occur early in the Qur'an: Surah 2:75–79. Look carefully at the words:

> ...*Seeing that a party of them heard the Word of Allah, and perverted it knowingly after they understood it. Behold! When they meet the men of Faith, they say: "We believe": But when they meet each other in private, they say...*

What this passage pertains to is a party of Jews who perverted the way they talked about the Word of Allah, not perversion of the text itself. It merely says that they spoke to Muslims one way in public and another way in private.

In the same passage, we have this other apparent disqualification:

---

173. Shlemon, *Ambassador's Guide to Islam,* 12.
174. Ibid., 10.

*Then woe to those who write the Book* [used here to refer to the Bible] *with their own hands, and then say: "This is from Allah," to traffic with it for miserable price!"- Woe to them for what their hands do write, and for the game they make thereby.*

The second portion of this excerpt does not indicate biblical text corruption, either. It deals with Jews who were inventing books, saying those books were from Allah, and then selling those books for profit. Conclusion: This whole section does not discredit the other authoritative books (of the Bible) that are recognized by the Qur'an.

Though this discussion may have you feeling as if you're swimming upstream, if the Qur'an does not definitively claim Bible corruption, then the others sources of Allah should be considered, especially the Gospel revelation given to Jesus. Mohammed and the early Muslims affirm a reliable Bible. In fact, in a dozen or so places, the Qur'an recognizes the Bible's divine pedigree.

*To thee We sent the Scripture in truth* [that's the Qur'an], *confirming the scripture that came before it* [that's the Bible], *and guarding it in safety: so judge between them what Allah has revealed, and follow not their vain desires, diverging from the Truth that hath come to thee* (surah 5:48).

This conversational track is meant to be used to construct a platform. It is one of the skills Christians need to develop in order to be effective in our pluralized world, where one must first lay down planks of knowledge and understanding in order to give the nonbeliever something solid to build upon. In this case, the Muslim must reconsider the other sources recognized by the Qur'an. Building a platform requires taking out wood, hammer, and nails for construction through multiple interactive conversations on what the Qur'an says about the Bible. Here is a list of some pertinent verses: surah 2:136; surah 4:136; surah 5:43, 47; surah 29:46; and surah 10:94.

One key question to ask a Muslim is, When was the Bible corrupted? We have tried to demonstrate that in the seventh century, Mohammed himself affirmed the Bible. Tracing forward from the seventh-century mark, historical and theological scholars affirm that the early manuscripts of the Bible are compatible with what we have today (granted, there is the filter of textual criticism to remove copyist errors or additions).[175] We can therefore conclude that its literalness has not been altered. To the contrary, the Bible possesses a unique internal consistency verifiable by historic record and prophetic fulfillment. And, unlike the Qur'an, the Bible was composed through multiple revelations over centuries of time. Another question: Why would Allah protect his Word (the Qur'an) in one case, and yet not be able to do the same thing with his other Revelations? Putting the answers together points to the logical conclusion that the divine sources affirmed in the Qur'an are not tainted. If Muslims still hold to the claim, it raises questions about the Qur'an's internal consistency and/or the truthful character of Allah.[176] Because of Muslims' nationalism (pride in their culture) and the romanticism of Islam (a highly exalted view of Mohammed as the messenger of God's final book), those are two conclusions they will not make, at least initially.

Can you see how treading into this conversation in a respectful, kind, and calm manner can open a line of inquisitiveness and questioning? Truth must be consistent. From my conversational experience, I can attest that Muslims tend toward logic, so you have that mentality to dig down on for leverage. (See footnote on logic fallacies pertaining to Islam.[177]) Is this angle always a slam dunk? No. Is it a good angle? Yes! This line of thought alone could ignite an openness in a Muslim to reconsider Jesus as he is portrayed in the Bible, God's Word. (For an in-depth view of how Islamic leaders justify the superiority of the Qur'an over the Old and New Testaments, see *The History of the Qur'anic Text* by M. Mustafa Al-A'zami.[178])

The downside is that once you establish that footing, what the Bible teaches about Jesus is contradictory to the main tenets of Islam. Muslims know this. So, eventually, you'll get to the issue of contradiction, with one religious source saying one thing about Jesus, and another source saying something entirely different. This is not bad; it is the nature of our gospel.

---

175. Bruce Manning Metzger, *The Text of the New Testament: Its Transmission, Corruption, and Restoration* (New York and Oxford: Oxford University Press, 1968), 149–246.
176. Shlemon, *Ambassador's Guide to Islam*, 16–17.
177. Four logic fallacies (errors of reason) pertain to Islam: (1) Authority, (2) Personal Incredulity, (3) Non-Sequitur, and (4) Tautology. Available at: http://www.cfimichigan.org/images/uploads/pdf/Top20LogicalFallacies-Tikkanen.pdf.
178. M. Mustafa al-A'zami, *The History of the Qur'anic Text: From Revelation to Compilation: A Comparative Study with the Old and New Testaments* (Chowk Urdu Bazar, Lahare, Pakistan: Suhail Academy, 2005).

If you don't broach the issue, you can't truly reach Muslims for Christ! Unless they assume a radically new and different belief system regarding Isa (Jesus), they cannot become Christians.

In that vein, I am offering several other apologetic lines of discussion to pursue. We seek to open Muslims' eyes to reconsider the Christian faith as being the true faith given to us from God. I need to reiterate that reaching a Muslim will take your full repertoire of skills. You need to build relationship first and then pick your spots with these kinds of conversations—open dialogues between friends who differ in their beliefs yet who both value God and truth. It is in this spirit that good conversations can take place, and the Spirit of God can do what he alone can do: draw men and women to himself. Rid yourself of the notion that this is a short-term relationship. No one wants to be someone else's project. It's a long-term genuine friendship that you are seeking to build.

One of the things that I want to do, perhaps after establishing common ground as to the Qur'an's favorable view of the Bible and Isa, is to examine the literal words of Christ. One of the four planks that establish the Christian faith is Jesus himself. Not only is he the only prophet born of a virgin and called "the Word of God," as their source affirms (surah 3:45–55); as we add the Gospel (Injeel) into the equation, a compelling view of Jesus arises. No one ever spoke or lived the way he did—not Mohammed, and not any other Old Testament prophet, for that matter. Just as we see internal inconsistencies with the Qur'an regarding Jesus' life and human history, the Bible contains internal consistencies that showcase Christ's authority and divinity.

When I interviewed an Iranian man who had converted from Islam to Christianity, I asked him to explain the appeal he made to other Muslims. He used simple logic. He asked me, "What is the best-selling book of all time? Who wrote it? Could fishermen alone have done that?" Not only is there a ring of divine authenticity in the Bible's influence, but there is an air of authenticity in Jesus' voice—an authority that no other man has ever demonstrated or could attempt to replicate. In fact, if we corralled all the wisest, smartest people on the planet together in one room, we would not be able to reproduce the authoritative wisdom in the words of Christ. What mere human talks like Jesus did in John's gospel alone?

[Jesus said,] *"If I told you earthly things and you do not believe, how will you believe if I tell you heavenly things? No one has ascended into heaven, but He who descended from heaven: the Son of Man."*
(John 3:12–13)

*Jesus answered them, "Destroy this temple, and in three days I will raise it up."* (John 2:19)

*I am the light of the world. Whoever follows me will never walk in darkness, but will have the light of life.* (John 8:12)

*You are from below; I am from above. You are of this world; I am not of this world. I told you that you would die in your sins; if you do not believe that I am the one I claim to be, you will indeed die in your sins.* (John 8:23–24)

*I am the resurrection and the life. The one who believes in me will live, even though they die; and whoever lives by believing in me will never die.* (John 11:25–26)

In Mark 2, Jesus' claim to forgive sins shocked the Jewish contingent. They knew what that meant. Only God forgives sins! Over and over again, Jesus speaks with divine authority, and exercises authority over everything in his path. (See, for example, Matthew 7:28–29; Mark 1:27–28; Luke 8:25.) Whether implicitly or explicitly, as "Son of God" and "Son of Man" (see Matthew 26:63–64; Daniel 7:13–14), Jesus was always asserting and exhibiting his divine nature, while at the same time having to avert human attempts to obstruct his ultimate mission. (His followers wanted to make him king, and his opponents wanted to make him dead, prematurely.) This Jesus, the Messiah, is the mediator of a restored relationship with God, a relationship that will bring enormous blessing by meeting every spiritual need. Be empowered to run down this line, planting seeds for Muslims to see Isa in a far greater way.

## #2 THE TESTS FOR DIVINE REVELATION

Rodney Stark's book *Discovering God: The Origins of the Great Religions and the Evolution of Belief* is significant because in it, the author devises specific criteria to discern whether a religious writing is divine revelation. His assessment, mind you, is made through a lens of sociology, not biblical theology. The benefit is its objective appeal. To pass the test, the revelatory source must meet three criteria: (1) It is a revelation from God himself, (2) It is consistent, and (3) It has progressive complexity. Stark's is a sound template to discern the authenticity of religious sources, and he uses it to come to several pointed conclusions: Judaism is revelation; Christianity is revelation of God, consistent with past revelation, and progressively complex in how much more is revealed; Islam, however, is none of the above.[179]

Consider Stark's rationale. He argues that Islam does not offer revelation from God himself. Though the Qur'an is splattered with beautiful poetic writings and many descriptive titles, words, and phrases for Allah, the bulk of the text is law stemming from the sixth-century world. Stark observes that, unlike the Old Testament and then the New Testament, the Qur'an does not provide revelation from God himself on who he is. To the contrary, it teaches that we cannot know God; he is, in essence, unknowable.[180] Here are three ayahs (verses) supporting this line of thought: "Glory be to your Lord, the Lord of inaccessibility, above what they describe" (surah 37:180), "Nothing is like Him" (surah 42:11), and "Never shall I give partners to God [a reference to his being beyond comparison]," surah 6:79).

Additionally, there is something different about the Qur'an that the casual reader is unlikely to pick up on. Reading through the text, one observes how, for the most part, it does not use direct voice but rather presents the content as conveyed by the messenger Mohammed. As you may know, Muslims believe that, over a course of 23 or so years, Allah conveyed his words through his final prophet. Yet, when you observe the way this occurs, you see that, suddenly, there is something distinctly different from what is found in the Old Testament and the New Testament, where God reveals himself directly. In the Old Testament, we find the refrain *"Thus says the LORD"* (see, for example, Exodus 5:1 NKJV). In the hundreds of verses that employ this refrain, God is speaking directly to us about

---

179. Rodney Stark, *Discovering God: The Origins of the Great Religions and the Evolution of Belief* (New York, NY: HarperCollins, 2007), 390–95.
180. Ibid., 390.

himself. In the New Testament, we have the Word coming to us in living form, the person of Christ, speaking the words of the Father, and revealing God in the most intimately personal of ways. In contrast, Allah does not reveal himself in that way.[181] This fact is suspect and disqualifying. Why the sudden change of voice?

Additionally, the Qur'an does not provide revelation that meets Stark's qualifications of either consistency or progressive complexity. In fact, instead of giving new information (revealing an aspect of God's identity that he had not previously conveyed), it puts forth content that is contradictory to God's prior revelation through Judaism and Christianity. Granted, Muslims readily dismiss this assertion by calling into question the authority of the Jewish and Christian Scriptures, saying these sources are corrupted. Yet inconsistency in the chain of revelations and manner of disclosure is a serious problem for a book that gives credence to the revelations that came before it. Is God, or "Allah," schizophrenic, divided, or oppositional with himself? Does he say something about himself at one point in history, only to say something different later on? Are portions of the Qur'an true in certain time periods but not later on? These possibilities are not logical, nor are they fitting or feasible for the exalted Creator God that Muslims believe in.

Please note: This type of apologetic technique needs to be set up in the right way, conversationally, to avoid or at least minimize offense. I typically will not pursue this particular line until there is a strong relationship and after we have had productive discussions about the Qur'an and how it affirms the biblical sources. The best way is to ask open-ended questions, such as: How is the Qur'an a revelation from Allah himself? And why does it categorize him as unknowable? (How different this is from Judeo-Christianity's holy, transcendent, yet still intimately personal and knowable, God.) Is it consistent with God's earlier revelations? How do we reconcile the inconsistency of what God revealed earlier through his prophets and what was revealed later in the seventh century?

## #3 THE CROSS VERSUS ISLAM'S DISMISSAL OF HISTORY

I have already illustrated this line of discussion, with the account of my conversation with my Muslim seatmate from Lebanon in the closing of

---

181. Ibid., 390–95.

Chapter 13. If you need to review the details of that exchange, please feel free to do so now. Here are two points I'd like to highlight:

(1) My asking Mahir whether he had seen the film *Schindler's List* was strategic. It tells the story of a German man helping Jewish people, and I wanted to see whether that fact would indicate Mahir's receptivity to the gospel message. Even though Mahir acknowledged the Middle East's animosity toward Israel, I perceived that he would be receptive to the story based on his openness and his global exposure. Now, I could have used another story found in this book that illustrates the accuracy of eyewitness testimony in the historic record. Do you recall the conclusion that was drawn after the investigation of the sinking of the *Titanic? Only the eyewitnesses got it right!* These popular stories underscore the gravity of the New Testament's four detailed eyewitness accounts on the public events surrounding the most significant person who ever walked the earth.

(2) Did you notice how I turned the point's relevance on Mahir by asking in a soft, earnest tone, "How would you feel if people started saying that Mohammed was not a real person? That all the big events in his story never happened?" Even if Mahir had previously tended to disregard what I was saying, it now became too personal for him to do so. He had to at least consider the magnitude of the Muslim claim that so flippantly disregards substantiated history.

In addition to four detailed Gospel accounts including everything prophesied and fulfilled by the death of Christ, we have two prominent nonbiblical historians, one of whom, a Hebrew named Josephus, wrote: "About this time there lived Jesus ... When Pilate, upon hearing him accused by men of the highest standing amongst us, had condemned him to be crucified".[182] The other, a Roman named Tacitus, wrote, "Christus, from whom the name had its origin, suffered the extreme penalty during the reign of Tiberius at the hands of one of our procurators, Pontius Pilatus."[183] Even the unorthodox non-literalist group of Bible scholars known as The Jesus Seminar recognized the weight of historicity's record here. Their leader, John Dominic Crossan, makes this definitive statement:

---

182. Josephus, *The Antiquities of the Jews*, XVIII.3.3.
183. Cornelius Tacitus, *Annals*, trans. Alfred John Church and William Jackson Brodribb, XV.44. Available at: http://classics.mit.edu/Tacitus/annals.11.xv.html.

"I take it absolutely for granted that Jesus was crucified under Pontius Pilate. Security about the fact of the Crucifixion derives not only from the unlikelihood that Christians would have invented it but also from the existence of two early and independent non-Christian witnesses to it, a Jewish one from 93–94 C.E. and a Roman one from the 110s or 120s C.E."[184] Now, certainly, Muslims can easily dismiss what we are saying, but the error they make in so doing is glaring. They dismiss what is confirmed by all credible historians, and this poses a massive, irreconcilable intellectual problem for Islam.

## #4 THE INFINITE TRINITY VERSUS FINITE HUMAN MINDS

Get alongside your Muslim friends to talk about Christianity, and you will quickly discover just how much the doctrine of the Trinity trips them up; after all, this doctrine defies the fundamental tenet of Islam—God's oneness. In the Qur'an, contradicting this particular quality of God, as Muslims understand him, is the ultimate sin! So, what do we do with this doctrine that is difficult for many Christians to understand, let alone explain to their West-leaning friends? Here is how former Muslim Nabeel Qureshi explains the Trinity to Muslims: "'God is one in being, and three in person.' A being is what you are, just like we use the term 'human being.' A person is who you are."[185] (Because Arab culture does not use middle names, you will have to use your own full name as an example, as I did with my imam friend, saying, "My full name is Gary Steven Comer. Am I one or three?") Christianity teaches that God is one, but three persons of the names Father, Son, and Spirit.

Many Muslims mistakenly humanize the relational language of the Trinity. They are confused and even offended by the terminology depicting God as capable of having a son or a wife (see surah 6:101), restricting such metaphorical concepts to biological and sexual implications.[186] Yet this is an egregious distortion by the Qur'an of what the New Testament

184. John Dominic Crossan, *The Historical Jesus: The Life of a Mediterranean Jewish Peasant* (New York, NY: HarperCollins, 1993), 372.

185. Nabeel Qureshi, "Understanding & Answering Islam" (video presentation of Ravi Zacharias International Ministries [RZIM] seminar, Corona, California, January 15-16, 2016).

186. Anonymous, "Qur'an Inconsistency: Can There Be a Son Without a Consort?" Available at: http://answering-islam.org/Quran/Contra/without_consort.html.

teaches. "Son of God" does not imply birth but rather being. In other words, the title is declaring God and his Son to be of the same kind. As Jesus said, *"I and the Father are one"* (John 10:30). What Nabeel Qureshi is doing, and what we are aiming for in our communication, is to convey that Christianity is not polytheistic but monotheistic, and that God's essence is in no way reduced by the idea of the incarnation. Interestingly, the Qur'an actually answers its own objection to God's lack of a consort (wife) by declaring that for Mary to have become pregnant outside sexual union would have presented "no problem" for Allah (surah 19:19–21). By the words of the Qur'an, we are halfway there. But the next jump for the Muslim mind to make, to God's incarnating himself, is huge!

This is why, in one sense, we must try to provide an explanation that helps clarify the Trinity as intellectually tenable (by the way, the logical fallacy of personal incredulity means, in a nutshell, "Just because we don't understand something, that does not mean it is false") and in no way irrational. Yet, in another sense, I want to question Islam's logical, lesser view of God—that is, challenge their rationally based conviction that God is no more sophisticated than human conceptualization. Ironically, the notion that we cannot fully know God is in the Qur'an: "For He (Allah) is greater than that the minds of men should delimit him through (their limited) thought" (surah 16:74; 42:11). Once you've established your common ground with a Muslim friend, you can cite these two references, saying, "Even your own source acknowledges the limits of understanding God Almighty." Our aim, then, is to take that accepted idea much further, philosophically speaking.

One thing I love about Christianity is that it is not what human beings would have created. The triune nature of God, his sacrifice, and the free gift of grace defy natural thinking. It is not that we can't understand the truths that God has revealed about himself and the necessary atonement to satisfy his righteous character; but if we were to create a God and a religion, would we have conceptualized the types of things we find in the Bible? Out of our human reasoning, we would have conjured something far different: God, the Creator, being one in person, just as we are; and mankind getting the justice they deserve, according to the deeds they have done (to honor God's way and submit to him). Couched within a system of ancient law, that, my friends, is Islam. The description also happens to fit other religions, generically speaking, whose adherents seek to appease God or their gods through good works or religious performance.

It is the very fact that Christianity defies human conception that cements my belief in its authenticity. It is intellectually arrogant for finite human minds to claim that we would have conceived of the infinite God exactly the way he is. In Judeo-Christianity, God has revealed himself to be divergent from what we thought. He is one being in three persons. Whether you agree with the Trinitarian doctrine or not, one thing we know: the Christian faith is not man-made. It is not man's attempt to reach God, unlike what is found in the vast evolutionary scope of world religions. To the contrary, it is more than we could have comprehended; God is greater than our limited human minds, and his way of salvation—grace showered upon us through a cross—is well beyond the bounds of man-centered ideology.

Unique among all rival faiths, Christianity bears the marks of divine origination, with God himself coming down from heaven and making a way for us to reach him. This is entirely different from man's weak and futile attempts to appease God through personal sacrifices and attempts at keeping the law. Only God's love, expressed through the cross of Christ, can usher human beings into a place of being assured of salvation, because that salvation is not based on human law or performance. Nor does the Christian faith exalt human effort or religious devotion, which cater to man's pride of accomplishment. Instead, the glory goes to God for what he has done in his substitutionary sacrifice on our behalf; in this, it is God-centered, not man-centered. You can use this philosophic appeal to delve deeper into the concept of the cross—God's only way to bring salvation and assurance.

In summary, God has not left us here without a corroboration of pointers to verify the most essential truths for belief and salvation. The challenge with our Muslim friends is to facilitate a shift from their pre-conditioned lens of rhetoric (what they have been taught) to independent critical thinking. These four conversational lines, along with the art and skill of a relational soul whisperer, can get you positioned for the Spirit's breakthrough.

As you enter the Muslim world—as you fall in love with these beautiful, God-loving people, and envisage their predicament without Christ—I will bet that it will rip your heart out. However, as we build relationships with Muslims, we must never lose sight of the truth that what we have in the gospel is what every Muslim desperately desires, deep down: the unconditional love of God, assurance of full atonement and salvation, and the grace and power to live free. They are currently living under the law, one in which they remain under the judgment of their unremitted sin. We possess the truth and the answer, as Christians saved and living under grace. Christ is their Messiah, too—the one who loved them by coming and dying on a cross for their sin, and the one who rose again to give them life and entrance to his heavenly kingdom!

Believe me, you will not become a friend and apologist to Muslims overnight. But do not discount the fact that the Lord may place an increasing number of Allah-adherents along your path. Can you take them a step or two closer to knowing the God who offers them freedom from the law through the grace of Jesus? If you are reading this book with an open heart, expect that God will have a Muslim for you to befriend and lead into the kingdom in your near future.

# —Addendum B—

## THE TOP 10 MISSION SKILLS

1. DISCOVERING THE GOSPEL KEY: This is a dynamic skill that involves reading the needs and storyline of an individual in order for you to convey the gospel to him or her in a resonant way. *Benefit:* It begins spiritual conversations in a meaningful, relevant sweet spot, and paves the way for sharing the full implications of the cross of Christ.

2. ESTABLISHING SAFETY: This is the skill of communicating that your friendship and its value will not be affected regardless of who the person is and what he or she believes or expresses. *Benefit:* It opens the door for candid spiritual conversations.

3. FRAMING UP: This is the skill of leveraging a relationship or a question/objection into an ongoing conversation where spiritual influence can eventually occur. *Benefit:* It leads people into influential relationships.

4. DRAWING OUT: This is the skill of asking second-, third-, and fourth-level questions in order to understand a person's thoughts, feelings, deeper needs, and story. *Benefit:* It deepens understanding and insight for faith-sharing.

5. THE DISCLOSURE WINDOW: This is the skill by which a Christian uses present personal sins and/or struggles to convey the grace and power of Christ. *Benefits:* (1) Empowers natural sharing. (2) Deepens the relationship bond. (3) Invites reciprocal sharing. (4) Shapes the heart toward humility, establishing the need for a Savior. (5) Conveys the essence of Christian dependence upon Christ.

6. PROGRESSION STEPS: This is the skill of working through the processing steps that nonbelievers naturally traverse in order to come to Christ: (1) Openness to, (2) Ability to, (3) Desire to, and (4) Choice to.

*Benefit:* It shows Christians where to focus, and sensitizes them to the journey needs of their friends.

7. PROJECTING: This is the skill of picturing, for the nonbeliever, how life could look for him or her as a Christian. *Benefit:* It helps the nonbeliever to envision and anticipate the decision to become a Christian.

8. PLATFORM-BUILDING: This is the skill of laying down solid planks of reason to give the searcher something to work from or stand upon. In my book *Soul Whisperer,* I develop four major planks in detail: (1) fulfilled prophecy, (2) historical authenticity, (3) the resurrection, and (4) Jesus himself. *Benefit:* It shows Christians what is necessary to reach those who are farther out: irreligious people, skeptics, atheists, and those professing a different faith.

9. HONOR: This skill respects and esteems the individual and his or her association or beliefs, enabling the Christian to make the point (to present the gospel truth) without losing the person. *Benefit:* It guides Christians in disarming the nonbeliever in order to engage conversationally in a productive way.

10. PATHS: This skill involves developing particular knowledge to reach distinct types of people: God-accusers, cultural Christians, pleasure-seekers, moralists, progressives, theistic skeptics, atheists, and followers of other faiths. *Benefit:* It gives believers keen insight on where Satan has snagged specific people, and how to release them.

PLUS-1 SKILL: CIRCLING BACK: This is the skill that one must employ once he or she has brought someone into the faith. It involves circling back with the individual to create a strong discipling projection. *Benefit:* It insures that Christians are fulfilling the Great Commission call to make disciples, not just render a salvation decision.

# –Addendum C–

## THE PATH MODEL

**E**ach stage of the path requires ample time—between 8 and 10 weeks—to be taught, so that the associated values may be reinforced. The extensions—phases following the class or group curriculum—are a means to apply and engage your people in the great story of God.

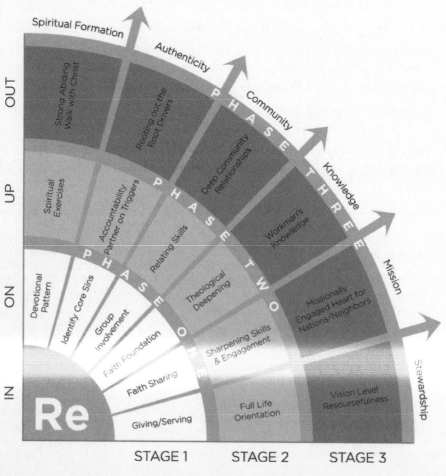

*Extensions, Phase #1:* Small groups launched from the class; devotional patterns practiced. Due to the unique positioning of newer believers, one opportunistic extension is to launch evangelistic "Discovery Circles" with newer believers and their unchurched friends.

*Extensions, Phase #2:* Reading assignments; elevated community engagement; mission-related projects.

*Extensions, Phase #3:* Gift-shape assessments; mission-statement creation; team assignments.

# ABOUT THE AUTHOR

**G**ary Comer is the founder of Soul Whisperer Ministries, an organization dedicated to helping churches develop missionally. After planting/pastoring two churches, Gary was hired as their outreach director by Sandals Church (a mega-sized congregation in Southern California). During that five-year stint he also served as a church planting coach for the Christian Missionary Alliance, and worked as an international mission trainer with Serve U International, while also completing his doctorate at Talbot Theological Seminary.

Spearheading the Soul Whisperer Ministries team, Gary offers multiple mission related services to churches. He is a motivational speaker, faith-sharing skills trainer, community group campaign catalyst, discipleship path designer, and development consultant. His ministry is national and international, involved in training leaders in the United Kingdom, Kenya, Egypt and India.

ReMission is Gary's sixth book. His other works:

*Soul Whisperer: Why the Church Must Change the Way It Views Evangelism* (2013)

*Launch Point: Moving Small Groups into Mission* (2014)

*Steps to Faith: Where Inquiring Friends Become Solid Followers* (2014)

*First Steps Discipleship Training: Turning Newer Believers into Missional Disciples* (with separate Leader's Guide) (2014)

Connect with Gary at: soulwhisperministry.com.